DATE DUE

OCT - 5 '04			
Feb 23 05			
FEB 1 1			
MAR 22 05			
APR 2 4 '06			
MAY 2 3 '06			
SEP 2 7 '06			
SEP 1 8 2008			
GAYLORD			PRINTED IN U.S.A.

The Devil's Dictionary

The Devil's
Dictionary
Ambrose Bierce

With an introduction by Roy Morris, Jr.

New York   Oxford
Oxford University Press
1999

Oxford University Press

Oxford   New York
Athens   Auckland   Bangkok   Bogotá   Buenos Aires   Calcutta
Cape Town   Chennai   Dar es Salaam   Delhi   Florence   Hong Kong   Istanbul
Karachi   Kuala Lumpur   Madrid   Melbourne   Mexico City   Mumbai
Nairobi   Paris   São Paulo   Singapore   Taipei   Tokyo   Toronto   Warsaw

and associated companies in
Berlin   Ibadan

Copyright © 1999 by Oxford University Press

Published by Oxford University Press, Inc.
198 Madison Avenue, New York, New York 10016

Oxford is a registered trademark of Oxford University Press

The Devil Alphabet from Bibliothèque Nationale de France, Paris.

Library of Congress Cataloging-in-Publication Data
Bierce, Ambrose, 1842-1914?
The devil's dictionary / by Ambrose Bierce: with an introduction by Roy Morris, Jr.
p. cm.
ISBN 0-19-512626-2 (cloth: alk. paper).—ISBN 0-19-512627-0 (paper: alk. paper).
1. English language—Dictionaries—Humor.
2. English Language—Semantics—Humor.
3. Vocabulary—Humor. I. Title
PS1097.D4   1998
423'.0207—dc21   98-22576

2004
25.00

CLOTH   10 9 8 7 6 5
PAPER   10 9 8

Printed in the United States of America
on acid-free paper

The Devil's Dictionary

Introduction

Of all the nicknames—mostly negative—that Ambrose Bierce acquired in the course of his career, one stands out as uniquely flattering: The West Coast Samuel Johnson. Most writers would have been pleased to find themselves mentioned, however briefly, in the same breath as the Great Cham, but Bierce was typically unimpressed. The problem, as he saw it, lay in Johnson's famous definition of patriotism as "the last refuge of a scoundrel." To Bierce's way of thinking, this was exactly wrong: "I beg to submit that it is the first." Nor would Bierce necessarily have agreed with Johnson's considered opinion that "no man but a blockhead ever wrote, except for money." While certainly not averse to being paid for his work, Bierce (like Johnson) wrote for many complex personal reasons, not least of which was a lifelong thirst for revenge upon a world that he felt—with some reason—had wounded him physically, spiritually, and emotionally. And while Johnson professed himself to be "more pained by ignorance than delighted by instruction," Bierce positively gloried in the ignorance of others, and he was only too happy to inflict upon "that immortal ass, the average man" a painful—if often hilarious—rod of correction.

The Devil's Dictionary was one of his most effective teaching tools. With the able assistance of "my scholarly friend, Mr. Satan," Bierce set out to challenge the most cherished institutions of American society: love, marriage, law, religion, politics, patriotism, and art. Wit was his weapon of choice, and The Devil's Dictionary remains one of the wittiest, if also one of the most deeply subversive, books in the English language. Readers would do well to keep in mind Kent's insightful warning to King Lear: "This is not altogether fool, my lord." For behind the word games and the mockery, the 998 definitions in *The Devil's Dictionary* comprise a deadly serious—and at times surprisingly personal—work of art. One modern critic has observed, with only slight exaggeration, that "each of these definitions, to some degree, may be said to define Bierce" himself. Certainly, the choice of words defined, as much as the definitions themselves, constitutes a sort of hidden autobiography, an indirect self-portrait of the artist as a not-so-young man at odds with his country, his family, his past, and himself. Such a reading, of course, requires a certain knowledge of the author's background. One does not become the devil's writing partner overnight.

In Bierce's case, the seeds of disquiet were planted early and deep. He was born on June 24, 1842, in the now-vanished frontier community of Horse Cave Creek, Ohio, the tenth of thirteen children (and the last to survive infancy) of intensely religious parents who had migrated west from Cornwall, Connecticut. When he was four the family moved again, to the tiny village of Warsaw in upstate Indiana, where Bierce spent the remainder of his distinctly unhappy childhood. From the start, his pious, sin-defying parents were as much an embarrassment to him as he was, no doubt, a puzzlement to them. His somewhat Dickensian father, Marcus Aurelius, was an odd mixture of religious zealot and closet aesthete, possessing along with a ramshackle farm and a forest of debts the largest collection of books in Kosciusko County. In fact, Bierce's own rather dandified name came from one of those books, a penny-dreadful play entitled *Ambrose Gwinett; or, A Sea-Side Story*, whose basic plot contrivance of the hero's surviving death by hanging would turn up again, albeit ironically, in Bierce's most famous story, "An Occurrence at Owl Creek Bridge." For reasons of his own, the elder Bierce gave all of his children names beginning with the letter *A*; Ambrose, true to form, always hated his.

For the most part, Bierce seems to have tolerated his father; his mother was another matter altogether. Laura Sherwood Bierce was a direct descendant of William Bradford, who had come over on the *Mayflower*. Besides having nine older children to care for—and three younger ones to bury—Mrs. Bierce faced the baffling and never-abating antipathy of blond-haired, blue-eyed Ambrose, who was as devilish-acting as he was angelic-looking. Both she and her husband seem to have made allowances for their youngest surviving child, excusing him from having to work in the fields and allowing him to attend school until the comparatively advanced age of fourteen. But if they expected anything in the way of filial gratitude, they were sorely disappointed. "Disobedience," Bierce would jeer forty years later, "is the silver lining to the cloud of servitude." And while he could occasionally find in his father "that severity of manner that so frequently conceals...a warm and affectionate nature," Bierce could never bring himself to say anything nice about his mother. She was "the pious old lady at home after service singing 'Plunged in a Gulf of Dark Despair,'" the unforgiven "deceiver" who had once had the gall to tell him that there was, indeed, a Santa Claus. "Even now," he would write after his mother's death, "I cannot say that I experience any consuming desire to renew my acquaintance with her in that other life to which, she also assured me, we hasten hence."

In a quartet of hair-raising short stories grouped under the all too apt title *The Parenticide Club*, Bierce would kill his parents again and again. "Having murdered my mother under circumstances of singular atrocity," he begins one story. Another opens: "Early one June morning in 1872 I murdered my father—an act which made a deep impression on me at the time." In "The Hypnotist," the title character mesmerizes his parents into thinking they are horses; after they kick and stomp each other to death in the grip of their delusion, he observes with smirking satisfaction that now "the author of the strife was an orphan."

Bierce's relations with his brothers and sisters were equally cold. Except for his brother Albert, the closest to him in age, he cared little for his siblings. They were, in their own ways, as eccentric as he was: one brother tipped the scales at 300 pounds; another ran off to be a strongman in a traveling circus; a third lived at home his entire life. Albert himself became something of a hermit late in life, while sister Almeda served as a missionary in Africa, where, it was said, she dropped dead of apoplexy after reading one of Ambrose's sacrilegious stories. (A second version has it that she was eaten by cannibals—either way, she may be said to have died a martyr's death.) When brother Aurelius bled to death in a carpentering accident, Bierce eulogized him—after a fashion—as "Mr. Bildad Snobblepopkin, whose life furnishes an instructive lesson for fast livers." His brother, wrote Bierce, "never tasted ardent spirits, ate spiced meats, or sat up later than nine o'clock. [He] rose, summer and winter, at two A.M., and passed an hour and three quarters immersed in ice water. For the last twenty years he has walked fifteen miles daily before breakfast, and then gone without breakfast. Up to the time of his death he had never spoken to a doctor, never had occasion to curse a dentist. If he had not been cut off by a circular saw at the early age of thirty-two there is no telling how long he might have weathered it through. A life like this is so bright and shining an example that we are almost sorry he died."

Outside the family Bierce found the pickings equally slim. He dutifully trudged three miles to school, but once there he stood apart from his rustic classmates, taking little interest in schoolyard play. He later observed, with a certain wistful defiance, that he could never tell the difference between tick-tac-toe, blind man's bluff, and Simon says; baseball and other team sports were "the last shifts of intellectual vacuity." One pert little jade named Bernice Wright inspired some vague adolescent yearnings, but for the most part Bierce kept to himself, taking long walks in the Warsaw woods and acquiring a lifelong affinity for small animals, particularly those, such as snakes and lizards, that were typically unloved. His nights were plagued by blood-soaked dreams and a Nietzschean sense of a God-abandoned universe. The only surviving relic from his isolate ramblings is a handwritten copy of a child's epitaph: "She tasted of life's bitter cup / Refused to drink her potion up / But turned her little head aside / Disgusted with the taste and died." No wonder he was friendless.

Given such a childhood, it is not surprising that Bierce left home as soon as he could, taking a job as an apprentice printer at the age of fifteen on the local newspaper, the *Northern Indianan*. It was his first brush with professional writing, a traditional step for literary-minded youths on the American frontier, but Bierce did not last long in the composing room—legend has it that he quit in a huff after being falsely accused of theft. His prospects dim, the troubled teen was taken in hand by his Uncle Lucius, the longtime mayor of Akron, Ohio, who somehow persuaded his nephew to enroll at the Kentucky Military Institute, near Frankfort. The school was one of many privately run soldier factories operating full-bore in the South in the years preceding the Civil War. At KMI, Bierce acquired his distinctive military bearing and the useful skills of draftsmanship and cartography that would serve him well in years to come. He seems to have thrived in the martial environment, but a disgruntled fellow cadet burned the school down around them in 1859, effectively ending Bierce's last experience with higher education. He returned to Indiana—but not to his hometown—and was waiting tables in an Elkhart saloon when the Civil War exploded in the spring of 1861. It was the best thing that ever happened to him.

The Civil War made Ambrose Bierce, even as it unmade some 600,000 other young Americans who did not share his good luck in surviving it. One week after the Confederate attack at Fort Sumter, he enlisted in Company C of the Ninth Indiana Infantry and marched off to fight in western Virginia, where in its opening battle the regiment had the unnerving experience of being shelled by its own artillery. Other battles quickly followed. In one, a luckless private named Abbott was killed when a stray cannonball rolled down the mountainside and struck him in the side while he was lying flat on the ground, presumably out of harm's way. When the dead man was rolled over it was discovered that the foundry imprint on the fatal shot was "Abbott." After another engagement, the regiment surprised a herd of wild pigs eating the faces off a pile of unburied corpses. Bierce always remembered the hideous sight and described it in his story "The Coup de Grace": "On the crest of a low, thinly wooded hill, he saw several dark objects moving about among the fallen men—a herd of swine. One stood with his back to him, its shoulders sharply elevated. Its forefeet were upon a human body, its head was depressed and invisible. The bristly ridge of its chine showed black against the red west. The swine, catching sight of him, threw up their crimson muzzles, regarding him suspiciously a second, and then with a gruff, concerted grunt, raced away out of sight." The soldiers shot the pigs but could not bring themselves to eat them.

That was bad enough, but much worse awaited the regiment upon its transfer to Tennessee in early 1862. There, under the command of Colonel William B. Hazen, the men marched south to join Major General Ulysses S. Grant's army at Pittsburg Landing, on the Tennessee-Mississippi border. At the Battle of Shiloh, April 6-7, Bierce and his comrades came face to face with war in all its terrifying variety. In two days of savage fighting in the marshy bottomlands between Owl Creek, Lick Creek, and the Tennessee River, more Americans were killed than had died in the Revolutionary War, the War of 1812, and the Mexican War put together. Bierce, not yet twenty, saw sights on the field that he would never forget: a dying sergeant, shot in the head, his brains oozing "creamily" down his cheeks; a ravine full of roasted bodies, "some swollen to double girth; others shriveled to manikins...their faces bloated and black or yellow and shrunken...each countenance [cursed] with a hideous grin"; panic-stricken soldiers drowning each other in their frenzy to escape across the river; officers shooting their own men in the back for deserting. He would later write it all down in "What I Saw of Shiloh," one of the earliest and best accounts of a soldier's initiation in the English language, and he would resurrect one of the battle's place names—Owl Creek—in the title and setting of his most celebrated short story.

After Shiloh, Bierce and his comrades were truly veterans, and they would prove their worth, individually and as a unit, on some of the war's most bitterly contested battlefields. Bierce, for his part, thrived in the army, winning promotion to first lieutenant and proudly taking his place among "hardened and impenitent man-killers, to whom death in its awfulest forms is a fact familiar to their every-day observation; who sleep on hills trembling with the thunder of great guns, dine in the midst of streaming missiles, and play cards among the dead faces of their dearest friends." Eventually he joined Hazen's personal staff as a topographical engineer, where his military school training, brief though it was, proved invaluable. His duties required him to scout ahead of the army, sketching and plotting the surrounding countryside. It was just the sort of solitary duty that most appealed to Bierce's nature, and it brought him into regular contact with Colonel Hazen, a gruff, somewhat argumentative officer who took the like-minded young lieutenant under his wing. Together they thrashed through the underbrush at Chickamauga, charged up the rocky slopes of Missionary Ridge, and dodged enemy bullets at Resaca and Pickett's Mill. To Bierce, Hazen was always "my commander and my friend, my master in the art of war. He was aggressive, arrogant, tyrannical, honorable, truthful, courageous, a skillful soldier,...and one of the most exasperating of men"—not a bad description of Bierce himself.

At Kenesaw Mountain, outside Atlanta, Bierce's luck ran out. Leading a Union skirmish line, he was shot in the head by a rebel sharpshooter. The bullet struck him in the left temple, fracturing the temporal bone and plowing a groove around the side of his skull before coming to rest behind his left ear. Praising Bierce in his after-battle report as "a brave and gallant fellow," Hazen described the wound as "very dangerous and complicated"; he seemed resigned to Bierce's death. But his young protégé was blessed with an extremely hard head—something that would not have come as news to the members of his family—and Bierce somehow managed to survive the wound. After several tedious months recuperating back home, during which time he first became engaged and then disengaged from his former schoolmate Bernice Wright, Bierce rejoined the army in Tennessee. However, he had become prone to splitting headaches and inconvenient fainting spells, and he resigned from the service in January 1865, three months' shy of having spent the entire war in uniform. Long afterwards he would recall his Civil War career with a characteristic mixture of pride and disgust: "It was once my fortune to command a company of soldiers—real soldiers," he wrote. "Not professional life-long fighters, the product of European militarism—just plain, ordinary American, volunteer soldiers, who loved their country and fought for it with never a thought of grabbing it for themselves; that is a trick which the survivors were taught later by gentlemen desiring their votes."

After a brief stint as a civilian treasury agent in Alabama, Bierce rejoined his mentor on a six-month tour of western forts. Hazen had been named assistant inspector general of the Department of the Platte, and his new duties required him to inspect conditions in the Powder River territory of Montana and Wyoming. He asked Bierce to come along and make a few sketches to accompany his report. In return, he could practically guarantee him a captain's bars in the regular army. The trip was not without its risks. The region's native inhabitants, the Sioux, Cheyenne, and other Plains Indians, were less than enchanted by the steady influx of white gold-seekers onto their land. They regularly made their objections known. A few days after the party arrived at Fort Reno, a pair of unwary travelers was murdered almost within sight of the fort. Bierce and Hazen managed to avoid a similar fate, although they dined with a number of fellow officers who would not be so lucky. Besides hostile Indians, the party faced the usual ardors of life on the trail: rattlesnakes, dust storms, dried-up watering holes, scorching temperatures, lack of food, and the unwelcome attention of foraging buffalo, one of which grabbed a sleeping teamster by the hair and came near to scalping him after mistaking the man's locks for a clump of grass. Not surprisingly, Bierce had unfond memories of the trip: "If in all that region there is a mountain that I have not climbed, a river that I have not swum, an alkali pool that I have not thrust my muzzle into, or an Indian that I have not shuddered to think about, I am ready to go back in a Pullman sleeper and do my duty."

Eventually, the party reached San Francisco, where Hazen was to catch a boat back to Washington and Bierce was to receive his captain's commission. Hazen made the boat, but Bierce discovered to his bitter disappointment that his commission was that of a second lieutenant. "Ingratitude, more strong than traitor's arms, quite vanquished me," he wrote. "I resigned, parted from Hazen more in sorrow than in anger and remained in California." He faced the immediate problem of finding a job. Acting on a tip from helpful army officers, Bierce secured work as a night watchman at the United States Mint. He moved in with a fellow employee and embarked on a dogged, year-long course of self-education, reading his way through such ponderous classics as Edward Gibbons's *Decline and Fall of the Roman Empire* and exploring the raucous boomtown in which he somewhat accidentally found himself living. It was a city of millionaires' mansions and waterfront dives, of four-star hotels and opium dens. Most of all, it was a city of readers. San Francisco in the mid-1860s boasted nearly 100 newspapers, more than had London or New York City, and a stable full of talented writers, led by Mark Twain and Bret Harte, to report on the zany antics of such homegrown individualists as Norton I, the self-proclaimed emperor of America; Money King, who conducted a brisk curbside savings and loan with hundred-dollar bills pinned to his coat; "Professor" Frederick Coombs, a sometime phrenologist who cavorted about town in a powdered wig and Revolutionary War uniform, styling himself Washington the Second; and the Great Unknown, an elegantly dressed older gentleman who silently promenaded down Montgomery Street each afternoon, ostentatiously nursing some private sorrow.

The journalists' favorite watering hole was the four-story Montgomery Block, a hotel and restaurant one street up from the Mint. Another popular meeting place was the office of the *Golden Era*, a weekly newspaper located just around the corner from Bierce's rooming house. The neophyte writer began frequenting both places, determined somehow to break into print. In the fall of 1867 he sold a handful of poems and essays to local publications, and by the next summer he had become a regular contributor to the *San Francisco News Letter and Commercial Advertiser*, commonly known as the *News Letter*, a sixteen-page weekly that offered literary criticism, theater reviews, and broad-brush political satire alongside its financial news. Under the generous tutelage of editor James W. Watkins, an urbane, well-traveled journalist who had worked in London and New York before coming west, Bierce caught on rapidly. In December 1868 he succeeded Watkins as editor of the *News Letter*, taking over the paper's "Town Crier" column and promising in his first issue to "chaff" local religious leaders.

From the start, Bierce's reign as Town Crier was both sensational and controversial. Not just men of the cloth but a wide range of local malefactors, public and private, felt the sting of his editorial lash. He began running a regular "Criminal Market Review" in which he reported jauntily that "Robberies are looking up; Assaults active; Forgeries dull...Juvenile delinquencies are lively; Election frauds, out of season; Perjuries brisk." Under the guise of simple reporting, he perfected his signature style, which mixed an innate cynicism with a deadpan, world-weary delivery: "Somebody has attempted to rob the safe in the office of the City and County Treasurer," he noted. "This is rushing matters; the impatient scoundrel ought to try his hand at being a Supervisor first. From Supervisor to Thief the transition is natural and easy." When an insurance company was robbed, he exulted, "Tit for tat." He sympathized with a local man who had just been committed to an insane asylum. "His idea is that the devil is in him, and he wishes to find the Virgin to cure him," joked Bierce. "It is just as well that he is gone to the Asylum; it is not likely that in San Francisco he would find any virgin of sufficient age to undertake his restoration to health." And when a candidate for the school board came under fire for consorting with a prostitute, Bierce immediately urged the man's election on the grounds that it would inevitably lead him to reform, since "no respectable harlot who cares for her reputation would continue her acquaintance with a man who had been elected to the Board of Education."

Crimes of all sorts, but particularly homicides, attracted his somewhat obsessive attention. The frequency with which he commented on men murdering their wives suggests that either the crime was more common in Victorian-era San Francisco than it is today, which seems doubtful, or else that it held an unhealthy fascination for the columnist himself, which seems all too likely. One typical example may stand for the general tone of his reporting: "Mr. John Beever, of St. Cloud, Minn., went to call upon his wife, from whom he had been some time separated, and before leaving took occasion to inveigle her into a back kitchen by the chignon.... He chopped away at the lady's head until he had made of it a basket of unsightly chips, hanging confusedly together by tangled skeins of hair, clogged with warm brain and smoking with blood—altogether a very discouraging spectacle for the hired girl who had to clean up after him. It doesn't seem right to treat a woman in this way after having left her. When one frees himself from the obligations of matrimony, he should be held to have renounced its privileges."

Suicide, too, fascinated Bierce. He fulsomely praised a German baker for following through on a sudden notion to blow off his head. "By this example," Bierce wrote, "we may be taught that when a man gets an idea in his head he may accomplish great results.... There is no use fooling about such things. Be sure you're right, then go ahead." Conversely, a poor devil named Linton was chided for his self-annihilating ineptitude. Said Bierce: "Linton cut his wind-pipe completely off with a very dull chisel because he could not get work. He immediately obtained all the work he wanted: he had to work very hard to breathe. There was a loaded pistol in the room, with which he might just as easily have taken himself off. There are some men who will play the fool even in fulfilling their most sacred obligations to society." As a public service, he cataloged the various means of killing oneself: "Razors are good in their own way, but some knowledge of the location of the jugular vein must precede their use.... A pistol is objectionable; it makes too much noise and wakes baby. If you must do it this way, take a revolver, put the muzzle in your mouth...close the lips to deaden the sound, and fire five barrels. Wait two minutes by the watch, and if you don't feel sick, pull off the other barrel and hold your head in a tub of water. Shotguns are vulgar. Besides, they must be fired with the toe, which is liable to slip off the trigger and hurt one's corns. Hanging will do on a stretch, and arsenic may be taken at a pinch. Asphyxiation by blowing out the gas should not be thought of; it makes the corpse smell bad."

Despite, or perhaps because of, his gory subject matter, Bierce quickly became a household name. From the lavish salons on Russian Hill to the lowest rumpots on the Barbary Coast, his bright, insolent columns were read with anger, amusement, horror, and shock—it did not matter to Bierce which emotion predominated. Newspapers as far away as New York and London began quoting his best lines and praising the "Rabelaisian audacity of his homicidal paragraphs." A rival columnist anointed him "the Mentor, whip, and Mirror of the town." Bierce scorned the praise. "We wish it distinctly understood," he said, "that we hold the press of this State in profound contempt....We are proud to confess that we have more in common with the average San Francisco jackass than with the average San Francisco journalist. You have never seen a jackass lick the feet of his master." Even the unoffending Mark Twain, whom he scarcely knew, attracted the Town Crier's pitiless gaze. "Mark Twain, who whenever he has been long enough sober to permit an estimate, has been uniformly found to bear a spotless character, has got married," Bierce wrote. "It was not the act of a desperate man—it was not committed while laboring under temporary insanity; his insanity is not of that type, nor does he ever labor—it was the cool, methodical, cumulative culmination of human nature, working in the breast of an orphan hankering for someone with a fortune to love—someone with a bank account to caress."

Ironically, Bierce would soon follow Twain's example, meeting and marrying a local beauty named Mary Ellen "Mollie" Day, the vivacious, dark-haired daughter of a wealthy mining engineer and his social-climbing wife. The two tied the knot on Christmas Day, 1871, an odd choice in itself, given Bierce's lifelong loathing for the holiday. Perhaps the timing of the nuptials jinxed the marriage; more likely, Bierce was not good marriage material whatever the date. Years later, he provided his own poetic version of the ceremony: "They stood before the altar and supplied/The fire themselves in which their fat was fried." Despite his misgivings, Bierce happily accepted his father-in-law's offer of an all-expenses-paid honeymoon trip to England. The couple left San Francisco in the spring of 1872, arriving in England in late April. Armed with letters of introduction from *News Letter* publisher Frederick Marriott, a native of London, Bierce fully intended to storm Fleet Street. He soon linked up with Thomas Hood, the gentle if hard-drinking editor of *Fun*, a weekly humor magazine modeled after the better-known *Punch*. Hood, of whom it was said that he had been christened in a punch bowl and thereafter was never far from one, obligingly introduced Bierce to his circle of London journalists and wits, including George Augustus Sala, the flamboyant columnist for the *Daily Telegraph*; novelist-adventurer Mayne Reid; and W. S. Gilbert, Arthur Sullivan's musical comedy collaborator. The group met regularly in the bar of the Ludgate Hill railway station to exchange gossip, harbor grudges, and trade insults. Bierce was in his element, living the life of a cultured man about town and acquiring a slight British accent that he would affect for the rest of his days. He and his companions "worked too hard, dined too well, frequented too many clubs, and went to bed too late in the forenoon," he remembered fondly. "In short, we diligently, conscientiously, and with a perverse satisfaction burned the candle of life at both ends and in the middle."

Somehow, in the midst of his clubbing and drinking, Bierce managed to churn out copy for *Fun* and other English magazines. He took to signing his articles "Dod Grile," hoping perhaps to create a memorable disyllabic pen name like Mark Twain's. But the name never really caught on in England, and neither did Bierce. Despite his publishing three books of rather forced humor with the notorious publisher-pornographer John Camden Hotten, most of Bierce's London work was decidedly second-rate. Only the titles of the books were any good: *The Fiend's Delight*, *Nuggets and Dust*, and *Cobwebs from an Empty Skull*. As for Mollie, she dutifully produced two sons in two years, Day and Leigh, but otherwise suffered the more or less benign neglect of her bon vivant husband. Not surprisingly, Bierce found fatherhood as unenchanting as marriage. "Of all the evils that flow from matrimony, the child is the greatest—except children," he told his friend Walter Neale many years later. "Both parents spend their entire adult lives in unrelieved slavery, quarreling with each other about their children the while, and unaware that the little miscreants will soon come to hold them in contempt, flout them, and probably never give them a thought after the final separation brought about by death." When a woman asked him his theory on child-rearing, he sternly advised her, "Study Herod, madam."

Mollie left England in May 1875, intending to visit her mother in San Francisco. A few months later, Bierce received the unwelcome news that she was six months' pregnant with their third child. He had never intended to return to San Francisco, but the recent deaths of Hood and Hotten, as much as Mollie's impending delivery, finally induced him to leave London. He arrived back on the West Coast in September 1875, after an absence of more than three years, and immediately mailed off two freelance submissions to the *News Letter*, one of which included the first forty-eight words of an embryonic "Demon's Dictionary." But if he was hoping to resume his old job with the newspaper, he was quickly disappointed. The *News Letter* no longer had an opening for the erstwhile Town Crier; nor were the city's other papers hiring just then. The entire country was in the grip of the worst depression in fifty years, occasioned by the failure of Jay Cooke's banking empire and the subsequent shock waves it sent through Wall Street. Bierce, for all his expensive tailoring and newfound accent, had to settle for a nonwriting job in the assayer's office at the U.S. Mint. It was not until early 1877 that he hooked up with a new San Francisco publication, *Argonaut*, and resumed writing a weekly column, which he modestly christened "Prattle." In most respects, it was virtually identical to his earlier Town Crier paragraphs. He whaled away remorselessly at rival journalists, would-be poets, and corrupt office-holders, while indulging his chronic obsession with the macabre. When one despondent San Franciscan committed suicide in St. Louis, Bierce wondered aloud why he had gone outside the city to shoot himself, since "no city in the world presents greater advantages to the suicide than San Francisco. We have an efficient and accommodating coroner, and a comfortable, though rather badly lighted, dead-house. Our undertakers have engaging manners, and their hearses easy springs. There is a charming view from every cemetery. In addition to these advantages, San Francisco itself is a very good motive."

Increasingly, Bierce was living apart from his wife and children, preferring the smoky haunts of the downtown Bohemian Club to the family home in San Rafael. By the summer of 1880, bored with the endless literary and political skirmishes that took up much of his time and energy, he somewhat impulsively joined an old army buddy in a gold-mining venture in South Dakota. The grandly named Black Hills Placer Mining Company looked good on paper, attracting thousands of dollars from outside investors, but on the ground it proved to be perhaps the only site in the entire Black Hills that did not contain any gold. Bierce labored manfully to turn the company into a paying proposition, but it was no use. Not even the assistance of a hired gunslinger, whom Bierce listed formally on the company payroll as "Boone May, Murderer," could turn up any gold. By the time he threw in the towel and returned to San Francisco in December 1880, Bierce was once again broke, frustrated, and unemployed. When his former employer at the *Argonaut*, Frank Pixley, declined to give him back his job, Bierce jumped to the new satirical journal *Wasp*, but not before developing an unassuageable hatred for the man he now referred to as "Mr. Pigsley of the Hogonaut." In this as in many things, Bierce eventually had the last word. After Pixley died he volunteered a suitable epitaph: "Here lies Frank Pixley, as usual."

Perhaps it was the failure of the Black Hills mining venture, or the endless wrangles with Pixley, or the absence of a satisfactory home life—whatever the reason, when Bierce assumed the editorship of the *Wasp* in January 1881, he brought along an old and valued ally: Satan. Beginning with his first issue, Bierce inaugurated a new feature, "The Devil's Dictionary," offering twisty new definitions of shopworn old words. The dictionary allowed him to range widely over all aspects of human endeavor. Under the guise of a purely disinterested study of words, he began a sort of undeclared guerrilla war on the most cherished—and often the least examined—values of American society. In a slippery world where, as the Dictionary succinctly put it, *white* was *black*, *his* was *hers*, and *once* was *enough*, Bierce challenged readers to rethink society and their place within it. There was a proud defiance in his definition of a cynic as "a blackguard whose faulty vision sees things as they are, not as they ought to be," and it is precisely this need to see things clearly that imbues the dictionary with its continuing, if ironic, moral authority. America in the Gilded Age was a rich melange of unparalleled prosperity and starvation wages, of oratorical platitudes and governmental malfeasance, of public morality and private vice. The nation as whole, Bierce advised his readers, was "a great, broad blackness with two or three small points of light struggling and flickering in the universal blank of ignorance, bigotry, crudity, conceit, tobacco-chewing, ill-dressing, unmannerly manners and general barbarity." Sounding more like his Calvinist forebears than his putative collaborator, he warned: "If our sins, which are scarlet, are to be washed as white as wool it must be in the tears of a genuine contrition: our crocodile deliverances will profit us nothing. We must stop chasing dollars, stop lying, stop cheating, stop ignoring art, literature, and all the refining agencies and instrumentalities of civilization. We must subdue our detestable habit of shaking hands with prosperous rascals and fawning upon the merely rich.... Until we amend our personal characters we shall amend our laws in vain."

Given his own personal and professional obsessions, it is not surprising that the most frequently defined words in *The Devil's Dictionary* deal with religion, politics, love, war, and death. However, it is not so much what Bierce defines as how he defines it that gives the dictionary its distinctive flavor. As he somewhat needlessly informed readers in December 1882: "We are not enamored of the world as it is. We think it peopled with a thousand-and-odd-millions of inhabitants, who are mostly fools, and it is our custom to set forth and illustrate this unsatisfactory state of affairs by instancing conspicuous examples." This dissatisfaction is echoed in his definition of *history* as "an account mostly false, of events mostly unimportant, which are brought about by rulers mostly knaves, and soldiers mostly fools." The largest of these events, *war*, is "a by-product of the arts of peace"; *peace* itself is merely "a period of cheating between two periods of fighting." *Battle*, the individual component of war, is "a method of untying with the teeth a political knot that would not yield to the tongue." As for the *patriot* who would attempt to untie these knots by force, he is "the dupe of statesmen and the tool of conquerors," induced to sacrifice himself by a mistaken emotion—*patriotism*—which is merely "combustible rubbish ready to the torch of anyone ambitious to illuminate his name." Nor does Bierce hold out much hope for the peaceable adjustment of events through democratic means. *Politics* is merely "a strife of interests masquerading as a contest of principles," while the *politician* is "an eel in the fundamental mud upon which the superstructure of organized society is reared." As for the *vote*, it is "the instrument and symbol of a freeman's power to make a fool of himself and a wreck of his country." The nation's highest elected official, the *president*, is nothing more than "the leading figure in a small group of men of whom—and of whom only— it is positively known that immense numbers of their countrymen did not want any of them for President."

This public pessimism is joined by a private bitterness that reveals— probably more clearly than Bierce intended—the unhappy man behind the pose. With the advantage of hindsight, one can almost chart Bierce's life chronologically in his definitions: "**Birth**, *n*. The first and direst of all disasters"; "**Childhood**, *n*. The period of human life intermediate between the idiocy of infancy and the folly of youth"; "**Religion**, *n*. A daughter of Hope and Fear, explaining to Ignorance the nature of the Unknowable"; "**Faith**, *n*. Belief without evidence in what is told by one who speaks without knowledge, of things without parallel"; "**Reverence**, *n*. The spiritual attitude of a man to a god and a dog to a man." An oppressive religious upbringing is succeeded by an equally oppressive courtship and marriage: "**Love**, *n*. A temporary insanity curable by marriage"; "**Intimacy**, *n*. A relationship into which fools are providentially drawn for their mutual destruction"; "**Affianced**, *pp*. Fitted with an ankle-ring for the ball-and-chain"; "**Wedding**, *n*. A ceremony at which two persons undertake to become one, one undertakes to become nothing, and nothing undertakes to become supportable"; "**Marriage**, *n*. The state or condition of a community consisting of a master, a mistress and two slaves, making in all, two"; "**Helpmate**, *n*. A wife, or bitter half"; "**Husband**, *n*. One who, having dined, is charged with the care of the plate"; "**Yoke**, *n*. A word that defines the matrimonial situation with precision, point and poignancy." As the disillusionment grows larger, the definitions become shorter: "**Hers**, *pron*. His"; "**White**, *adj*. and *n*. Black"; "**Once**, *adv*. Enough"; "**Twice**, *adv*. Once too often"; "**Alone**, *adj*. In bad company." Over all hangs a pervasive emptiness: "**Day**, *n.* A period of twenty-four hours, mostly misspent"; "**November**, *n.* The eleventh twelfth of a weariness"; "**Year**, *n.* A period of 365 disappointments"; "**Tomb**, *n.* The House of Indifference."

The Devil's Dictionary, he noted later, was addressed specifically to those "enlightened souls who prefer dry wines to sweet, sense to sentiment, wit to humor and clear English to slang." The distinction between wit and humor is important, as Bierce made clear in a late essay. "Humor is tolerant, tender," he wrote, "its ridicule caresses. Wit stabs, begs pardon—and turns the weapon in the wound." Most Americans were naturally humorous, he said, but "if any are born witty heaven help them to emigrate." As for the would-be writer, he must live with "an ever-present consciousness that this is a world of fools and rogues, blind with superstition, tormented with envy, consumed with vanity, selfish, false, cruel, cursed with illusions—frothing mad! He must be a sinner and in turn a saint, a hero, a wretch." As a job description, it had more in common with Baudelaire's *poete maudit* than with such homegrown American humorists as Mark Twain, Artemus Ward, and Peter Finley Dunne, and Bierce carefully cultivated a public image that, in keeping with the dictionary's title, was overtly satanic. He habitually dressed in black, carried a loaded revolver under his coat, and displayed a human skull and a box of ashes on his desk—the remains, he said, of former friends. His overall philosophy he summed up in two words: "Nothing matters."

After five years as editor-*cum*-lexicographer, Bierce resigned from the *Wasp* in December 1885 and withdrew from the hubbub of San Francisco journalism, relocating himself and his family to St. Helena, a small resort town at the northern end of the Napa Valley. A recurrence of his chronic asthma forced him to seek a cure at Angwin's, a health spa in the mountains above St. Helena that he sourly christened "the place of last resort." By March of 1887 he had recovered sufficiently to accept an offer from William Randolph Hearst, the twenty-three-year-old publisher of the San Francisco *Examiner*, to come to work for his newspaper. He stopped writing "The Devil's Dictionary," perhaps in protest of the feature's being renamed "The Cynic's Dictionary" to protect the tender feelings of religious subscribers, but his criticism of American society continued unabated. When Benjamin Harrison was elected president in 1888, Bierce marveled at the public's seemingly imperishable faith in the political system. "You can effect a change of robbers every four years," he wrote. "Inestimable privilege to pull off the glutted leech and attach the lean one! And you cannot even choose among the lean leeches, but must accept those designated by the programmers and showmen who have the reptiles on tap." The American people as a whole were "a nation of blockheads and scoundrels," and the country itself was "the home of political heresy, the paradise of robbers and the hell of true men." He even regretted his "youthful indiscretion" of fighting to preserve the Union, declaring, "I am of the conviction that the country's institutions ought not to be preserved and that the slaves were not fit to be freed." In general, he advised, "Murder, but do not vote."

In 1889, Bierce suffered a pair of personal tragedies that further darkened his worldview. The first was the breakup of his seventeen-year marriage to Mollie, occasioned by his accidental discovery of a packet of love letters to her from a Danish visitor to St. Helena. Despite her protestations that the letters were innocent, Bierce stormed out of the house, and her life, forever, declaring with crushing finality, "I don't take part in competitions—even in love." The two would meet one last time the following summer to bury their firstborn son, Day, who at age sixteen had shot and killed his best friend and himself in a foolish quarrel over a girl. The twin tragedies devastated Bierce emotionally, but they did not prevent him from continuing to work on a series of remarkable short stories, published first in the *Sunday Examiner* and then brought out in 1892 in book form under the title *Tales of Soldiers and Civilians*. The stories alternated among genres; some were ghost stories, some were horror stories, others were ostensibly realistic stories set in the Civil War. All shared a common theme: the fatal consequences of failing to see the world clearly. Again and again, the stories feature protagonists—they could scarcely be called heroes—who die as a direct result of misconceiving the world. The Union soldier trapped in a collapsed house in "One of the Missing" dies of fright after failing to realize that the gun pointing at his head has already discharged. The cowardly officer in "One Officer, One Man" kills himself because he cannot face the great battle he sees looming; the battle never comes. In "The Man and the Snake," an overwrought intellectual manages to scare himself to death after mistaking a toy snake for a real one. The old soldier in "A Resumed Identity" dies of shock after realizing that he has lost the past forty years to amnesia. And in "Chickamauga," a young deaf-mute thinks the gruesome battle taking place in the woods around his home is something of a lark—until he finds his mother lying dead in their yard. In Bierce's world, death is random and arbitrary, and whether one is a hero or a coward is almost secondary—certainly, it does not effect the workings of Chance, "a brutal, blind design, like the unconscious malevolence of an idiot."

This point is made most brilliantly in Bierce's best-known story, "An Occurrence at Owl Creek Bridge." In it a feckless Southern planter named Peyton Farquhar, deluded by dreams of military glory, allows himself to be suborned into committing an act of sabotage that immediately leads to his arrest and execution. Not only does Farquhar misinterpret the situation—his supposed conspirator is a Union spy—but in his last fleeting seconds of life he continues to see the world through a prism of wishful thinking. The entire middle section of the story is a perfectly rendered trompe l'oeil in which Farquhar (and by extension the reader) imagines his miraculous, last-second escape from hanging. Bierce carefully and subtly misleads the reader into accepting Farquhar's self-delusion. In this way the surprise ending, perhaps the most famous in American literature, both underscores and embodies the story's message that human perception is often fatally self-deluding. After several pages given over to Farquhar's supposed escape—complete with heroic feats of derring-do and a romantic happy ending—the story suddenly snaps back into real time: "Peyton Farquhar was dead; his body, with a broken neck, swung gently from side to side beneath the timbers of the Owl Creek Bridge." It had all been a dream. Farquhar's senses, preternaturally heightened by fear and anguish, had inflated a split second of wishful thinking into a fully imagined eleventh-hour escape—until he reached the end of his rope.

The war stories in *Tales of Soldiers and Civilians* are now considered among the finest in world literature, but at the time they did not even win Bierce a national audience. Their effects were too sensational, their meanings too dark, and their insights too subtle for a generation of readers weaned on the teacup tragedies of William Dean Howells and the neurasthenic heiresses of Henry James. The dominant literary movement of the day was realism, contemned by Bierce as "the art of depicting nature as it is seen by toads," dealing exclusively with "the acts, thoughts, feelings of commonplace people, the lives and loves of noodles, nobodies, ignoramuses and millionaires." He publicly derided "Miss Nancy Howells" and "Miss Nancy James"—*nancy* being slang for homosexual—and when Howells generously praised him as one of the country's three best writers, Bierce immediately responded, "I suppose

Mr. Howells is the other two." As for Stephen Crane, whose astonishing novel *The Red Badge of Courage* was enjoying the sort of widespread popular and critical acclaim that Bierce's own Civil War stories never would, he shrugged off Crane's effusive praise of "An Occurrence at Owl Creek Bridge," calling the younger writer a "freak" and challenging a friendly critic's opinion that two minor writers were even worse than Stephen Crane. "I had thought that there could be only two worse writers than Stephen Crane," Bierce groused, "namely, two Stephen Cranes."

But though he may have been out of step artistically, Bierce was still, on occasion, an effective political columnist. In 1896 he enjoyed the supreme satisfaction of helping to defeat California railroad tycoon Collis P. Huntington's blatant efforts to bully Congress into postponing his repayment of a $75 million federal loan. Following Huntington to Washington, Bierce directed a small army of Hearst reporters and cartoonists in derailing the magnate's heavy-handed efforts. He kept up a remorseless barrage, characterizing the old railroader as "an inflated old pigskin," "a veteran calumniator," and "the swine of the century." "Of our modern Forty Thieves," he wrote, "Mr. Huntington is the remaining thirty-six." When the thoroughly exasperated robber baron confronted Bierce on the steps of the Capitol one day and publicly invited him to name his price, Bierce responded with a quote picked up by newspapers across the country. "My price," he thundered, "is seventy-five million dollars. If, when you are ready to pay, I happen to be out of town, you may hand it over to my friend, the Treasurer of the United States." Needless to say, Huntington did not get his debt extension.

Bierce had less success in preventing his own publisher from single-handedly starting a war with Spain. After a full year of sensational, one-sided, and often fictitious reporting of alleged Spanish atrocities in freedom-loving Cuba, Hearst got his way. A battalion of reporters, photographers, and illustrators rushed off to Cuba, while Bierce, the only veteran in the bunch, stayed home. He was content to snipe at the war from a distance, perceptively seeing it as being less about freedom and democracy than power and territory. In "the Land of the Comparatively Free," he observed, "the passion for territory...rages like a lion." He savagely mocked President William McKinley for admitting that he had fallen to his knees and asked God to tell him what to do about Cuba. "Wholesale slaughter of our fellow men in this or any war should, I think, be regarded rather as a political than a religious duty," Bierce wrote, adding that he had difficulty "conceiving Jesus Christ in command of a battleship." The Yanko-Spanko War, as he styled it, was "a freak war...distinctly inferior to cholera and hardly more exciting than the bubonic plague." When the United States sent troops into the Philippines to quell Filipino resistance to American rule, he jeered at a senator's pious reasoning that the country could not in good conscience return to a policy of isolation. Bierce translated the statement "into the language of common sense, that having taken a few sips of the wine of conquest and glory we like the taste of it and want more." History, of course, has proven him right.

Convinced that the Hearst newspapers had become "indistinguishable from circus posters," Bierce went to work for *Cosmopolitan* magazine in 1905, writing a column entitled "The Curmudgeon Philosopher." He complained ceaselessly about his editors, his coworkers, and the new title of the column, saying, "The title so handicaps me that I can do nothing right." He was right about the title: Bierce was no philosopher, except perhaps by negation of all other philosophies, and in his increasingly enervated state he was scarcely a curmudgeon, although he was something of a crank. He spent most of his time sniping at homegrown socialists, newfangled inventions like the airplane, and politicians such as Theodore Roosevelt, whom he had always despised. He could still occasionally get off a crisp one, as he did when he was forced to admit that much of his own work was "sadly antiquated. My checks, though are always up to date." He angrily rejected Hearst's suggestion that he use the column to attack newspaper rival Joseph Pulitzer, grousing, "I don't like the job of chained bulldog to be let loose only to tear the panties off the boys who throw rocks at you. Henceforth I won't bite anybody." Still, he admitted to a friend, "I'm a wage-slave for Hearst. But then the negro quarters are fairly comfortable, the corn and bacon tolerable and the overseer's whip can't reach me here in Washington."

There was one unexpected bonus in writing for *Cosmopolitan*: it brought his work to the attention of New York publishers. In 1906, he met with editors at Doubleday, Page & Company, one of whom was Robert Lanier, the son of Georgia poet Sidney Lanier, the only Civil War veteran besides Bierce to achieve literary prominence after the war. The editors liked the idea of bringing out a collection of Bierce's demonic definitions, although they were nervous about the title *The Devil's Dictionary*. They settled, instead, on the less sulphorus heading *The Cynic's Word Book*. Bierce agreed, however grudgingly, to the change, although he later complained that "the country already had been flooded by a score of 'cynic' books—*The Cynic's This, The Cynic's That,* and *The Cynic's t'Other.* Among them, they brought the word 'cynic' into disfavor so deep that any book bearing it was discredited in advance." Discredited or not, *The Cynic's Word Book* somewhat surprisingly failed to make much of an impact on the world of New York letters. "The book is getting me a little glory," he wrote to his friend George Sterling, "but it will have no sale, for it has no slang, no 'dialect' and no grinning through a horse collar." As it was, the 500-word edition, which included only the first half of the alphabet (A-L), sank without a trace, and Doubleday declined to publish the second half. Bierce undoubtedly was disappointed, but he shrugged it off with a characteristic joke. "Here in the East," he said, "the Devil is a sacred personage (the Fourth Person of the Trinity, as an Irishman might say) and his name must not be taken in vain."

In 1909 he resigned from *Cosmopolitan,* ending a twenty-two-year connection with Hearst and forty-one-year career as a practicing journalist. For the next three years he devoted himself to compiling and publishing the twelve-volume *Collected Works of Ambrose Bierce,* a project suggested to him by publisher-friend Walter Neale. One of his first tasks was to reprint *The Devil's Dictionary* in its entirety, restoring its preferred title and including the missing definitions from the second half of the alphabet. For the first—but certainly not the last—time, the 998 definitions were brought together in one place, giving readers who had long savored the Biercian wordplay in his newspaper columns the opportunity to read the Dictionary in all its prickly variety. The collection as a whole was handsomely printed on high-grade paper and bound in rich morocco leather, but inside it was a hodgepodge that mixed brilliant short stories and matchless definitions with pedestrian poetry, tedious essays, and flaccid philosophizing. Perversely, Bierce did not include a single line of his journalism, ignoring entirely four decades' worth of insightful, hilarious, and frequently courageous reporting. The *Collected Works* was a critical disaster, derided as much for its pretentious wrappings as its admittedly jumbled contents. Critics called the collection "potatoes set in platinum," "turnips in Tiffany's window," and "pure piffle in plush pants." Bierce feigned indifference to the harsh reception, but nevertheless it hurt him badly. When he revisited California in the summer of 1912, friends found him suddenly aged; he walked with a stoop and leaned on a cane. To one acquaintance he confided that he was "sleepy for death." He paid a last visit to the family cemetery at St. Helena, where Mollie (who died in 1905) and Day had been joined in death by Bierce's other son, Leigh, dead of alcoholism and pneumonia at the age of twenty-six. According to the cemetery sexton, Bierce said something about "going into Mexico."

In the autumn of 1913, he made good on his promise to the sexton. To the surprise and concern of his family and friends, the seventy-one-year-old Bierce set out abruptly for Mexico, then in the midst of a ferocious revolution that eventually would claim over a million lives. "This fighting in Mexico interests me," he told his daughter, Helen. "I want to go down and see if these Mexicans can shoot straight." He signed over ownership of the family burial plot to her, telling her not to worry about his mortal remains, since "that matter is all arranged." Prior to leaving, he wrote a number of letters to old associates, all saying the same thing: that he was going into Mexico and that given the violent state of Mexican affairs, he might not be coming back. To his niece Lora he wrote: "Good-bye—if you hear of my being stood up against a Mexican stone wall and shot to rags please know that I think that a pretty good way to depart this life. It beats old age, disease, or falling down the cellar stairs. To be a Gringo in Mexico—ah, that is euthanasia!" At the same time, he wrote to longtime friend Josephine McCrackin: "I expect to go to, perhaps across, South America—possibly via Mexico, if I can get through without being stood up against a wall and shot as a Gringo. But that is better than dying in bed, is it not?" After a last nostalgic tour of his old Civil War battlefields, Bierce arrived on the border in early November. He spent a few days in San Antonio, where he allowed himself to be disappointed in the Alamo and dined with cavalry officers at Fort Sam Houston. His last surviving letter, mailed to his niece from San Antonio on November 6, concludes: "I shall not be here long enough to hear from you, and don't know where I shall be next. Guess it doesn't matter much. Adios."

Whether or not Bierce knew where he was going, no one in the ensuing eighty-five years has been able to say conclusively where he went. He simply disappeared. "Nobody will find my bones," he promised, and nobody ever has. An impressive slate of investigators, including the chief of staff of the United States Army, the secretary of the interior, the American consul in Chihuahua, and numerous official and unofficial sources within the American and Mexican governments, began looking for Bierce in early 1914, after it became obvious that he was missing. They failed to turn up any trace of the famous writer. Rumor had it that he had been killed by Pancho Villa or one of his henchmen. Villa, for his part, denied the charges, saying that he had never even met Bierce. Nor did anyone else in the large coterie of journalists traveling with Villa see Bierce in the bandit's camp, which strongly suggests that he was never there. This flies in the face of the popular but unverified theory that he died in the fighting at Ojinaga between Villa's forces and federalist troops. A more likely scenario, first advanced by his friend Walter Neale, maintains that Bierce had purposely misled people into thinking he was going to Mexico. According to Neale, Bierce had shown him photographs taken at the Grand Canyon the year before and strongly implied that there would be his final resting place. He even showed him the German revolver he intended to use to shoot himself. There is no hard evidence to support Neale's theory—or any of the other outlandish theories surrounding Bierce's mysterious disappearance—but given the writer's lifelong fascination with suicide and his well-known taste for practical jokes, it is at least psychologically plausible.

Whatever became of Ambrose Bierce the man, he remains a distinctly unquiet ghost. His best short stories, particularly "An Occurrence at Owl Creek Bridge" and "Chickamauga," are fixtures in the college curriculum, and new collections of his poetry, his Civil War stories, and his humorous writings appear with increasing regularity. Battalions of red-eyed graduate students continue to slave away in poorly lighted libraries, each intent on proving comprehensively that Bierce is either a major minor or a minor major writer; while at the most rarefied level of literary theory, he is now seen as the godfather of "magical realism." A French-language version of "An Occurrence at Owl Creek Bridge" won an Academy Award in 1963, and in 1989, Hollywood produced a star-studded movie of Latin American novelist Carlos Fuentes' bestselling novel *The Old Gringo*, based on Bierce's supposed last days in Mexico. In his own country, writers as diverse as H.L. Mencken, Ring Lardner, Ernest Hemingway, Joseph Heller, Kurt Vonnegut, Thomas Pynchon, and T.C. Boyle have all felt the pull of his derisive style; comedians such as Groucho Marx and W.C. Fields have extended the range of his wiseguy humor.

Bierce, no doubt, would have enjoyed the attention—he was not overburdened by humility—but one suspects that he would have been most gratified by the cultic popularity of *The Devil's Dictionary*. Since its initial publication in volume 7 of the *Collected Works*, the acrid little lexicon has remained continuously in print. Today, with the possible exceptions of Dorothy Parker and Oscar Wilde, he is probably the world's most frequently quoted wit. His famous one-sentence book review—"The covers of this book are too far apart"—does not apply to *The Devil's Dictionary*. Nor does its eternally jeering author conform to Samuel Johnson's modest definition of a *lexicographer* as "a harmless drudge." There was nothing harmless about Ambrose Bierce, and—with or without the devil's help—the words he sharpened into verbal pitchforks a hundred years ago can still draw blood today.

Roy Morris, Jr.

The Devil's Dictionary

Abasement, *n.* A decent and customary mental attitude in the presence of wealth or power. Peculiarly appropriate in an employee when addressing an employer.

Abatis, *n.* Rubbish in front of a fort, to prevent the rubbish outside from molesting the rubbish inside.

Abdication, *n.* An act whereby a sovereign attests his sense of the high temperature of the throne.

> Poor Isabella's dead, whose abdication
> Set all tongues wagging in the Spanish nation.
> For that performance 'twere unfair to scold her
> She wisely left a throne too hot to hold her.
> To History she'll be no royal riddle—
> Merely a plain parched pea that jumped the griddle.
>
> *G.J.*

Abdomen, *n.* The temple of the god Stomach, in whose worship, with sacrificial rights, all true men engage. From women this ancient faith commands but a stammering assent. They sometimes minister at the altar in a half-hearted and ineffective way, but true reverence for the one deity that men really adore they know not. If woman had a free hand in the world's marketing the race would become graminivorous.

Ability, *n.* The natural equipment to accomplish some small part of the

meaner ambitions distinguishing able men from dead ones. In the
last analysis ability is commonly found to consist mainly in a high
degree of solemnity. Perhaps, however, this impressive quality is
rightly appraised; it is no easy task to be solemn.

Abnormal, *adj.* Not conforming to standard. In matters of thought and
conduct, to be independent is to be abnormal, to be abnormal is to
be detested. Wherefore the lexicographer adviseth a striving
toward a straiter resemblance to the Average Man than he hath to
himself. Whoso attaineth thereto shall have peace, the prospect of
death and the hope of Hell.

Aborigines, *n.* Persons of little worth found cumbering the soil of a
newly discovered country. They soon cease to cumber; they fertil-
ize.

Abracadabra.

> By *Abracadabra* we signify
>   An infinite number of things.
> 'Tis the answer to What? and How? and Why?
> And Whence? and Whither?—a word whereby
>   The Truth (with the comfort it brings)
> Is open to all who grope in night,
> Crying for Wisdom's holy light.
>
> Whether the word is a verb or a noun
>   Is knowledge beyond my reach.
> I only know that 'tis handed down
>   From sage to sage,
>   From age to age—
>   An immortal part of speech!
>
> Of an ancient man the tale is told
> That he lived to be ten centuries old,
>   In a cave on a mountain side.
>   (True, he finally died.)
> The fame of his wisdom filled the land,
> For his head was bald, and you'll understand
>   His beard was long and white
>   And his eyes uncommonly bright.

Philosophers gathered from far and near
To sit at his feet and hear and hear,
  Though he never was heard
  To utter a word
 But *"Abracadabra, abracadab,*
 Abracada, abracad,
 Abraca, abrac, abra, ab!"
  'Twas all he had,
'Twas all they wanted to hear, and each
Made copious notes of the mystical speech,
  Which they published next—
  A trickle of text
In a meadow of commentary.
 Mighty big books were these,
 In number, as leaves of trees;
In learning, remarkable—very!

  He's dead,
  As I said,
And the books of the sages have perished,
But his wisdom is sacredly cherished.
In *Abracadabra* it solemnly rings,
Like an ancient bell that forever swings.
  O, I love to hear
  That word make clear
Humanity's General Sense of Things.

          Jamrach Holobom

Abridge, *v.t.* To shorten.

When in the course of human events it becomes necessary for
a people to abridge their king, a decent respect for the opinions of mankind requires that they should declare the causes
which impel them to the separation.—*Oliver Cromwell.*

Abrupt, *adj.* Sudden, without ceremony, like the arrival of a cannon-
shot and the departure of the soldier whose interests are most
affected by it. Dr. Samuel Johnson beautifully said of another
author's ideas that they were "concatenated without abruption."

Abscond, *v.i.* To "move in a mysterious way," commonly with the property of another.

Spring beckons! All things to the call respond;
The trees are leaving and cashiers abscond.

Phela Orm

Absent, *adj.* Peculiarly exposed to the tooth of detraction; vilified; hopelessly in the wrong; superseded in the consideration and affection of another.

To men a man is but a mind. Who cares
What face he carries or what form he wears?
But woman's body is the woman. O,
Stay thou, my sweetheart, and do never go,
But heed the warning the sage hath said:
A woman absent is a woman dead.

Jogo Tyree

Absentee, *n.* A person with an income who has had the forethought to remove himself from the sphere of exaction.

Absolute, *adj.* Independent, irresponsible. An absolute monarchy is one in which the sovereign does as he pleases so long as he pleases the assassins. Not many absolute monarchies are left, most of them having been replaced by limited monarchies, where the sovereign's power for evil (and for good) is greatly curtailed, and by republics, which are governed by chance.

Abstainer, *n.* A weak person who yields to the temptation of denying himself a pleasure. A total abstainer is one who abstains from everything but abstention, and especially from inactivity in the affairs of others.

Said a man to a crapulent youth: "I thought
   You a total abstainer, my son."
"So I am, so I am," said the scapegrace caught—
   "But not, sir, a bigoted one."

G.J.

Absurdity, *n.* A statement of belief manifestly inconsistent with one's own opinion.

Academe, *n.* An ancient school where morality and philosophy were taught.

Academy, *n.* (from academe). A modern school where football is taught.

Accident, *n.* An inevitable occurrence due to the action of immutable natural laws.

Accomplice, *n.* One associated with another in a crime, having guilty knowledge and complicity, as an attorney who defends a criminal, knowing him guilty. This view of the attorney's position in the matter has not hitherto commanded the assent of attorneys, no one having offered them a fee for assenting.

Accord, *n.* Harmony.

Accordion, *n.* An instrument in harmony with the sentiments of an assassin.

Accountability, *n.* The mother of caution.

> "My accountability, bear in mind,"
>   Said the Grand Vizier: "Yes, yes,"
> Said the Shah: "I do—'tis the only kind
>   Of ability you possess."
>
> *Joram Tate*

Accuse, *v.t.* To affirm another's guilt or unworth; most commonly as a justification of ourselves for having wronged him.

Acephalous, *adj.* In the surprising condition of the Crusader who absently pulled at his forelock some hours after a Saracen scimitar had, unconsciously to him, passed through his neck, as related by de Joinville.

Achievement, *n.* The death of endeavor and the birth of disgust.

Acknowledge, *v.t.* To confess. Acknowledgment of one another's faults is the highest duty imposed by our love of truth.

Acquaintance, *n.* A person whom we know well enough to borrow from, but not well enough to lend to. A degree of friendship called slight when its object is poor or obscure, and intimate when he is rich or famous.

Actually, *adv.* Perhaps; possibly.

Adage, *n.* Boned wisdom for weak teeth.

Adamant, *n.* A mineral frequently found beneath a corset. Soluble in solicitate of gold.

Adder, *n.* A species of snake. So called from its habit of adding funeral outlays to the other expenses of living.

Adherent, *n.* A follower who has not yet obtained all that he expects to get.

Administration, *n.* An ingenious abstraction in politics, designed to receive the kicks and cuffs due to the premier or president. A man of straw, proof against bad-egging and dead-catting.

Admiral, n. That part of a war-ship which does the talking while the figure-head does the thinking.

Admiration, *n.* Our polite recognition of another's resemblance to ourselves.

Admonition, *n.* Gentle reproof, as with a meat-axe. Friendly warning.

> Consigned, by way of admonition,
> His soul forever to perdition.
>
> *Judibras*

Adore, *v.t.* To venerate expectantly.

Advice, *n.* The smallest current coin.

> "The man was in such deep distress,"
> Said Tom, "that I could do no less
> Than give him good advice." Said Jim:
> "If less could have been done for him
> I know you well enough, my son,
> To know that's what you would have done."
>
> *Jebel Jocordy*

Affianced, *pp.* Fitted with an ankle-ring for the ball-and-chain.

Affliction, *n.* An acclimatizing process preparing the soul for another and bitter world.

African, *n.* A nigger that votes our way.

Age, *n.* That period of life in which we compound for the vices that we still cherish by reviling those that we have no longer the enterprise to commit.

Agitator, *n.* A statesman who shakes the fruit trees of his neighbors—to dislodge the worms.

Aim, *n.* The task we set our wishes to.

> "Cheer up! Have you no aim in life?"
> She tenderly inquired.
> "An aim? Well, no, I haven't, wife;
> The fact is—I have fired."
>
> G.J.

Air, *n.* A nutritious substance supplied by a bountiful Providence for the fattening of the poor.

Alderman, *n.* An ingenious criminal who covers his secret thieving with a pretence of open marauding.

Alien, *n.* An American sovereign in his probationary state.

Allah, *n.* The Mahometan Supreme Being, as distinguished from the Christian, Jewish, and so forth.

> Allah's good laws I faithfully have kept,
> And ever for the sins of man have wept;
>   And sometimes kneeling in the temple I
> Have reverently crossed my hands and slept.
>
> Junker Barlow

Allegiance, *n.*

> This thing Allegiance, as I suppose,
> Is a ring fitted in the subject's nose,
> Whereby that organ is kept rightly pointed
> To smell the sweetness of the Lord's anointed.
>
> G.J.

Alliance, *n.* In international politics, the union of two thieves who have their hands so deeply inserted in each other's pocket that they cannot separately plunder a third.

Alligator, *n.* The crocodile of America, superior in every detail to the crocodile of the effete monarchies of the Old World. Herodotus says the Indus is, with one exception, the only river that produces crocodiles, but they appear to have gone West and grown up with the other rivers. From the notches on his back the alligator is called a sawrian.

Alone, *adj.* In bad company.

> In contact, lo! the flint and steel,
> By spark and flame, the thought reveal
> That he the metal, she the stone,
> Had cherished secretly alone.
>
> *Booley Fito*

Altar, *n.* The place whereon the priest formerly raveled out the small intestine of the sacrificial victim for purposes of divination and cooked its flesh for the gods. The word is now seldom used, except with reference to the sacrifice of their liberty and peace by a male and a female fool.

> They stood before the altar and supplied
> The fire themselves in which their fat was fried.
> In vain the sacrifice!—no god will claim
> An offering burnt with an unholy flame.
>
> *M.P. Nopput*

Ambidextrous, *adj.* Able to pick with equal skill a right-hand pocket or a left.

Ambition, *n.* An overmastering desire to be vilified by enemies while living and made ridiculous by friends when dead.

Amnesty, *n.* The state's magnanimity to those offenders whom it would be too expensive to punish.

Anoint, *v.t.* To grease a king or other great functionary already sufficiently slippery.

> As sovereigns are anointed by the priesthood,
> So pigs to lead the populace are greased good.
>
> *Judibras*

Antipathy, *n.* The sentiment inspired by one's friend's friend.

Aphorism, *n.* Predigested wisdom.

> The flabby wine-skin of his brain
> Yields to some pathologic strain,
> And voids from its unstored abysm
> The driblet of an aphorism.
>
> *"The Mad Philosopher," 1697*

Apologize, *v.i.* To lay the foundation for a future offence.

Apostate, *n.* A leech who, having penetrated the shell of a turtle only to find that the creature has long been dead, deems it expedient to form a new attachment to a fresh turtle.

Apothecary, *n.* The physician's accomplice, undertaker's benefactor and grave worm's provider.

> When Jove sent blessings to all men that are,
> And Mercury conveyed them in a jar,
> That friend of tricksters introduced by stealth
> Disease for the apothecary's health,
> Whose gratitude impelled him to proclaim:
> "My deadliest drug shall bear my patron's name!"
>
> *G.J.*

Appeal, *v.t.* In law, to put the dice into the box for another throw.

Appetite, *n.* An instinct thoughtfully implanted by Providence as a solution to the labor question.

Applause, *n.* The echo of a platitude.

April Fool, *n.* The March fool with another month added to his folly.

Archbishop, *n.* An ecclesiastical dignitary one point holier than a bishop.

> If I were a jolly archbishop,
> On Fridays I'd eat all the fish up—
> Salmon and flounders and smelts;
> On other days everything else.
>
> *Joho Rem*

Architect, *n.* One who drafts a plan of your house, and plans a draft of your money.

Ardor, *n.* The quality that distinguishes love without knowledge.

Arena, *n.* In politics, an imaginary rat-pit in which the statesman wrestles with his record.

Aristocracy, *n.* Government by the best men. (In this sense the word is obsolete; so is that kind of government.) Fellows that wear downy hats and clean shirts—guilty of education and suspected of bank accounts.

Armor, *n.* The kind of clothing worn by a man whose tailor is a blacksmith.

Arrayed, *pp.* Drawn up and given an orderly disposition, as a rioter hanged to a lamp-post.

Arrest, *v.t.* Formally to detain one accused of unusualness.
     God made the world in six days and was arrested on the seventh.— *The Unauthorized Version.*

Arsenic, *n.* A kind of cosmetic greatly affected by the ladies, whom it greatly affects in turn.

> "Eat arsenic? Yes, all you get,"
>   Consenting, he did speak up;
> "'Tis better you should eat it, pet,
>   Than put it in my teacup."
>
>   *Joel Huck*

Art, *n.* This word has no definition. Its origin is related as follows by the ingenious Father Gassalasca Jape, S.J.

> One day a wag—what would the wretch be at?—
> Shifted a letter of the cipher RAT,
> And said it was a god's name! Straight arose
> Fantastic priests and postulants (with shows,
> And mysteries, and mummeries, and hymns,
> And disputations dire that lamed their limbs)
> To serve his temple and maintain the fires,
> Expound the law, manipulate the wires.

Amazed, the populace the rites attend,
Believe whate'er they cannot comprehend,
And, inly edified to learn that two
Half-hairs joined so and so (as Art can do)
Have sweeter values and a grace more fit
Than Nature's hairs that never have been split,
Bring cates and wines for sacrificial feasts,
And sell their garments to support the priests.

Artlessness, *n.* A certain engaging quality to which women attain by long study and severe practice upon the admiring male, who is pleased to fancy it resembles the candid simplicity of his young.

Asperse, *v.t.* Maliciously to ascribe to another vicious actions which one has not had the temptation and opportunity to commit.

Ass, *n.* A public singer with a good voice but no ear. In Virginia City, Nevada, he is called the Washoe Canary, in Dakota, the Senator, and everywhere the Donkey. The animal is widely and variously celebrated in the literature, art and religion of every age and country; no other so engages and fires the human imagination as this noble vertebrate. Indeed, it is doubted by some (Ramasilus, *lib. II., De Clem.,* and C. Stantatus, *De Temperamente*) if it is not a god; and as such we know it was worshiped by the Etruscans, and, if we may believe Macrobious, by the Cupasians also. Of the only two animals admitted into the Mahometan Paradise along with the souls of men, the ass that carried Balaam is one, the dog of the Seven Sleepers the other. This is no small distinction. From what has been written about this beast might be compiled a library of great splendor and magnitude, rivaling that of the Shakspearean cult, and that which clusters about the Bible. It may be said, generally, that all literature is more or less Asinine.

"Hail, holy Ass!" the quiring angels sing;
"Priest of Unreason, and of Discords King!
Great co-Creator, let Thy glory shine:
God made all else; the Mule, the Mule is thine!"

G.J.

Auctioneer, *n.* The man who proclaims with a hammer that he has picked a pocket with his tongue.

Ambrose Bierce

Australia, *n.* A country lying in the South Sea, whose industrial and commercial development has been unspeakably retarded by an unfortunate dispute among geographers as to whether it is a continent or an island.

Avernus, *n.* The lake by which the ancients entered the infernal regions. The fact that access to the infernal regions was obtained by a lake is believed by the learned Marcus Ansello Scrutator to have suggested the Christian rite of baptism by immersion. This, however, has been shown by Lactantius to be an error.

> *Facilis descensus Averni,*
>   The poet remarks; and the sense
> Of it is that when down-hill I turn I
>   Will get more of punches than pence.
>
> *Jehal Dai Lupe*

Baal, *n*. An old deity formerly much worshiped under various names. As Baal he was popular with the Phoenicians; as Belus or Bel he had the honor to be served by the priest Berosus, who wrote the famous account of the Deluge; as Babel he had a tower partly erected to his glory on the Plain of Shinar. From Babel comes our English word "Babble." Under whatever name worshiped, Baal is the Sun-god. As Beelzebub he is the god of flies, which are begotten of the sun's rays on stagnant water. In Physicia Baal is still worshiped as Bolus, and as Belly he is adored and served with abundant sacrifice by the priests of Guttledom.

Babe or **Baby,** *n*. A misshapen creature of no particular age, sex, or condition, chiefly remarkable for the violence of the sympathies and antipathies it excites in others, itself without sentiment or emotion. There have been famous babes; for example, little Moses, from whose adventure in the bulrushes the Egyptian hierophants of seven centuries before doubtless derived their idle tale of the child Osiris being preserved on a floating lotus leaf.

> Ere babes were invented
> The girls were contented.
> Now man is tormented
> Until to buy babes he has squandered
> His money. And so I have pondered
> This thing, and thought may be

'T were better that Baby
The First had been eagled or condored.

Ro Amil

Bacchus, *n.* A convenient deity invented by the ancients as an excuse for getting drunk.

Is public worship, then, a sin,
    That for devotions paid to Bacchus
The lictors dare to run us in,
    And resolutely thump and whack us?

Jorace

Back, *n.* That part of your friend which it is your privilege to contemplate in your adversity.

Backbite, *v.t.* To speak of a man as you find him when he can't find you.

Bait, *n.* A preparation that renders the hook more palatable. The best kind is beauty.

Baptism, *n.* A sacred rite of such efficacy that he who finds himself in heaven without having undergone it will be unhappy forever. It is performed with water in two ways—by immersion, or plunging, and by aspersion, or sprinkling.

But whether the plan of immersion
Is better than simple aspersion
    Let those immersed
    And those aspersed
Decide by the Authorized Version,
And by matching their agues tertian.

G.J.

Barometer, *n.* An ingenious instrument which indicates what kind of weather we are having.

Barrack, *n.* A house in which soldiers enjoy a portion of that of which it is their business to deprive others.

Basilisk, *n.* The cockatrice. A sort of serpent hatched from the egg of a cock. The basilisk had a bad eye, and its glance was fatal. Many infidels deny this creature's existence, but Semprello Aurator saw and handled one that had been blinded by lightning as a punishment for having fatally gazed on a lady of rank whom Jupiter loved. Juno afterward restored the reptile's sight and hid it in a cave. Nothing is so well attested by the ancients as the existence of the basilisk, but the cocks have stopped laying.

Bastinado, *n.* The act of walking on wood without exertion.

Bath, *n.* A kind of mystic ceremony substituted for religious worship, with what spiritual efficacy has not been determined.

> The man who taketh a steam bath
> He loseth all the skin he hath,
> And, for he's boiled a brilliant red,
> Thinketh to cleanliness he's wed,
> Forgetting that his lungs he's soiling
> With dirty vapors of the boiling.
>
> *Richard Gwow*

Battle, *n.* A method of untying with the teeth a political knot that would not yield to the tongue.

Beard, *n.* The hair that is commonly cut off by those who justly execrate the absurd Chinese custom of shaving the head.

Beauty, *n.* The power by which a woman charms a lover and terrifies a husband.

Befriend, *v.t.* To make an ingrate.

Beg, *v.* To ask for something with an earnestness proportioned to the belief that it will not be given.

> Who is that, father?
>
>> A mendicant, child,
>> Haggard, morose, and unaffable—wild!
>> See how he glares through the bars of his cell!
>> With Citizen Mendicant all is not well.
>
> Why did they put him there, father?
>
>> Because
>> Obeying his belly he struck at the laws.
>
> His belly?

Oh, well, he was starving, my boy—
A state in which, doubtless, there's little of joy.
No bite had he eaten for days, and his cry
Was "Bread!" ever "Bread!"

What's the matter with pie?

With little to wear, he had nothing to sell;
To beg was unlawful—improper as well.

Why didn't he work?

He would even have done that,
But men said: "Get out!" and the State remarked:
"Scat!"
I mention these incidents merely to show
That the vengeance he took was uncommonly low.
Revenge, at the best, is the act of a Siou,
But for trifles—

Pray what did bad Mendicant do?

Stole two loaves of bread to replenish his lack
And tuck out the belly that clung to his back.

Is that *all*, father dear?

There is little to tell:
They sent him to jail, and they'll send him to—well,
The company's better than here we can boast,
And there's—

Bread for the needy, dear father?

Um—toast.

Atka Mip

Beggar, *n.* One who has relied on the assistance of his friends.

Behavior, *n.* Conduct, as determined, not by principle, but by breeding.
The word seems to be somewhat loosely used in Dr. Jamrach
Holobom's translation of the following lines in the *Dies Iræ*:

> Recordare, Jesu pie,
> Quod sum causa tuæ viæ.
> Ne me perdas illa die.

> Pray remember, sacred Savior,
> Whose the thoughtless hand that gave your
> Death-blow. Pardon such behavior.

Belladonna, *n.* In Italian a beautiful lady; in English a deadly poison. A striking example of the essential identity of the two tongues.

Benedictines, *n.* An order of monks otherwise known as black friars.

> She thought it a crow, but it turned out to be
> A monk of St. Benedict croaking a text.
> "Here's one of an order of cooks," said she—
> "Black friars in this world, fried black in the next."
> > *"The Devil on Earth" (London, 1712)*

Benefactor, *n.* One who makes heavy purchases of ingratitude, without, however, materially affecting the price, which is still within the means of all.

Berenice's Hair, *n.* A constellation (*Coma Berenices*) named in honor of one who sacrificed her hair to save her husband.

> Her locks an ancient lady gave
> Her loving husband's life to save;
> And men—they honored so the dame—
> Upon some stars bestowed her name.

> But to our modern married fair,
> Who'd give their lords to save their hair,
> No stellar recognition's given.
> There are not stars enough in heaven.
> > *G.J.*

Bigamy, *n.* A mistake in taste for which the wisdom of the future will adjudge a punishment called trigamy.

Bigot, *n.* One who is obstinately and zealously attached to an opinion that you do not entertain.

Billingsgate, *n.* The invective of an opponent.

Birth, *n.* The first and direst of all disasters. As to the nature of it there appears to be no uniformity. Castor and Pollux were born from the egg. Pallas came out of a skull. Galatea was once a block of stone. Peresilis, who wrote in the tenth century, avers that he grew up out of the ground where a priest had spilled holy water. It is known that Arimaxus was derived from a hole in the earth, made by a stroke of lightning. Leucomedon was the son of a cavern in Mount Ætna, and I have myself seen a man come out of a wine cellar.

Blackguard, *n.* A man whose qualities, prepared for display like a box of berries in a market—the fine ones on top—have been opened on the wrong side. An inverted gentleman.

Blank-verse, *n.* Unrhymed iambic pentameters—the most difficult kind of English verse to write acceptably; a kind, therefore, much affected by those who cannot acceptably write any kind.

Body-snatcher, *n.* A robber of grave-worms. One who supplies the young physicians with that with which the old physicians have supplied the undertaker. The hyena.

> "One night," a doctor said, "last fall,
> I and my comrades, four in all,
>   When visiting a graveyard stood
> Within the shadow of a wall.
>
> "While waiting for the moon to sink
> We saw a wild hyena slink
>   About a new-made grave, and then
> Begin to excavate its brink!
>
> "Shocked by the horrid act, we made
> A sally from our ambuscade,
>   And, falling on the unholy beast,
> Dispatched him with a pick and spade."
>
> *Bettel K. Jhones*

Bondsman, *n.* A fool who, having property of his own, undertakes to become responsible for that entrusted by another to a third.

Philippe of Orleans wishing to appoint one of his favorites, a dissolute nobleman, to a high office, asked him what security he would be able to give. "I need no bondsmen," he replied, "for I can give you my word of honor." "And pray what may be the value of that?" inquired the amused Regent. "Monsieur, it is worth its weight in gold."

Bore, *n.* A person who talks when you wish him to listen.

Botany, *n.* The science of vegetables—those that are not good to eat, as well as those that are. It deals largely with their flowers, which are commonly badly designed, inartistic in color, and ill-smelling.

Bottle-nosed, *adj.* Having a nose created in the image of its maker.

Boundary, *n.* In political geography, an imaginary line between two nations, separating the imaginary rights of one from the imaginary rights of the other.

Bounty, *n.* The liberality of one who has much, in permitting one who has nothing to get all that he can.

> A single swallow, it is said, devours ten millions of insects every year. The supplying of these insects I take to be a signal instance of the Creator's bounty in providing for the lives of His creatures.
>
> *Henry Ward Beecher*

Brahma, *n.* He who created the Hindoos, who are preserved by Vishnu and destroyed by Siva—a rather neater division of labor than is found among the deities of some other nations. The Abracadabranese, for example, are created by Sin, maintained by Theft and destroyed by Folly. The priests of Brahma, like those of the Abracadabranese, are holy and learned men who are never naughty.

> O Brahma, thou rare old Divinity,
> First Person of the Hindoo Trinity,
> You sit there so calm and securely,
> With feet folded up so demurely—
> You're the First Person Singular, surely.
>
> *Polydore Smith*

Brain, *n.* An apparatus with which we think that we think. That which distinguishes the man who is content to *be* something from the man who wishes to *do* something. A man of great wealth, or one who has been pitchforked into high station, has commonly such a headful of brain that his neighbors cannot keep their hats on. In our civilization, and under our republican form of government, brain is so highly honored that it is rewarded by exemption from the cares of office.

Brandy, *n.* A cordial composed of one part thunder-and-lightning, one part remorse, two parts bloody murder, one part death-hell-and-the-grave and four parts clarified Satan. Dose, a headful all the time. Brandy is said by Dr. Johnson to be the drink of heroes. Only a hero will venture to drink it.

Bride, *n.* A woman with a fine prospect of happiness behind her.

Brute, *n.* See HUSBAND.

Caaba, *n.* A large stone presented by the archangel Gabriel to the patriarch Abraham, and preserved at Mecca. The patriarch had perhaps asked the archangel for bread.

Cabbage, *n.* A familiar kitchen-garden vegetable about as large and wise as a man's head.

The cabbage is so called from Cabagius, a prince who on ascending the throne issued a decree appointing a High Council of Empire consisting of the members of his predecessor's Ministry and the cabbages in the royal garden. When any of his Majesty's measures of state policy miscarried conspicuously it was gravely announced that several members of the High Council had been beheaded, and his murmuring subjects were appeased.

Calamity, *n.* A more than commonly plain and unmistakable reminder that the affairs of this life are not of our own ordering. Calamities are of two kinds: misfortune to ourselves, and good fortune to others.

Callous, *adj.* Gifted with great fortitude to bear the evils afflicting another.

When Zeno was told that one of his enemies was no more he was observed to be deeply moved. "What!" said one of his disciples, "you weep at the death of an enemy?" "Ah, 'tis true," replied the great Stoic; "but you should see me smile at the death of a friend."

Calumnus, *n.* A graduate of the School for Scandal.

Camel, *n.* A quadruped (the *Splaypes humpidorsus*) of great value to the show business. There are two kinds of camels—the camel proper and the camel improper. It is the latter that is always exhibited.

Cannibal, *n.* A gastronome of the old school who preserves the simple tastes and adheres to the natural diet of the pre-pork period.

Cannon, *n.* An instrument employed in the rectification of national boundaries.

Canonicals, *n.* The motley worn by Jesters of the Court of Heaven.

Capital, *n.* The seat of misgovernment. That which provides the fire, the pot, the dinner, the table and the knife and fork for the anarchist; the part of the repast that himself supplies is the disgrace before meat. *Capital Punishment*, a penalty regarding the justice and expediency of which many worthy persons—including all the assassins—entertain grave misgivings.

Carmelite, *n.* A mendicant friar of the order of Mount Carmel.

> As Death was a-riding out one day,
> Across Mount Carmel he took his way,
>   Where he met a mendicant monk,
>   Some three or four quarters drunk,
> With a holy leer and a pious grin,
> Ragged and fat and as saucy as sin,
>   Who held out his hands and cried:
> "Give, give in Charity's name, I pray.
> Give in the name of the Church. O give,
> Give that her holy sons may live!"
>   And Death replied,
>   Smiling long and wide:
> "I'll give, holy father, I'll give thee—a ride."
>
>   With a rattle and bang
>   Of his bones, he sprang
> From his famous Pale Horse, with his spear;
>   By the neck and the foot
>   Seized the fellow, and put
> Him astride with his face to the rear.

The Monarch laughed loud with a sound that fell
Like clods on the coffin's sounding shell:
"Ho, ho! A beggar on horseback, they say,
   Will ride to the devil!"—and *thump*
   Fell the flat of his dart on the rump
Of the charger, which galloped away.

Faster and faster and faster it flew,
Till the rocks and the flocks and the trees that grew
By the road were dim and blended and blue
   To the wild, wide eyes
   Of the rider—in size

   Resembling a couple of blackberry pies.
Death laughed again, as a tomb might laugh
   At a burial service spoiled,
   And the mourners' intentions foiled
   By the body erecting
   Its head and objecting
To further proceedings in its behalf.

Many a year and many a day
Have passed since these events away.
The monk has long been a dusty corse,
And Death has never recovered his horse.
   For the friar got hold of its tail,
   And steered it within the pale
Of the monastery gray,
Where the beast was stabled and fed
With barley and oil and bread
Till fatter it grew than the fattest friar,
And so in due course was appointed Prior.

                                         G.J.

Carnivorous, *adj.* Addicted to the cruelty of devouring the timorous vegetarian, his heirs and assigns.

Cartesian, *adj.* Relating to Descartes, a famous philosopher, author of the celebrated dictum, *Cogito ergo sum*—whereby he was pleased to suppose he demonstrated the reality of human existence. The dictum might be improved, however, thus: *Cogito cogito ergo cogito sum*—"I think that I think, therefore I think that I am;" as close an approach to certainty as any philosopher has yet made.

Cat, *n.* A soft, indestructible automaton provided by nature to be kicked when things go wrong in the domestic circle.

> This is a dog,
>   This is a cat,
> This is a frog,
>   This is a rat.
> Run, dog, mew, cat,
> Jump, frog, gnaw, rat.
>
> *Elevenson*

Caviler, *n.* A critic of our own work.

Cemetery, *n.* An isolated suburban spot where mourners match lies, poets write at a target and stone-cutters spell for a wager. The inscriptions following will serve to illustrate the success attained in these Olympian games:

> His virtues were so conspicuous that his enemies, unable to overlook them, denied them, and his friends, to whose loose lives they were a rebuke, represented them as vices. They are here commemorated by his family, who shared them.

> In the earth we here prepare a
> Place to lay our little Clara.
>   *—Thomas M. and Mary Frazer*
> P.S.—Gabriel will raise her.

Centaur, *n.* One of a race of persons who lived before the division of labor had been carried to such a pitch of differentiation, and who followed the primitive economic maxim, "Every man his own horse." The best of the lot was Chiron, who to the wisdom and virtues of the horse added the fleetness of man. The scripture story of the head of John the Baptist on a charger shows that pagan myths have somewhat sophisticated sacred history.

Cerberus, *n.* The watch-dog of Hades, whose duty it was to guard the entrance—against whom or what does not clearly appear; everybody, sooner or later, had to go there, and nobody wanted to carry off the entrance. Cerberus is know to have had three heads, and some of the poets have credited him with as many as a hundred. Professor Graybill, whose clerky erudition and profound knowl-

edge of Greek give his opinion great weight, has averaged all the
estimates, and makes the number twenty-seven—a judgment that
would be entirely conclusive if Professor Graybill had known *(a)*
something about dogs, and *(b)* something about arithmetic.

Childhood, *n.* The period of human life intermediate between the idiocy of infancy and the folly of youth—two removes from the sin of
manhood and three from the remorse of age.

Christian, *n.* One who believes that the New Testament is a divinely
inspired book admirably suited to the spiritual needs of his neighbor. One who follows the teachings of Christ in so far as they are
not inconsistent with a life of sin.

> I dreamed I stood upon a hill, and, lo!
> The godly multitudes walked to and fro
> Beneath, in Sabbath garments fitly clad,
> With pious mien, appropriately sad,
> While all the church bells made a solemn din—
> A fire-alarm to those who lived in sin.
> Then saw I gazing thoughtfully below,
> With tranquil face, upon that holy show
> A tall, spare figure in a robe of white,
> Whose eyes diffused a melancholy light.
> "God keep you, stranger," I exclaimed. "You are
> No doubt (your habit shows it) from afar;
> And yet I entertain the hope that you,
> Like these good people, are a Christian too."
> He raised his eyes and with a look so stern
> It made me with a thousand blushes burn
> Replied—his manner with disdain was spiced:
> "What! I a Christian? No, indeed! I'm Christ."
>
>   *G.J.*

Circus, *n.* A place where horses, ponies and elephants are permitted to
see men, women and children acting the fool.

Clairvoyant, *n.* A person, commonly a woman, who has the power of
seeing that which is invisible to her patron—namely, that he is a
blockhead.

Clarionet, *n.* An instrument of torture operated by a person with cotton in his ears. There are two instruments that are worse than a clarionet—two clarionets.

Clergyman, *n.* A man who undertakes the management of our spiritual affairs as a method of bettering his temporal ones.

Clio, *n.* One of the nine Muses. Clio's function was to preside over history—which she did with great dignity, many of the prominent citizens of Athens occupying seats on the platform, the meetings being addressed by Messrs. Xenophon, Herodotus and other popular speakers.

Clock, *n.* A machine of great moral value to man, allaying his concern for the future by reminding him what a lot of time remains to him.

> A busy man complained one day:
> "I get no time!" "What's that you say?"
> Cried out his friend, a lazy quiz;
> "You have, sir, all the time there is.
> There's plenty, too, and don't you doubt it—
> We're never for an hour without it."
>
> *Purzil Crofe*

Close-fisted, *adj.* Unduly desirous of keeping that which many meritorious persons wish to obtain.

> "Close-fisted Scotchman!" Johnson cried
>   To thrifty J. Macpherson;
> "See me—I'm ready to divide
>   With any worthy person."
>
> Said Jamie: "That is very true—
>   The boast requires no backing;
> And all are worthy, sir, to you,
>   Who have what you are lacking."
>
> *Anita M. Bobe*

Cœnobite, *n.* A man who piously shuts himself up to meditate upon the sin of wickedness; and to keep it fresh in his mind joins a brotherhood of awful examples.

> O Cœnobite, O cœnobite,
>   Monastical gregarian,
> You differ from the anchorite,

That solitudinarian:
With vollied prayers you wound Old Nick;
With dropping shots he makes him sick.

Quincy Giles

Comfort, *n.* A state of mind produced by contemplation of a neighbor's uneasiness.

Commendation, *n.* The tribute that we pay to achievements that resemble, but do not equal, our own.

Commerce, *n.* A kind of transaction in which A plunders from B the goods of C, and for compensation B picks the pocket of D of money belonging to E.

Commonwealth, *n.* An administrative entity operated by an incalculable multitude of political parasites, logically active but fortuitously efficient.

This commonwealth's capitol's corridors view,
So thronged with a hungry and indolent crew
Of clerks, pages, porters and all attachés
Whom rascals appoint and the populace pays
That a cat cannot slip through the thicket of shins
Nor hear its own shriek for the noise of their chins.
On clerks and on pages, and porters, and all,
Misfortune attend and disaster befall!
May life be to them a succession of hurts;
May fleas by the bushel inhabit their shirts;
May aches and diseases encamp in their bones,
Their lungs full of tubercles, bladders of stones;
May microbes, bacilli, their tissues infest,
And tapeworms securely their bowels digest;
May corn-cobs be snared without hope in their hair,
And frequent impalement their pleasure impair.
Disturbed be their dreams by the awful discourse
Of audible sofas sepulchrally hoarse,
By chairs acrobatic and wavering floors—
The mattress that kicks and the pillow that snores!
Sons of cupidity, cradled in sin!
Your criminal ranks may the death angel thin,
Avenging the friend whom I couldn't work in.

K.Q.

Compromise, *n.* Such an adjustment of conflicting interests as gives each adversary the satisfaction of thinking he has got what he ought not to have, and is deprived of nothing except what was justly his due.

Compulsion, *n.* The eloquence of power.

Condole, *v.i.* To show that bereavement is a smaller evil than sympathy.

Confidant, Confidante, *n.* One entrusted by A with the secrets of B, confided by *him* to C.

Congratulation, *n.* The civility of envy.

Congress, *n.* A body of men who meet to repeal laws.

Connoisseur, *n.* A specialist who knows everything about something and nothing about anything else.

    An old wine-bibber having been smashed in a railway collision, some wine was poured upon his lips to revive him. "Pauillac, 1873," he murmured and died.

Conservative, *n.* A statesman who is enamored of existing evils, as distinguished from the Liberal, who wishes to replace them with others.

Consolation, *n.* The knowledge that a better man is more unfortunate than yourself.

Consul, *n.* In American politics, a person who having failed to secure an office from the people is given one by the Administration on condition that he leave the country.

Consult, *v.t.* To seek another's approval of a course already decided on.

Contempt, *n.* The feeling of a prudent man for an enemy who is too formidable safely to be opposed.

Controversy, n. A battle in which spittle or ink replaces the injurious cannonball and the inconsiderate bayonet.

      In controversy with the facile tongue—
      That bloodless warfare of the old and young—
      So seek your adversary to engage

That on himself he shall exhaust his rage,
And, like a snake that's fastened to the ground,
With his own fangs inflict the fatal wound.
You ask me how this miracle is done?
Adopt his own opinions, one by one,
And taunt him to refute them; in his wrath
He'll sweep them pitilessly from his path.
Advance then gently all you wish to prove,
Each proposition prefaced with, "As you've
So well remarked," or, "As you wisely say,
And I cannot dispute," or, "By the way,
This view of it which, better far expressed,
Runs through your argument." Then leave the rest
To him, secure that he'll perform his trust
And prove your views intelligent and just.

Conmore Apel Brune

Convent, *n.* A place of retirement for women who wish for leisure to meditate upon the vice of idleness.

Conversation, *n.* A fair for the display of the minor mental commodities, each exhibitor being too intent upon the arrangement of his own wares to observe those of his neighbor.

Coronation, *n.* The ceremony of investing a sovereign with the outward and visible signs of his divine right to be blown skyhigh with a dynamite bomb.

Corporal, *n.* A man who occupies the lowest rung of the military ladder.

Fiercely the battle raged and, sad to tell,
Our corporal heroically fell!
Fame from her height looked down upon the brawl
And said: "He hadn't very far to fall."

Giacomo Smith

Corporation, *n.* An ingenious device for obtaining individual profit without individual responsibility.

Corsair, *n.* A politician of the seas.

Court Fool, *n.* The plaintiff.

Coward, *n.* One who in a perilous emergency thinks with his legs.

Craft, *n.* A fool's substitute for brains.

Crayfish, *n.* A small crustacean very much resembling the lobster, but less indigestible.

> In this small fish I take it that human wisdom is admirably fig-
> ured and symbolized; for whereas the crayfish doth move only
> backward, and can have only retrospection, seeing naught but
> the perils already passed, so the wisdom of man doth not
> enable him to avoid the follies that beset his course, but only
> to apprehend their nature afterward.—*Sir James Merivale*

Creditor, *n.* One of a tribe of savages dwelling beyond the Financial Straits and dreaded for their desolating incursions.

Cremona, *n.* A high-priced violin made in Connecticut.

Critic, *n.* A person who boasts himself hard to please because nobody tries to please him.

> There is a land of pure delight,
>   Beyond the Jordan's flood,
> Where saints, apparelled all in white,
>   Fling back the critic's mud.
>
> And as he legs it through the skies,
>   His pelt a sable hue,
> He sorrows sore to recognize
>   The missiles that he threw.
>
> *Orrin Goof*

Cross, *n.* An ancient religious symbol erroneously supposed to owe its significance to the most solemn event in the history of Christianity, but really antedating it by thousands of years. By many it has been believed to be identical with the *crux ansata* of the ancient phallic worship, but it has been traced even beyond all that we know of that, to the rites of primitive peoples. We have to-day the White Cross as a symbol of chastity, and the Red Cross as a badge of benevolent neutrality in war. Having in mind the for-

mer, the reverend Father Gassalasca Jape smites the lyre to the
effect following:

> "Be good, be good!" the sisterhood
>   Cry out in holy chorus,
> And, to dissuade from sin, parade
>   Their various charms before us.
>
> But why, O why, has ne'er an eye
>   Seen her of winsome manner
> And youthful grace and pretty face
>   Flaunting the White Cross banner?
>
> Now where's the need of speech and screed
>   To better our behaving?
> A simpler plan for saving man
>   (But, first, is he worth saving?)
>
> Is, dears, when he declines to flee
>   From bad thoughts that beset him,
> Ignores the Law as 't were a straw,
>   And wants to sin—don't let him.

Cui Bono? (Latin). What good would that do *me*?

Cunning, *n.* The faculty that distinguishes a weak animal or person
from a strong one. It brings its possessor much mental satisfaction
and great material adversity. An Italian proverb says: "The furrier
gets the skins of more foxes than asses."

Cupid, *n.* The so-called god of love. This bastard creation of a barbarous fancy was no doubt inflicted upon mythology for the sins
of its deities. Of all unbeautiful and inappropriate conceptions this
is the most reasonless and offensive. The notion of symbolizing
sexual love by a semisexless babe, and comparing the pains of passion to the wounds of an arrow—of introducing this pudgy
homunculus into art grossly to materialize the subtle spirit and
suggestion of the work—this is eminently worthy of the age that,
giving its birth, laid it on the doorstep of posterity.

Curiosity, *n.* An objectionable quality of the female mind. The desire to know whether or not a woman is cursed with curiosity is one of the most active and insatiable passions of the masculine soul.

Curse, *v.t.* Energetically to belabor with a verbal slap-stick. This is an operation which in literature, particularly in the drama, is commonly fatal to the victim. Nevertheless, the liability to a cursing is a risk that cuts but a small figure in fixing the rates of life insurance.

Cynic, *n.* A blackguard whose faulty vision sees things as they are, not as they ought to be. Hence the custom among the Scythians of plucking out a cynic's eyes to improve his vision.

Damn, *v.* A word formerly much used by the Paphlagonians, the meaning of which is lost. By the learned Dr. Dolabelly Gak it is believed to have been a term of satisfaction, implying the highest possible degree of mental tranquillity. Professor Groke, on the contrary, thinks it expressed an emotion of tumultuous delight, because it so frequently occurs in combination with the word *jod or god,* meaning "joy." It would be with great diffidence that I should advance an opinion conflicting with that of either of these formidable authorities.

Dance, *v.i.* To leap about to the sound of tittering music, preferably with arms about your neighbor's wife or daughter. There are many kinds of dances, but all those requiring the participation of the two sexes have two characteristics in common: they are conspicuously innocent, and warmly loved by the vicious.

Danger, *n.*

> A savage beast which, when it sleeps,
>   Man girds at and despises,
> But takes himself away by leaps
>   And bounds when it arises.

Ambat Delaso

Daring, *n.* One of the most conspicuous qualities of a man in security.

Datary, *n.* A high ecclesiastic official of the Roman Catholic Church, whose important function is to brand the Pope's bulls with the words *Datum Romæ.* He enjoys a princely revenue and the friendship of God.

Dawn, *n.* The time when men of reason go to bed. Certain old men prefer to rise at about that time, taking a cold bath and a long walk with an empty stomach, and otherwise mortifying the flesh. They then point with pride to these practices as the cause of their sturdy health and ripe years; the truth being that they are hearty and old, not because of their habits, but in spite of them. The reason we find only robust persons doing this thing is that it has killed all the others who have tried it.

Day, *n.* A period of twenty-four hours, mostly misspent. This period is divided into two parts, the day proper and the night, or day improper—the former devoted to sins of business, the latter consecrated to the other sort. These two kinds of social activity overlap.

Dead, *adj.*

> Done with the work of breathing; done
> With all the world; the mad race run
> Through to the end; the golden goal
> Attained and found to be a hole!
>
> *Squatol Johnes*

Debauchee, *n.* One who has so earnestly pursued pleasure that he has had the misfortune to overtake it.

Debt, *n.* An ingenious substitute for the chain and whip of the slave-driver.

> As, pent in an aquarium, the troutlet
> Swims round and round his tank to find an outlet,
> Pressing his nose against the glass that holds him,
> Nor ever sees the prison that enfolds him;
> So the poor debtor, seeing naught around him,
> Yet feels the narrow limits that impound him,

Grieves at his debt and studies to evade it,
And finds at last he might as well have paid it.

Barlow S. Vode

Decalogue, *n.* A series of commandments, ten in number—just enough
to permit an intelligent selection for observance, but not enough
to embarrass the choice. Following is the revised edition of the
Decalogue, calculated for this meridian.

Thou shalt no God but me adore:
'Twere too expensive to have more.

No images nor idols make
For Robert Ingersoll to break.

Take not God's name in vain; select
A time when it will have effect.

Work not on Sabbath days at all,
But go to see the teams play ball.

Honor thy parents. That creates
For life insurance lower rates.

Kill not, abet not those who kill;
Thou shalt not pay thy butcher's bill.

Kiss not thy neighbor's wife, unless
Thine own thy neighbor doth caress.

Don't steal; thou'lt never thus compete
Successfully in business. Cheat.

Bear not false witness—that is low—
But "hear 'tis rumored so and so."

Covet thou naught that thou hast not
By hook or crook, or somehow, got.

G.J.

Decide, *v.i.* To succumb to the preponderance of one set of influences
over another set.

A leaf was riven from a tree,
"I mean to fall to earth," said he.

The west wind, rising, made him veer.
"Eastward," said he, "I now shall steer."

The east wind rose with greater force.
Said he: " 'Twere wise to change my course."

With equal power they contend.
He said: "My judgment I suspend."

Down died the winds; the leaf, elate,
Cried: "I've decided to fall straight."

"First thoughts are best?" That's not the moral;
Just choose your own and we'll not quarrel.

Howe'er your choice may chance to fall,
You'll have no hand in it at all.

G.J.

Defame, *v.t.* To lie about another. To tell the truth about another.

Defenceless, *adj.* Unable to attack.

Degenerate, *adj.* Less conspicuously admirable than one's ancestors. The contemporaries of Homer were striking examples of degeneracy; it required ten of them to raise a rock or a riot that one of the heroes of the Trojan war could have raised with ease. Homer never tires of sneering at "men who live in these degenerate days," which is perhaps why they suffered him to beg his bread—a marked instance of returning good for evil, by the way, for if they had forbidden him he would certainly have starved.

Degradation, *n.* One of the stages of moral and social progress from private station to political preferment.

Deinotherium, *n.* An extinct pachyderm that flourished when the Pterodactyl was in fashion. The latter was a native of Ireland, its name being pronounced Terry Dactyl or Peter O'Dactyl, as the man pronouncing it may chance to have heard it spoken or seen it printed.

Dejeuner, *n.* The breakfast of an American who has been in Paris. Variously pronounced.

Delegation, *n.* In American politics, an article of merchandise that comes in sets.

Deliberation, *n.* The act of examining one's bread to determine which side it is buttered on.

Deluge, *n.* A notable first experiment in baptism which washed away the sins (and sinners) of the world.

Delusion, *n.* The father of a most respectable family, comprising Enthusiasm, Affection, Self-denial, Faith, Hope, Charity and many other goodly sons and daughters.

> All hail, Delusion! Were it not for thee
> The world turned topsy-turvy we should see;
> For Vice, respectable with cleanly fancies,
> Would fly abandoned Virtue's gross advances.
> *Mumfrey Mappel*

Dentist, *n.* A prestidigitator who, putting metal into your mouth, pulls coins out of your pocket.

Dependent, *adj.* Reliant upon another's generosity for the support which you are not in a position to exact from his fears.

Deputy, *n.* A male relative of an office-holder, or of his bondsman. The deputy is commonly a beautiful young man, with a red necktie and an intricate system of cobwebs extending from his nose to his desk. When accidentally struck by the janitor's broom, he gives off a cloud of dust.

> "Chief Deputy," the Master cried,
> "To-day the books are to be tried
> By experts and accountants who
> Have been commissioned to go through
> Our office here, to see if we
> Have stolen injudiciously.
> Please have the proper entries made,
> The proper balances displayed,
> Conforming to the whole amount

Of cash on hand—which they will count.
I've long admired your punctual way—
Here at the break and close of day,
Confronting in your chair the crowd
Of business men, whose voices loud
And gestures violent you quell
By some mysterious, calm spell—
Some magic lurking in your look
That brings the noisiest to book
And spreads a holy and profound
Tranquillity o'er all around.
So orderly all's done that they
Who came to draw remain to pay.
But now the time demands, at last,
That you employ your genius vast
In energies more active. Rise
And shake the lightnings from your eyes;
Inspire your underlings, and fling
Your spirit into everything!"
The Master's hand here dealt a whack
Upon the Deputy's bent back,
When straightway to the floor there fell
A shrunken globe, a rattling shell,
A blackened, withered, eyeless head!
The man had been a twelvemonth dead.

Jamrach Holobom

Destiny, *n.* A tyrant's authority for crime and a fool's excuse for failure.

Diagnosis, *n.* A physician's forecast of disease by the patient's pulse and
purse.

Diaphragm, *n.* A muscular partition separating disorders of the chest
from disorders of the bowels.

Diary, *n.* A daily record of that part of one's life, which he can relate to
himself without blushing.

Hearst kept a diary wherein were writ
All that he had of wisdom and of wit.
So the Recording Angel, when Hearst died,
Erased all entries of his own and cried:
"I'll judge you by your diary." Said Hearst:
"Thank you; 'twill show you I am Saint the First"—

Straightway producing, jubilant and proud,
That record from a pocket in his shroud.
The Angel slowly turned the pages o'er,
Each stupid line of which he knew before,
Glooming and gleaming as by turns he hit
On shallow sentiment and stolen wit;
Then gravely closed the book and gave it back.
"My friend, you've wandered from your proper track:
You'd never be content this side the tomb—
For big ideas Heaven has little room,
And Hell's no latitude for making mirth,"
He said, and kicked the fellow back to earth.

"The Mad Philosopher"

Dictator, n. The chief of a nation that prefers the pestilence of despotism to the plague of anarchy.

Dictionary, n. A malevolent literary device for cramping the growth of a language and making it hard and inelastic. This dictionary, however, is a most useful work.

Die, n. The singular of "dice." We seldom hear the word, because there is a prohibitory proverb, "Never say die." At long intervals, however, some one says: "The die is cast," which is not true, for it is cut. The word is found in an immortal couplet by that eminent poet and domestic economist, Senator Depew:

A cube of cheese no larger than a die
May bait the trap to catch a nibbling mie.

Digestion, n. The conversion of victuals into virtues. When the process is imperfect, vices are evolved instead—a circumstance from which that wicked writer, Dr. Jeremiah Blenn, infers that the ladies are the greater sufferers from dyspepsia.

Diplomacy, n. The patriotic art of lying for one's country.

Disabuse, v.t. To present your neighbor with another and better error than the one which he has deemed it advantageous to embrace.

Discriminate, v.i. To note the particulars in which one person or thing is, if possible, more objectionable than another.

Discussion, n. A method of confirming others in their errors.

Disobedience, *n.* The silver lining to the cloud of servitude.

Disobey, *v.t.* To celebrate with an appropriate ceremony the maturity of a command.

> His right to govern me is clear as day,
> My duty manifest to disobey;
> And if that fit observance e'er I shun
> May I and duty be alike undone.
>
> *Israfel Brown*

Dissemble, *v.i.* To put a clean shirt upon the character.

> Let us dissemble.—Adam.

Distance, *n.* The only thing that the rich are willing for the poor to call theirs, and keep.

Distress, *n.* A disease incurred by exposure to the prosperity of a friend.

Divination, *n.* The art of nosing out the occult. Divination is of as many kinds as there are fruit-bearing varieties of the flowering dunce and the early fool.

Dog, *n.* A kind of additional or subsidiary Deity designed to catch the overflow and surplus of the world's worship. This Divine Being in some of his smaller and silkier incarnations, takes, in the affection of Woman, the place to which there is no human male aspirant. The Dog is a survival—an anachronism. He toils not, neither does he spin, yet Solomon in all his glory never lay upon a door-mat all day long, sun-soaked and fly—fed and fat, while his master worked for the means wherewith to purchase an idle wag of the Solomonic tail, seasoned with a look of tolerant recognition.

Dragoon, *n.* A soldier who combines dash and steadiness in so equal measure that he makes his advances on foot and his retreats on horseback.

Dramatist, *n.* One who adapts plays from the French.

Druids, *n.* Priests and ministers of an ancient Celtic religion which did not disdain to employ the humble allurement of human sacrifice. Very little is now known about the Druids and their faith. Pliny says their religion, originating in Britain, spread eastward as far as Persia. Cæsar says those who desired to study its mysteries went to Britain. Cæsar himself went to Britain, but does not appear to have obtained any high preferment in the Druidical Church, although his talent for human sacrifice was considerable.

Druids performed their religious rites in groves, and knew nothing of church mortgages and the season-ticket system of pew rents. They were, in short, heathens and—as they were once complacently catalogued by a distinguished prelate of the Church of England—Dissenters.

Duck-bill, *n.* Your account at your restaurant during the canvas-back season.

Duel, *n.* A formal ceremony preliminary to the reconciliation of two enemies. Great skill is necessary to its satisfactory observance; if awkwardly performed the most unexpected and deplorable consequences sometimes ensue. A long time ago a man lost his life in a duel.

> That dueling's a gentlemanly vice
>   I hold; and wish that it had been my lot
>   To live my life out in some favored spot—
> Some country where it is considered nice
> To split a rival like a fish, or slice
>   A husband like a spud, or with a shot
>   Bring down a debtor doubled in a knot
> And ready to be put upon the ice.
> Some miscreants there are, whom I do long
>   To shoot, or stab, or some such way reclaim
> The scurvy rogues to better lives and manners,
> I seem to see them now—a mighty throng.
>   It looks as if to challenge me they came,
> Jauntily marching with brass bands and banners!
>   *Xamba Q. Dar*

Dullard, *n.* A member of the reigning dynasty in letters and life. The Dullards came in with Adam, and being both numerous and sturdy have overrun the habitable world. The secret of their power is their insensibility to blows; tickle them with a bludgeon and they laugh with a platitude. The Dullards came originally from Bœotia,

whence they were driven by stress of starvation, their dulness having blighted the crops. For some centuries they infested Philistia,
and many of them are called Philistines to this day. In the turbulent
times of the Crusades they withdrew thence and gradually over-
spread all Europe, occupying most of the high places in politics,
art, literature, science and theology. Since a detachment of
Dullards came over with the Pilgrims in the *Mayflower* and made a
favorable report of the country, their increase by birth, immigra-
tion, and conversion has been rapid and steady. According to the
most trustworthy statistics the number of adult Dullards in the
United States is but little short of thirty millions, including the sta-
tisticians. The intellectual centre of the race is somewhere about
Peoria, Illinois, but the New England Dullard is the most shock-
ingly moral.

Duty, *n.* That which sternly impels us in the direction of profit, along
the line of desire.

> Sir Lavender Portwine, in favor at court,
> Was worth at his master, who'd kissed Lady Port.
> His anger provoked him to take the king's head,
> But duty prevailed, and he took the king's bread,
>   Instead.
>
>   G.J.

Eat, *v.i.* To perform successively (and successfully) the functions of mastication, humectation, and deglutition.

"I was in the drawing-room, enjoying my dinner," said Brillat-Savarin, beginning an anecdote. "What!" interrupted Rochebriant; "eating dinner in a drawing-room?" "I must beg you to observe, monsieur," explained the great gastronome, "that I did not say I was eating my dinner, but enjoying it. I had dined an hour before."

Eavesdrop, *v.i.* Secretly to overhear a catalogue of the crimes and vices of another or yourself.

> A lady with one of her ears applied
> To an open keyhole heard, inside,
> Two female gossips in converse free—
> The subject engaging them was she.
> "I think," said one, "and my husband thinks
> That she's a prying, inquisitive minx!"
> As soon as no more of it she could hear
> The lady, indignant, removed her ear.
> "I will not stay," she said, with a pout,
> "To hear my character lied about!"
>
> *Gopete Sherany*

Eccentricity, *n.* A method of distinction so cheap that fools employ it to accentuate their incapacity.

Economy, *n.* Purchasing the barrel of whiskey that you do not need for the price of the cow that you cannot afford.

Edible, *adj.* Good to eat, and wholesome to digest, as a worm to a toad, a toad to a snake, a snake to a pig, a pig to a man, and a man to a worm.

Editor, *n.* A person who combines the judicial functions of Minos, Rhadamanthus and Æacus, but is placable with an obolus; a severely virtuous censor, but so charitable withal that he tolerates the virtues of others and the vices of himself; who flings about him the splintering lightning and sturdy thunders of admonition till he resembles a bunch of firecrackers petulantly uttering its mind at the tail of a dog; then straightway murmurs a mild, melodious lay, soft as the cooing of a donkey intoning its prayer to the evening star. Master of mysteries and lord of law, high-pinnacled upon the throne of thought, his face suffused with the dim splendors of the Transfiguration, his legs intertwisted and his tongue a-cheek, the editor spills his will along the paper and cuts it off in lengths to suit. And at intervals from behind the veil of the temple is heard the voice of the foreman demanding three inches of wit and six lines of religious meditation, or bidding him turn off the wisdom and whack up some pathos.

> O, the Lord of Law on the Throne of Thought,
>   A gilded impostor is he.
> Of shreds and patches his robes are wrought,
>   His crown is brass,
>   Himself is an ass,
> And his power is fiddle-dee-dee.
> Prankily, crankily prating of naught,
> Silly old quilly old Monarch of Thought.
>   Public opinion's camp-follower he,
>   Thundering, blundering, plundering free.
>   Affected,
>   Ungracious,
>   Suspected,
>   Mendacious,
> Respected contemporaree!
>
>   *J.H. Bumbleshook*

Education, *n.* That which discloses to the wise and disguises from the foolish their lack of understanding.

Effect, *n.* The second of two phenomena which always occur together in the same order. The first, called a Cause, is said to generate the other—which is no more sensible than it would be for one who has never seen a dog except in pursuit of a rabbit to declare the rabbit the cause of the dog.

Egotist, *n.* A person of low taste, more interested in himself than in me.

> Megaceph, chosen to serve the State
> In the halls of legislative debate,
> One day with all his credentials came
> To the capitol's door and announced his name.
> The doorkeeper looked, with a comical twist
> Of the face, at the eminent egotist,
> And said: "Go away, for we settle here
> All manner of questions, knotty and queer,
> And we cannot have, when the speaker demands
> To be told how every member stands,
> A man who to all things under the sky
> Assents by eternally voting 'I'."

Ejection, *n.* An approved remedy for the disease of garrulity. It is also much used in cases of extreme poverty.

Elector, *n.* One who enjoys the sacred privilege of voting for the man of another man's choice.

Electricity, *n.* The power that causes all natural phenomena not known to be caused by something else. It is the same thing as lightning, and its famous attempt to strike Dr. Franklin is one of the most picturesque incidents in that great and good man's career. The memory of Dr. Franklin is justly held in great reverence, particularly in France, where a waxen effigy of him was recently on exhibition, bearing the following touching account of his life and services to science:

> "Monsieur Franqulin, inventor of electricity. This illustrious savant, after having made several voyages around the world, died on the Sandwich Islands and was devoured by savages, of whom not a single fragment was ever recovered."

Electricity seems destined to play a most important part in the arts and industries. The question of its economical application to some purposes is still unsettled, but experiment has already proved that it will propel a street car better than a gas jet and give more light than a horse.

Elegy, *n.* A composition in verse, in which, without employing any of the methods of humor, the writer aims to produce in the reader's mind the dampest kind of dejection. The most famous English example begins somewhat like this:

> The cur foretells the knell of parting day;
> The loafing herd winds slowly o'er the lea;
> The wise man homeward plods; I only stay
> To fiddle-faddle in a minor key.

Eloquence, *n.* The art of orally persuading fools that white is the color that it appears to be. It includes the gift of making any color appear white.

Elysium, *n.* An imaginary delightful country which the ancients foolishly believed to be inhabited by the spirits of the good. This ridiculous and mischievous fable was swept off the face of the earth by the early Christians—may their souls be happy in Heaven!

Emancipation, *n.* A bondman's change from the tyranny of another to the despotism of himself.

> He was a slave: at word he went and came;
> His iron collar cut him to the bone.
> Then Liberty erased his owner's name,
> Tightened the rivets and inscribed his own.
>
> G.J.

Embalm, *v.t.* To cheat vegetation by locking up the gases upon which it feeds. By embalming their dead and thereby deranging the natural balance between animal and vegetable life, the Egyptians made their once fertile and populous country barren and incapable of supporting more than a meagre crew. The modern metallic burial casket is a step in the same direction, and many a dead man who ought now to be ornamenting his neighbor's lawn as a tree, or enriching his table as a bunch of radishes, is doomed to a long inutility. We shall get him after awhile if we are spared, but in the meantime the violet and rose are languishing for a nibble at his *glutæus maximus.*

Emotion, *n.* A prostrating disease caused by a determination of the heart to the head. It is sometimes accompanied by a copious discharge of hydrated chloride of sodium from the eyes.

Encomiast, *n.* A special (but not particular) kind of liar.

End, *n.* The position farthest removed on either hand from the Interlocutor.

> The man was perishing apace
>   Who played the tambourine:
> The seal of death was on his face—
>   'Twas pallid, for 'twas clean.
>
> "This is the end," the sick man said
>   In faint and failing tones.
> A moment later he was dead,
>   And Tambourine was Bones.
>
>   *Tinley Roquot*

Enough, *pro.* All there is in the world if you like it.

> Enough is as good as a feast—for that matter
> Enougher's as good as a feast and the platter.
>   *Arbely C. Strunk*

Entertainment, *n.* Any kind of amusement whose inroads stop short of death by dejection.

Enthusiasm, *n.* A distemper of youth, curable by small doses of repentance in connection with outward applications of experience. Byron, who recovered long enough to call it "entuzy-muzy," had a relapse which carried him off—to Missolonghi.

Envelope, *n.* The coffin of a document; the scabbard of a bill; the husk of a remittance; the bed-gown of a love-letter.

Envy, *n.* Emulation adapted to the meanest capacity.

Epaulet, *n.* An ornamented badge, serving to distinguish a military officer from the enemy—that is to say, from the officer of the lower rank to whom his death would give promotion.

Epicure, *n.* An opponent of Epicurus, an abstemious philosopher who, holding that pleasure should be the chief aim of man, wasted no time in gratification of the senses.

Epigram, *n.* A short, sharp saying in prose or verse, frequently characterized by acidity or acerbity and sometimes by wisdom. Following are some of the more notable epigrams of the learned and ingenious Dr. Jamrach Holobom:

> We know better the needs of ourselves than of others. To serve oneself is economy of administration.
>
> In each human heart are a tiger, a pig, an ass and a nightingale. Diversity of character is due to their unequal activity.
>
> There are three sexes; males, females and girls.
>
> Beauty in women and distinction in men are alike in this: they seem to the unthinking a kind of credibility.
>
> Women in love are less ashamed than men. They have less to be ashamed of.
>
> While your friend holds you affectionately by both your hands you are safe, for you can watch both his.

Epitaph, *n.* An inscription on a tomb, showing that virtues acquired by death have a retroactive effect. Following is a touching example:

> Here lie the bones of Parson Platt,
> Wise, pious, humble and all that,
> Who showed us life as all should live it;
> Let that be said—and God forgive it!

Erudition, *n.* Dust shaken out of a book into an empty skull.

> So wide his erudition's mighty span,
> He knew Creation's origin and plan
> And only came by accident to grief—
> He thought, poor man, 'twas right to be a thief.
>
> *Romach Pute*

Esoteric, *adj.* Very particularly abstruse and consummately occult. The ancient philosophies were of two kinds,—*exoteric*, those that the philosophers themselves could partly understand, and *esoteric*, those that nobody could understand. It is the latter that have most profoundly affected modern thought and found greatest acceptance in our time.

Ethnology, *n.* The science that treats of the various tribes of Man, as robbers, thieves, swindlers, dunces, lunatics, idiots and ethnologists.

Eucharist, *n.* A sacred feast of the religious sect of Theophagi.

A dispute once unhappily arose among the members of this sect as to what it was that they ate. In this controversy some five hundred thousand have already been slain, and the question is still unsettled.

Eulogy, *n.* Praise of a person who has either the advantages of wealth and power, or the consideration to be dead.

Evangelist, *n.* A bearer of good tidings, particularly (in a religious sense) such as assure us of our own salvation and the damnation of our neighbors.

Everlasting, *adj.* Lasting forever. It is with no small diffidence that I venture to offer this brief and elementary definition, for I am not unaware of the existence of a bulky volume by a sometime Bishop of Worcester, entitled, *A Partial Definition of the Word "Everlasting," as Used in the Authorized Version of the Holy Scriptures.* His book was once esteemed of great authority in the Anglican Church, and is still, I understand, studied with pleasure to the mind and profit to the soul.

Exception, *n.* A thing which takes the liberty to differ from other things of its class, as an honest man, a truthful woman, etc. "The exception proves the rule" is an expression constantly upon the lips of the ignorant, who parrot it from one another with never a thought of its absurdity. In the Latin, *"Exceptio probat regulam"* means that the exception *tests* the rule, puts it to the proof, not *confirms* it. The malefactor who drew the meaning from this excellent dictum and substituted a contrary one of his own exerted an evil power which appears to be immortal.

Excess, *n.* In morals, an indulgence that enforces by appropriate penalties the law of moderation.

Hail, high Excess—especially in wine.
  To thee in worship do I bend the knee
  Who preach abstemiousness unto me—
My skull thy pulpit, as my paunch thy shrine.
Precept on precept, aye, and line on line,
  Could ne'er persuade so sweetly to agree
  With reason as thy touch, exact and free,
Upon my forehead and along my spine.
At thy command eschewing pleasure's cup,
  With the hot grape I warm no more my wit;
  When on thy stool of penitence I sit
I'm quite converted, for I can't get up.
Ungrateful he who afterward would falter
To make new sacrifices at thine altar!

Excommunication, *n.*

This "excommunication" is a word
In speech ecclesiastical oft heard,
And means the damning, with bell, book and candle,
Some sinner whose opinions are a scandal—
A rite permitting Satan to enslave him
Forever, and forbidding Christ to save him.

                       Gat Huckle

Executive, *n.* An officer of the Government, whose duty it is to enforce the wishes of the legislative power until such time as the judicial department shall be pleased to pronounce them invalid and of no effect. Following is an extract from an old book entitled, *The Lunarian Astonished*—Pfeiffer & Co., Boston, 1803:

LUNARIAN: Then when your Congress has passed a law it goes directly to the Supreme Court in order that it may at once be known whether it is constitutional?

TERRESTRIAN: O no; it does not require the approval of the Supreme Court until having perhaps been enforced for many years somebody objects to its operation against himself—I mean his client. The President, if he approves it, begins to execute it at once.

LUNARIAN: Ah, the executive power is a part of the legislative. Do your policemen also have to approve the local ordinances that they enforce?

TERRESTRIAN: Not yet—at least not in their character of constables. Generally speaking, though, all laws require the approval of those whom they are intended to restrain.

LUNARIAN: I see. The death warrant is not valid until signed by the murderer.

TERRESTRIAN: My friend, you put it too strongly; we are not so consistent.

LUNARIAN: But this system of maintaining an expensive judicial machinery to pass upon the validity of laws only after they have long been executed, and then only when brought before the court by some private person—does it not cause great confusion?

TERRESTRIAN: It does.

LUNARIAN: Why then should not your laws, previously to being executed, be validated, not by the signature of your President, but by that of the Chief Justice of the Supreme Court?

TERRESTRIAN: There is no precedent for any such course.

LUNARIAN: Precedent. What is that?

TERRESTRIAN: It has been defined by five hundred lawyers in three volumes each. So how can anyone know?

Exhort, *v.t.* In religious affairs, to put the conscience of another upon the spit and roast it to a nut-brown discomfort.

Exile, *n.* One who serves his country by residing abroad, yet is not an ambassador.

An English sea-captain being asked if he had read "The Exile of Erin," replied: "No, sir, but I should like to anchor on it." Years afterwards, when he had been hanged as a pirate after a career of unparalleled atrocities, the following memorandum was found in the ship's log that he had kept at the time of his reply:

Aug. 3d, 1842. Made a joke on the ex-Isle of Erin. Coldly received. War with the whole world!

Existence, *n.*

A transient, horrible fantastic dream,
Wherein is nothing yet all do seem:
From which we're wakened by a friendly nudge
Of our bedfellow Death, and cry: "O fudge!"

Experience, *n.* The wisdom that enables us to recognize as an undesirable old acquaintance the folly that we have already embraced.

> To one who, journeying through night and fog,
> Is mired neck-deep in an unwholesome bog,
> Experience, like the rising of the dawn,
> Reveals the path that he should not have gone.
>
> *Joel Frad Bink*

Expostulation, *n.* One of the many methods by which fools prefer to lose their friends.

Extinction, *n.* The raw material out of which theology created the future state.

Fairy, *n.* A creature, variously fashioned and endowed, that formerly inhabited the meadows and forests. It was nocturnal in its habits, and somewhat addicted to dancing and the theft of children. The fairies are now believed by naturalists to be extinct, though a clergyman of the Church of England saw three near Colchester as lately as 1855, while passing through a park after dining with the lord of the manor. The sight greatly staggered him, and he was so affected that his account of it was incoherent. In the year 1807 a troop of fairies visited a wood near Aix and carried off the daughter of a peasant, who had been seen to enter it with a bundle of clothing. The son of a wealthy *bourgeois* disappeared about the same time, but afterward returned. He had seen the abduction and been in pursuit of the fairies. Justinian Gaux, a writer of the fourteenth century, avers that so great is the fairies' power of transformation that he saw one change itself into two opposing armies and fight a battle with great slaughter, and that the next day, after it had resumed its original shape and gone away, there were seven hundred bodies of the slain which the villagers had to bury. He does not say if any of the wounded recovered. In the time of Henry III, of England, a law was made which prescribed the death penalty for "Kyllinge, wowndynge, or mamynge" a fairy, and it was universally respected.

Faith, *n.* Belief without evidence in what is told by one who speaks without knowledge, of things without parallel.

Famous, *adj.* Conspicuously miserable.

> Done to a turn on the iron, behold
>   Him who to be famous aspired.
> Content? Well, his grill has a plating of gold,
>   And his twistings are greatly admired.
>
> > *Hassan Brubuddy*

Fashion, *n.* A despot whom the wise ridicule and obey.

> A king there was who lost an eye
>   In some excess of passion;
> And straight his courtiers all did try
>   To follow the new fashion.
>
> Each dropped one eyelid when before
>   The throne he ventured, thinking
> 'Twould please the king. That monarch swore
>   He'd slay them all for winking.
>
> What should they do? They were not hot
>   To hazard such disaster;
> They dared not close an eye—dared not
>   See better than their master.
>
> Seeing them lacrymose and glum,
>   A leech consoled the weepers:
> He spread small rags with liquid gum
>   And covered half their peepers.
>
> The court all wore the stuff, the flame
>   Of royal anger dying.
> That's how court-plaster got its name
>   Unless I'm greatly lying.
>
> > *Naramy Oof*

Feast, *n.* A festival. A religious celebration usually signalized by glut-
tony and drunkenness, frequently in honor of some holy person
distinguished for abstemiousness. In the Roman Catholic Church
feasts are "movable" and "immovable," but the celebrants are uniformly immovable until they are full. In their earliest development
these entertainments took the form of feasts for the dead; such

were held by the Greeks, under the name of *Nemeseia*, by the
Aztecs and Peruvians, as in modern times they are popular with
the Chinese; thought it is believed that the ancient dead, like the
modern, were light eaters. Among the many feasts of the Romans
was the *Novemdiale*, which was held, according to Livy, whenever
stones fell from heaven.

Felon, *n.* A person of greater enterprise than discretion, who in embrac-
ing an opportunity has formed an unfortunate attachment.

Female, *n.* One of the opposing, or unfair, sex.

> The Maker, at Creation's birth,
> With living things had stocked the earth.
> From elephants to bats and snails,
> They all were good, for all were males.
> But when the Devil came and saw
> He said: "By Thine eternal law
> Of growth, maturity, decay,
> These all must quickly pass away
> And leave untenanted the earth
> Unless Thou dost establish birth"—
> Then tucked his head beneath his wing
> To laugh—he had no sleeve—the thing
> With deviltry did so accord,
> That he'd suggested to the Lord.
> The Master pondered this advice,
> Then shook and threw the fateful dice
> Wherewith all matters here below
> Are ordered and observed the throw;
> Then bent His head in awful state,
> Confirming the decree of Fate.
> From every part of earth anew
> The conscious dust consenting flew,
> While rivers from their courses rolled
> To make it plastic for the mould.
> Enough collected (but no more,
> For niggard Nature hoards her store)
> He kneaded it to flexile clay,
> While Nick unseen threw some away.
> And then the various forms He cast,
> Gross organs first and finer last;

No one at once evolved, but all
By even touches grew and small
Degrees advanced, till, shade by shade,
To match all living things He'd made
Females, complete in all their parts
Except (His clay gave out) the hearts.
"No matter," Satan cried; "with speed
I'll fetch the very hearts they need"—
So flew away and soon brought back
The number needed, in a sack.
That night earth rang with sounds of strife—
Ten million males had each a wife
That night sweet Peace her pinions spread
O'er Hell—ten million devils dead!

G.J.

Fib, *n.* A lie that has not cut its teeth. An habitual liar's nearest approach to truth: the perigee of his eccentric orbit.

When David said: "All men are liars," Dave,
    Himself a liar, fibbed like any thief.
    Perhaps he thought to weaken disbelief
By proof that even himself was not a slave
To Truth; though I suspect the aged knave
    Had been of all her servitors the chief
    Had he but known a fig's reluctant leaf
Is more than e'er she wore on land or wave.
No, David served not Naked Truth when he
    Struck that sledge-hammer blow at all his race;
        Nor did he hit the nail upon the head:
For reason shows that it could never be,
    And the facts contradict him to his face.
        Men are not liars all, for some are dead.

Bartle Quinker

Fickleness, *n.* The iterated satiety of an enterprising affection.

Fiddle, *n.* An instrument to tickle human ears by friction of a horse's tail on the entrails of a cat.

To Rome said Nero: "If to smoke you turn
I shall not cease to fiddle while you burn."

> To Nero Rome replied: "Pray do your worst,
> 'Tis my excuse that you were fiddling first."
>
> *Orm Pludge*

Fidelity, *n.* A virtue peculiar to those who are about to be betrayed.

Finance, *n.* The art or science of managing revenues and resources for the best advantage of the manager. The pronunciation of this word with the i long and the accent on the first syllable is one of America's most precious discoveries and possessions.

Flag, *n.* A colored rag borne above troops and hoisted on forts and ships. It appears to serve the same purpose as certain signs that one sees on vacant lots in London—"Rubbish may be shot here."

Flesh, *n.* The Second Person of the secular Trinity.

Flop, *v.* Suddenly to change one's opinions and go over to another party. The most notable flop on record was that of Saul of Tarsus, who has been severely criticised as a turn-coat by some of our partisan journals.

Fly-Speck, *n.* The prototype of punctuation. It is observed by Garvinus that the systems of punctuation in use by the various literary nations depended originally upon the social habits and general diet of the flies infesting the several countries. These creatures, which have always been distinguished for a neighborly and companionable familiarity with authors, liberally or niggardly embellish the manuscripts in process of growth under the pen, according to their bodily habit, bringing out the sense of the work by a species of interpretation superior to, and independent of, the writer's powers. The "old masters" of literature—that is to say, the early writers whose work is so esteemed by later scribes and critics in the same language—never punctuated at all, but worked right along free-handed, without that abruption of the thought which comes from the use of points. (We observe the same thing in children to-day, whose usage in this particular is a striking and beautiful instance of the law that the infancy of individuals reproduces the methods and stages of development characterizing the infancy of races.) In the work of these primitive scribes all the punctuation is found, by the modern investigator with his optical instrument and chemical tests, to have been inserted by the writers' ingenious and serviceable collaborator, the common house-fly—*Musca maledicta*. In transcribing these ancient MSS, for the purpose of either making the work their own or preserving what they naturally regard as divine revelations, later writers reverently and accurately copy whatever marks they find upon the papyrus or parchment, to the unspeakable enhancement of the lucidity of the thought and value of the work. Writers contemporary with the copyists naturally avail themselves of the obvious advantages of these marks in their own work, and with such assistance as the flies of their own household may be willing to grant, frequently rival and sometimes surpass the older compositions, in respect at least of punctuation, which is no small glory. Fully to understand the important services that flies perform to literature it is only necessary to lay a page of some popular novelist alongside a saucer of cream-and-molasses in a sunny room and observe "how the wit brightens and the style refines" in accurate proportion to the duration of exposure.

Folly, *n.* That "gift and faculty divine" whose creative and controlling energy inspires Man's mind, guides his actions and adorns his life.

> Folly! although Erasmus praised thee once
>   In a thick volume, and all authors known,
>   If not thy glory yet thy power have shown,
> Deign to take homage from thy son who hunts
> Through all thy maze his brothers, fool and dunce,
>   To mend their lives and to sustain his own,
>   However feebly be his arrows thrown,
>
> Howe'er each hide the flying weapons blunts.
> All-Father Folly! be it mine to raise,
>   With lusty lung, here on this western strand
>   With all thine offspring thronged from every land,
> Thyself inspiring me, the song of praise.
> And if too weak, I'll hire, to help me bawl,
> Dick Watson Gilder, gravest of us all.

Aramis Loto Frope

Fool, *n.* A person who pervades the domain of intellectual speculation and diffuses himself through the channels of moral activity. He is omnific, omniform, omnipercipient, omniscient, omnipotent. He it was who invented letters, printing, the railroad, the steamboat, the telegraph, the platitude, and the circle of the sciences. He created patriotism and taught the nations war—founded theology, philosophy, law, medicine and Chicago. He established monarchical and republican government. He is from everlasting to everlasting—such as creation's dawn beheld he fooleth now. In the morning of time he sang upon primitive hills, and in the noonday of existence headed the procession of being. His grandmotherly hand has warmly tucked—in the set sun of civilization, and in the twilight he prepares Man's evening meal of milk-and-morality and turns down the covers of the universal grave. And after the rest of us shall have retired for the night of eternal oblivion he will sit up to write a history of human civilization.

Force, *n.*

> "Force is but might," the teacher said—
>   "That definition's just."
> The boy said naught but thought instead,
> Remembering his pounded head:
>   "Force is not might but must!"

Forefinger, *n.* The finger commonly used in pointing out two malefactors.

Foreordination, *n.* This looks like an easy word to define, but when I consider that pious and learned theologians have spent long lives in explaining it, and written libraries to explain their explanations; when I remember that nations have been divided and bloody battles caused by the difference between foreordination and predestination, and that millions of treasure have been expended in the effort to prove and disprove its compatibility with freedom of the will and the efficacy of prayer, praise, and a religious life—recalling these awful facts in the history of the word, I stand appalled before the mighty problem of its signification, abase my spiritual eyes, fearing to contemplate its portentous magnitude, reverently uncover and humbly refer it to His Eminence Cardinal Gibbons and His Grace Bishop Potter.

Forgetfulness, *n.* A gift of God bestowed upon debtors in compensation for their destitution of conscience.

Fork, *n.* An instrument used chiefly for the purpose of putting dead animals into the mouth. Formerly the knife was employed for this purpose, and by many worthy persons is still thought to have many advantages over the other tool, which, however, they do not altogether reject, but use to assist in charging the knife. The immunity of these persons from swift and awful death is one of the most striking proofs of God's mercy to those that hate Him.

Forma Pauperis (Latin). In the character of a poor person—a method by which a litigant without money for lawyers is considerately permitted to lose his case.

> When Adam long ago in Cupid's awful court
>   (For Cupid ruled ere Adam was invented)
> Sued for Eve's favor, says an ancient law report,
>   He stood and pleaded unhabilimented.
>
> "You sue *in forma pauperis,* I see," Eve cried;
>   "Actions can't here be that way prosecuted."
> So all poor Adam's motions coldly were denied:
>   He went away—as he had come—nonsuited.
>
>   G.J.

Frankalmoigne, *n.* The tenure by which a religious corporation holds land on condition of praying for the soul of the donor. In mediæval times many of the wealthiest fraternities obtained their estates in this simple and cheap manner, and once when Henry VIII of England sent an officer to confiscate certain vast possessions which a fraternity of monks held by frankalmoigne, "What!" said the Prior, "would your master stay our benefactor's soul in Purgatory?" "Ay," said the officer, coldly, "an ye will not pray him thence for naught he must e'en roast." "But look you, my son," persisted the good man, "this act hath rank as robbery of God!" "Nay, nay, good father, my master the king doth but deliver Him from the manifold temptations of too great wealth."

Freebooter, *n.* A conqueror in a small way of business, whose annexations lack the sanctifying merit of magnitude.

Freedom, *n.* Exemption from the stress of authority in a beggarly half dozen of restraint's infinite multitude of methods. A political condition that every nation supposes itself to enjoy in virtual monopoly. Liberty. The distinction between freedom and liberty is not accurately known; naturalists have never been able to find a living specimen of either.

> Freedom, as every schoolboy knows,
>   Once shrieked as Kosciusko fell;
> On every wind, indeed, that blows
>   I hear her yell.
>
> She screams whenever monarchs meet,
>   And parliaments as well,
> To bind the chains about her feet
>   And toll her knell.
>
> And when the sovereign people cast
>   The votes they cannot spell,
> Upon the pestilential blast
>   Her clamors swell.
>
> For all to whom the power's given
>   To sway or to compel,
> Among themselves apportion Heaven
>   And give her Hell.
>
> *Blary O'Gary*

Freemasons, *n.* An order with secret rites, grotesque ceremonies and fantastic costumes, which, originating in the reign of Charles II, among working artisans of London, has been joined successively by the dead of past centuries in unbroken retrogression until now it embraces all the generations of man on the hither side of Adam and is drumming up distinguished recruits among the pre-Creational inhabitants of Chaos and the Formless Void. The order was founded at different times by Charlemagne, Julius Cæsar, Cyrus, Solomon, Zoroaster, Confucius, Thothmes, and Buddha. Its emblems and symbols have been found in the Catacombs of Paris and Rome, on the stones of the Parthenon and the Chinese Great Wall, among the temples of Karnak and Palmyra and in the Egyptian Pyramids—always by a Freemason.

Friendless, *adj.* Having no favors to bestow. Destitute of fortune. Addicted to utterance of truth and common sense.

Friendship, *n.* A ship big enough to carry two in fair weather, but only one in foul.

> The sea was calm and the sky was blue;
> Merrily, merrily sailed we two.
> (High barometer maketh glad.)
> On the tipsy ship, with a dreadful shout,
> The tempest descended and we fell out.
> (O the walking is nasty bad!)
>
> *Armit Huff Bettle*

Frog, *n.* A reptile with edible legs. The first mention of frogs in profane literature is in Homer's narrative of the war between them and the mice. Skeptical persons have doubted Homer's authorship of the work, but the learned, ingenious and industrious Dr. Schliemann has set the question forever at rest by uncovering the bones of the slain frogs. One of the forms of moral suasion by which Pharaoh was besought to favor the Israelites was a plague of frogs, but Pharaoh, who liked them *fricasées*, remarked, with truly oriental stoicism, that he could stand it as long as the frogs and the Jews could; so the programme was changed. The frog is a diligent songster, having a good voice but no ear. The libretto of his favorite opera, as written by Aristophanes, is brief, simple and effective— "brekekex-koäx"; the music is apparently by that eminent composer, Richard Wagner. Horses have a frog in each hoof—a thoughtful provision of nature, enabling them to shine in a hurdle race.

Frying-Pan, *n.* One part of the penal apparatus employed in that punitive institution, a woman's kitchen. The frying-pan was invented by Calvin, and by him used in cooking span-long infants that had died without baptism; and observing one day the horrible torment of a tramp who had incautiously pulled a fried babe from the waste-dump and devoured it, it occurred to the great divine to rob death of its terrors by introducing the frying-pan into every household in Geneva. Thence it spread to all corners of the world, and has been of invaluable assistance in the propagation of his sombre faith. The following lines (said to be from the pen of his Grace Bishop Potter) seem to imply that the usefulness of this utensil is not limited to this world; but as the consequences of its employment in this life reach over into the life to come, so also itself may be found on the other side, rewarding its devotees:

Old Nick was summoned to the skies.
  Said Peter: "Your intentions
Are good, but you lack enterprise
  Concerning new inventions.

"Now, broiling is an ancient plan
  Of torment, but I hear it
Reported that the frying-pan
  Sears best the wicked spirit.

"Go get one—fill it up with fat—
  Fry sinners brown and good in't."
"I know a trick worth two o' that,"
  Said Nick—"I'll cook their food in't."

Funeral, *n.* A pageant whereby we attest our respect for the dead by enriching the undertaker, and strengthen our grief by an expenditure that deepens our groans and doubles our tears.

The savage dies—they sacrifice a horse
  To bear to happy hunting-grounds the corse.
Our friends expire—we make the money fly
  In hope their souls will chase it to the sky.

Jex Wopley

Future, *n.* That period of time in which our affairs prosper, our friends are true and our happiness is assured.

Gallows, *n.* A stage for the performance of miracle plays, in which the leading actor is translated to heaven. In this country the gallows is chiefly remarkable for the number of persons who escape it.

> Whether on the gallows high
>   Or where blood flows the reddest,
> The noblest place for man to die—
>   Is where he died the deadest.

Old Play

Gargoyle, *n.* A rain-spout projecting from the eaves of mediæval buildings, commonly fashioned into a grotesque caricature of some personal enemy of the architect or owner of the building. This was especially the case in churches and ecclesiastical structures generally, in which the gargoyles presented a perfect rogues' gallery of local heretics and controversialists. Sometimes when a new dean and chapter were installed the old gargoyles were removed and others substituted having a closer relation to the private animosities of the new incumbents.

Garter, *n.* An elastic band intended to keep a woman from coming out of her stockings and desolating the country.

Generous, *adj.* Originally this word meant noble by birth and was rightly applied to a great multitude of persons. It now means noble by nature and is taking a bit of a rest.

Genealogy, *n.* An account of one's descent from an ancestor who did not particularly care to trace his own.

Genteel, *adj.* Refined, after the fashion of a gent.

> Observe with care, my son, the distinction I reveal:
> A gentleman is gentle and a gent genteel.
> Heed not the definitions your "unabridged" presents,
> For dictionary makers are generally gents.
>
> *G.J.*

Geographer, *n.* A chap who can tell you offhand the difference between the outside of the world and the inside.

> Habeam, geographer of wide renown,
> Native of Abu-Keber's ancient town,
> In passing thence along the river Zam
> To the adjacent village of Xelam,
> Bewildered by the multitude of roads,
> Got lost, lived long on migratory toads,
> Then from exposure miserably died,
> And grateful travelers bewailed their guide.
>
> *Henry Haukhorn*

Geology, *n.* The science of the earth's crust—to which, doubtless, will be added that of its interior whenever a man shall come up garrulous out of a well. The geological formations of the globe already noted are catalogued thus: The Primary, or lower one, consists of rocks, bones of mired mules, gas-pipes, miners' tools, antique statues minus the nose, Spanish doubloons and ancestors. The Secondary is largely made up of red worms and moles. The Tertiary comprises railway tracks, patent pavements, grass, snakes, mouldy boots, beer bottles, tomato cans, intoxicated citizens, garbage, anarchists, snap-dogs and fools.

Ghost, *n.* The outward and visible sign of an inward fear.

> He saw a ghost.
> It occupied—that dismal thing!—
> The path that he was following.
> Before he'd time to stop and fly,
> An earthquake trifled with the eye

That saw a ghost.
He fell as fall the early good;
Unmoved that awful vision stood.
The stars that danced before his ken
He wildly brushed away, and then
    He saw a post.

Jared Macphester

    Accounting for the uncommon behavior of ghosts, Heine mentions somebody's ingenious theory to the effect that they are as much afraid of us as we of them. Not quite, if I may judge from such tables of comparative speed as I am able to compile from memories of my own experience.

    There is one insuperable obstacle to a belief in ghosts. A ghost never comes naked: he appears either in a winding-sheet or "in his habit as he lived." To believe in him, then, is to believe that not only have the dead the power to make themselves visible after there is nothing left of them, but that the same power inheres in textile fabrics. Supposing the products of the loom to have this ability, what object would they have in exercising it? And why does not the apparition of a suit of clothes sometimes walk abroad without a ghost in it? These be riddles of significance. They reach away down and get a convulsive grasp on the very tap-root of this flourishing faith.

Ghoul, *n.* A demon addicted to the reprehensible habit of devouring the dead. The existence of ghouls has been disputed by that class of controversialists who are more concerned to deprive the world of comforting beliefs than to give it anything good in their place. In 1640 Father Secchi saw one in a cemetery near Florence and frightened it away with the sign of the cross. He describes it as gifted with many heads and an uncommon allowance of limbs, and he saw it in more than one place at a time. The good man was coming away from dinner at the time and explains that if he had not been "heavy with eating" he would have seized the demon at all hazards. Atholston relates that a ghoul was caught by some sturdy peasants in a churchyard at Sudbury and ducked in a horsepond. (He appears to think that so distinguished a criminal should have been ducked in a tank of rose-water.) The water turned at once to blood "and so contynues unto ys daye." The pond has since been bled with a ditch. As late as the beginning of the fourteenth century a ghoul was cornered in the crypt of the cathedral at Amiens and the whole population surrounded the place. Twenty armed men with a priest at their head, bearing a crucifix, entered and captured the ghoul, which, thinking to escape by the stratagem, had transformed itself to the semblance of a well known citizen, but was nevertheless hanged, drawn and quartered in the midst of hideous popular orgies. The citizen whose shape the demon had assumed was so affected by the sinister occurrence that he never again showed himself in Amiens and his fate remains a mystery.

Glutton, *n.* A person who escapes the evils of moderation by committing dyspepsia.

Gnome, *n.* In North-European mythology, a dwarfish imp inhabiting the interior parts of the earth and having special custody of mineral treasures. Bjorsen, who died in 1765, says gnomes were common enough in the southern parts of Sweden in his boyhood, and he frequently saw them scampering on the hills in the evening twilight. Ludwig Binkerhoof saw three as recently as 1792 in the Black Forest, and Sneddeker avers that in 1803 they drove a party of miners out of a Silesian mine. Basing our computations upon data supplied by these statements, we find that gnomes were probably extinct as early as 1764.

Gnostics, *n.* A sect of philosophers who tried to engineer a fusion between the early Christians and the Platonists. The former would not go into the caucus and the combination failed, greatly to the chagrin of the fusion managers.

Gnu, *n.* An animal of South Africa, which in its domesticated state resembles a horse, a buffalo and a stag. In its wild condition it is something like a thunderbolt, an earthquake and a cyclone.

> A hunter from Kew caught a distant view
>   Of a peacefully meditative gnu,
> And he said: "I'll pursue, and my hands imbrue
>   In its blood at a closer interview."
> But that beast did ensue and the hunter it threw
> O'er the top of a palm that adjacent grew;
> And he said as he flew: "It is well I withdrew
>   Ere, losing my temper, I wickedly slew
>   That really meritorious gnu."

Jarn Leffer

Good, *adj.* Sensible, madam, to the worth of this present writer. Alive, sir, to the advantages of letting him alone.

Goose, *n.* A bird that supplies quills for writing. These, by some occult process of nature, are penetrated and suffused with various degrees of the bird's intellectual energies and emotional character, so that when inked and drawn mechanically across paper by a person called an "author," there results a very fair and accurate transcript of the fowl's thought and feeling. The difference in geese, as discovered by this ingenious method, is considerable: many are found to have only trivial and insignificant powers, but some are seen to be very great geese indeed.

Gorgon, *n.*

> The Gorgon was a maiden bold
> Who turned to stone the Greeks of old
> That looked upon her awful brow.
> We dig them out of ruins now,
> And swear that workmanship so bad
> Proves all the ancient sculptors mad.

Gout, *n.* A physician's name for the rheumatism of a rich patient.

Graces, *n.* Three beautiful goddesses, Aglaia, Thalia and Euphrosyne, who attended upon Venus, serving without salary. They were at no expense for board and clothing, for they ate nothing to speak of and dressed according to the weather, wearing whatever breeze happened to be blowing.

Grammar, *n.* A system of pitfalls thoughtfully prepared for the feet of the self-made man, along the path by which he advances to distinction.

Grape, *n.*

> Hail noble fruit!—by Homer sung,
>   Anacreon and Khayyam;
> Thy praise is ever on the tongue
>   Of better men than I am.
>
> The lyre my hand has never swept,
>   The song I cannot offer:

My humbler service pray accept—
    I'll help to kill the scoffer.

The water-drinkers and the cranks
    Who load their skins with liquor—
I'll gladly bare their belly-tanks
    And tap them with my sticker.

Fill up, fill up, for wisdom cools
    When e'er we let the wine rest.
Here's death to Prohibition's fools,
    And every kind of vine-pest!

Jamrach Holobom

Grapeshot, *n.* An argument which the future is preparing in answer to the demands of American Socialism.

Grave, *n.* A place in which the dead are laid to await the coming of the medical student.

Beside a lonely grave I stood—
    With brambles 'twas encumbered;
The winds were moaning in the wood,
    Unheard by him who slumbered.

A rustic standing near, I said:
    "He cannot hear it blowing!"
" 'Course not," said he: "the feller's dead—
    He can't hear nowt that's going."

"Too true," I said; "alas, too true—
    No sound his sense can quicken!"
"Well, mister, wot is that to you?—
    The deadster ain't a-kickin'."

I knelt and prayed: "O Father, smile
    On him, and mercy show him!"
That countryman looked on the while,
    And said: "Ye didn't know him."

Pobeter Dunk

Gravitation, *n.* The tendency of all bodies to approach one another with a strength proportioned to the quantity of matter they contain—the quantity of matter they contain being ascertained by the strength of their tendency to approach one another. This is a lovely and edifying illustration of how science, having made A the proof of B, makes B the proof of A.

Great, *adj.*

> "I'm great," the Lion said—"I reign
> The monarch of the wood and plain!"
>
> The Elephant replied: "I'm great—
> No quadruped can match my weight!"
>
> "I'm great—no animal has half
> So long a neck!" said the Giraffe.
>
> "I'm great," the Kangaroo said—"see
> My femoral muscularity!"
>
> The 'Possum said: "I'm great—behold,
> My tail is lithe and bald and cold!"
>
> An Oyster fried was understood
> To say: "I'm great because I'm good!"
>
> Each reckons greatness to consist
> In that in which he heads the list,
>
> And Vierick thinks he tops his class
> Because he is the greatest ass.
>
> *Arion Spurl Doke*

Guillotine, *n.* A machine which makes a Frenchman shrug his shoulders with good reason.

In his great work on *Divergent Lines of Racial Evolution*, the learned Professor Brayfugle argues from the prevalence of this gesture—the shrug—among Frenchmen, that they are descended from turtles and it is simply a survival of the habit of retracting the head inside the shell. It is with reluctance that I differ with so eminent an authority, but in my judgment (as more elaborately set forth and enforced in my work entitled *Hereditary Emotions*—lib. II, c. XI) the shrug is a poor foundation upon which to build so important a theory, for previously to the Revolution the gesture was unknown. I have not a doubt that it is directly referable to the terror inspired by the guillotine during the period of that instrument's activity.

Gunpowder, *n.* An agency employed by civilized nations for the settlement of disputes which might become troublesome if left unadjusted. By most writers the invention of gunpowder is ascribed to the Chinese, but not upon very convincing evidence. Milton says it was invented by the devil to dispel angels with, and this opinion seems to derive some support from the scarcity of angels. Moreover, it has the hearty concurrence of the Hon. James Wilson, Secretary of Agriculture.

Secretary Wilson became interested in gunpowder through an event that occurred on the Government experimental farm in the District of Columbia. One day, several years ago, a rogue imperfectly reverent of the Secretary's profound attainments and personal character presented him with a sack of gunpowder, representing it as the seed of the *Flashawful flabbergastor,* a Patagonian cereal of great commercial value, admirably adapted to this climate. The good Secretary was instructed to spill it along in a furrow and afterward inhume it with soil. This he at once proceeded to do, and had made a continuous line of it all the way across a ten-acre field, when he was made to look backward by a shout from the generous donor, who at once dropped a lighted match into the furrow at the starting-point. Contact with the earth had somewhat dampened the powder, but the startled functionary saw himself pursued by a tall moving pillar of fire and smoke in fierce evolution. He stood for a moment paralyzed and speechless, then he recollected an engagement and, dropping all, absented himself thence with such surprising celerity that to the eyes of spectators along the route selected he appeared like a long, dim streak prolonging itself with inconceivable rapidity through seven villages, and audibly refusing to be comforted. "Great Scott! what is that?" cried a surveyor's chainman, shading his eyes and gazing at the fading line of agriculturist which bisected his visible horizon. "That," said the surveyor, carelessly glancing at the phenomenon and again centering his attention upon his instrument, "is the Meridian of Washington."

Habeas Corpus. A writ by which a man may be taken out of jail when confined for the wrong crime.

Habit, *n.* A shackle for the free.

Hades, *n.* The lower world; the residence of departed spirits; the place where the dead live.

Among the ancients the idea of Hades was not synonymous with our Hell, many of the most respectable men of antiquity residing there in a very comfortable kind of way. Indeed, the Elysian Fields themselves were a part of Hades, though they have since been removed to Paris. When the Jacobean version of the New Testament was in process of evolution the pious and learned men engaged in the work insisted by a majority vote on translating the Greek word Αιδης as "Hell"; but a conscientious minority member secretly possessed himself of the record and struck out the objectionable word wherever he could find it. At the next meeting, the Bishop of Salisbury, looking over the work, suddenly sprang to his feet and said with considerable excitement: "Gentlemen, somebody has been razing 'Hell' here!" Years afterward the good prelate's death was made sweet by the reflection that he had been the means (under Providence) of making an important, serviceable and immortal addition to the phraseology of the English tongue.

Hag, *n.* An elderly lady whom you do not happen to like; sometimes called, also, a hen, or cat. Old witches, sorceresses, etc., were called hags from the belief that their heads were surrounded by a kind of baleful lumination or nimbus—hag being the popular name of that peculiar electrical light sometimes observed in the hair. At one time hag was not a word of reproach: Drayton speaks of a "beautiful hag, all smiles," much as Shakespeare said, "sweet wench." It would not now be proper to call your sweetheart a hag—that compliment is reserved for the use of her grandchildren.

Half, *n.* One of two equal parts into which a thing may be divided, or considered as divided. In the fourteenth century a heated discussion arose among theologians and philosophers as to whether Omniscience could part an object into three halves; and the pious Father Aldrovinus publicly prayed in the cathedral at Rouen that God would demonstrate the affirmative of the proposition in some signal and unmistakable way, and particularly (if it should please Him) upon the body of that hardy blasphemer, Manutius Procinus, who maintained the negative. Procinus, however, was spared to die of the bite of a viper.

Halo, *n.* Properly, a luminous ring encircling an astronomical body, but not infrequently confounded with "aureola," or "nimbus," a somewhat similar phenomenon worn as a head-dress by divinities and saints. The halo is a purely optical illusion, produced by moisture in the air, in the manner of a rainbow; but the aureola is conferred as a sign of superior sanctity, in the same way as a bishop's mitre, or the Pope's tiara. In the painting of the Nativity, by Szedgkin, a pious artist of Pesth, not only do the Virgin and the Child wear the nimbus, but an ass nibbling hay from the sacred manger is similarly decorated and, to his lasting honor be it said, appears to bear his unaccustomed dignity with a truly saintly grace.

Hand, *n.* A singular instrument worn at the end of a human arm and commonly thrust into somebody's pocket.

Handkerchief, *n.* A small square of silk or linen, used in various ignoble offices about the face and especially serviceable at funerals to conceal the lack of tears. The handkerchief is of recent invention; our ancestors knew nothing of it and intrusted its duties to the sleeve. Shakespeare's introducing it into the play of "Othello" is an anachronism: Desdemona dried her nose with her skirt, as Dr.

Mary Walker and other reformers have done with their coat-tails in our own day—an evidence that revolutions sometimes go backward.

Hangman, *n.* An officer of the law charged with duties of the highest dignity and utmost gravity, and held in hereditary disesteem by a populace having a criminal ancestry. In some of the American States his functions are now performed by an electrician, as in New Jersey, where executions by electricity have recently been ordered—the first instance known to this lexicographer of anybody questioning the expediency of hanging Jerseymen.

Happiness, *n.* An agreeable sensation arising from contemplating the misery of another.

Harangue, *n.* A speech by an opponent, who is known as an harangue-outang.

Harbor, *n.* A place where ships taking shelter from storms are exposed to the fury of the customs.

Harmonists, *n.* A sect of Protestants, now extinct, who came from Europe in the beginning of the last century and were distinguished for the bitterness of their internal controversies and dissensions.

Hash, *x.* There is no definition for this word—nobody knows what hash is.

Hatchet, *n.* A young axe, known among Indians as a Thomashawk.

> "O bury the hatchet, irascible Red,
> For peace is a blessing," the White Man said.
> The Savage concurred, and that weapon interred,
> With imposing rites, in the White Man's head.
> *John Lukkus*

Hatred, *n.* A sentiment appropriate to the occasion of another's superiority.

Head-Money, *n.* A capitation tax, or poll-tax.

> In ancient times there lived a king
> Whose tax-collectors could not wring
> From all his subjects gold enough
> To make the royal way less rough.

For pleasure's highway, like the dames
Whose premises adjoin it, claims
Perpetual repairing. So
The tax-collectors in a row
Appeared before the throne to pray
Their master to devise some way
To swell the revenue. "So great,"
Said they, "are the demands of state
A tithe of all that we collect
Will scarcely meet them. Pray reflect:
How, if one-tenth we must resign,
Can we exist on t'other nine?"
The monarch asked them in reply:
"Has it occurred to you to try
The advantage of economy?"
"It has," the spokesman said: "we sold
All of our gay garrotes of gold;
With plated-ware we now compress
The necks of those whom we assess.
Plain iron forceps we employ
To mitigate the miser's joy
Who hoards, with greed that never tires,
That which your Majesty requires."
Deep lines of thought were seen to plow
Their way across the royal brow.
"Your state is desperate, no question;
Pray favor me with a suggestion."
"O King of Men," the spokesman said,
"If you'll impose upon each head
A tax, the augmented revenue
We'll cheerfully divide with you."
As flashes of the sun illume
The parted storm-cloud's sullen gloom,
The king smiled grimly. "I decree
That it be so—and, not to be
In generosity outdone,
Declare you, each and every one,
Exempted from the operation
Of this new law of capitation.
But lest the people censure me
Because they're bound and you are free,
'Twere well some clever scheme were laid

By you this poll-tax to evade.
I'll leave you now while you confer
With my most trusted minister."
The monarch from the throne-room walked
And straightway in among them stalked
A silent man, with brow concealed,
Bare-armed—his gleaming axe revealed!

G.J.

Hearse, n. Death's baby-carriage.

Heart, n. An automatic, muscular blood-pump. Figuratively, this useful organ is said to be the seat of emotions and sentiments—a very pretty fancy which, however, is nothing but a survival of a once universal belief. It is now known that the sentiments and emotions reside in the stomach, being evolved from food by chemical action of the gastric fluid. The exact process by which a beefsteak becomes a feeling—tender or not, according to the age of the animal from which it was cut; the successive stages of elaboration through which a caviar sandwich is transmuted to a quaint fancy and reappears as a pungent epigram; the marvelous functional methods of converting a hard-boiled egg into religious contrition, or a cream-puff into a sigh of sensibility—these things have been patiently ascertained by M. Pasteur, and by him expounded with convincing lucidity. (See, also, my monograph, *The Essential Identity of the Spiritual Affections and Certain Intestinal Gases Freed in Digestion*—4to, 687 pp.) In a scientific work entitled, I believe, *Delectatio Demonorum* (John Camden Hotton, London, 1873) this view of the sentiments receives a striking illustration; and for further light consult Professor Dam's famous treatise on *Love as a Product of Alimentary Maceration.*

Heat, n.

Heat, says Professor Tyndall, is a mode
    Of motion, but I know now how he's proving
His point; but this I know—hot words bestowed
    With skill will set the human fist a-moving,
And where it stops the stars burn free and wild.
Crede expertum—I have seen them, child.

Gorton Swope

Heathen, *n.* A benighted creature who has the folly to worship something that he can see and feel. According to Professor Howison, of the California State University, Hebrews are heathens.

> "The Hebrews are heathens!" says Howison. He's
> A Christian philosopher. I'm
> A scurril agnostical chap, if you please,
> Addicted too much to the crime
> Of religious discussion in rhyme.
>
> Though Hebrew and Howison cannot agree
> On a *modus vivendi*—not they!—
> Yet Heaven has had the designing of me,
> And I haven't been reared in a way
> To joy in the thick of the fray.
>
> For this of my creed is the soul and the gist,
> And the truth of it I aver:
> Who differs from me in his faith is an 'ist,
> An 'ite, an 'ic, or an 'er—
> And I'm down upon him or her!
>
> Let Howison urge with perfunctory chin
> Toleration—that's all very well,
> But a roast is "nuts" to his nostril thin,
> And he's running—I know by the smell—
> A secret and personal Hell!
>
> *Bissell Gip*

Heaven, *n.* A place where the wicked cease from troubling you with talk of their personal affairs, and the good listen with attention while you expound your own.

Hebrew, *n.* A male Jew, as distinguished from the Shebrew, an altogether superior creation.

Helpmate, *n.* A wife, or bitter half.

> "Now, why is yer wife called a helpmate, Pat?"
> Says the priest. "Since the time o' yer wooin'
> She's niver assisted in what ye were at—
> For it's naught ye are ever doin'."

"That's true of yer Riverence," Patrick replies,
And no sign of contrition evinces;
"But, bedad, it's a fact which the word implies,
For she helps to mate the expinses!"

Marley Wottel

Hemp, *n.* A plant from whose fibrous bark is made an article of neck-wear which is frequently put on after public speaking in the open air and prevents the wearer from taking cold.

Hermit, *n.* A person whose vices and follies are not sociable.

Hers, *pron.* His.

Hibernate, *v.i.* To pass the winter season in domestic seclusion. There have been many singular popular notions about the hibernation of various animals. Many believe that the bear hibernates during the whole winter and subsists by mechanically sucking its paws. It is admitted that it comes out of its retirement in the spring so lean that it has to try twice before it can cast a shadow. Three or four centuries ago, in England, no fact was better attested than that swallows passed the winter months in the mud at the bottoms of the brooks, clinging together in globular masses. They have apparently been compelled to give up the custom on account of the foulness of the brooks. Sotus Escobius discovered in Central Asia a whole nation of people who hibernate. By some investigators, the fasting of Lent is supposed to have been originally a modified form of hibernation, to which the Church gave a religious significance; but this view was strenuously opposed by that eminent authority, Bishop Kip, who did not wish any honours denied to the memory of the Founder of his family.

Hippogriff, *n.* An animal (now extinct) which was half horse and half griffin. The griffin was itself a compound creature, half lion and half eagle. The hippogriff was actually, therefore, only one-quarter eagle, which is two dollars and fifty cents in gold. The study of zoology is full of surprises.

Historian, *n.* A broad-gauge gossip.

History, *n.* An account mostly false, of events mostly unimportant, which are brought about by rulers mostly knaves, and soldiers mostly fools.

> Of Roman history, great Niebuhr's shown
> 'Tis nine-tenths lying. Faith, I wish 'twere known,
> Ere we accept great Niebuhr as a guide,
> Wherein he blundered and how much he lied.
>
> *Salder Bupp*

Hog, *n.* A bird remarkable for the catholicity of its appetite and serving to illustrate that of ours. Among the Mahometans and Jews, the hog is not in favor as an article of diet, but is respected for the delicacy of its habits, the beauty of its plumage and the melody of its voice. It is chiefly as a songster that the fowl is esteemed; a cage of him in full chorus has been known to draw tears from two persons at once. The scientific name of this dicky-bird is *Porcus Rockefelleri.* Mr. Rockefeller did not discover the hog, but it is considered his by right of resemblance.

Homœopathist, *n.* The humorist of the medical profession.

Homœopathy, *n.* A school of medicine midway between Allopathy and Christian Science. To the last both the others are distinctly inferior, for Christian Science will cure imaginary diseases, and they can not.

Homicide, *n.* The slaying of one human being by another. There are four kinds of homicide: felonious, excusable, justifiable and praiseworthy, but it makes no great difference to the person slain whether he fell by one kind or another—the classification is for advantage of the lawyers.

Homiletics, *n.* The science of adapting sermons to the spiritual needs, capacities and conditions of the congregation.

> So skilled the parson was in homiletics
> That all his moral purges and emetics
> To medicine the spirit were compounded
> With a most just discrimination founded
> Upon a rigorous examination
> Of tongue and pulse and heart and respiration.
> Then, having diagnosed each one's condition,

His scriptural specifics this physician
Administered—his pills so efficacious
And pukes of disposition so vivacious
That souls afflicted with ten kinds of Adam
Were convalescent ere they knew they had 'em.
But Slander's tongue—itself all coated—uttered
Her bilious mind and scandalously muttered
That in the case of patients having money
The pills were sugar and the pukes were honey.

Biography of Bishop Potter

Honorable, *adj.* Afflicted with an impediment in one's reach. In legislative bodies it is customary to mention all members as honorable; as, "the honorable gentleman is a scurvy cur."

Hope, *n.* Desire and expectation rolled into one.

Delicious Hope! when naught to man is left—
Of fortune destitute, of friends bereft;
When even his dog deserts him, and his goat
With tranquil disaffection chews his coat
While yet it hangs upon his back; then thou,
The star far-flaming on thine angel brow,
Descendest, radiant, from the skies to hint
The promise of a clerkship in the Mint.

Fogarty Weffing

Hospitality, *n.* The virtue which induces us to feed and lodge certain persons who are not in need of food and lodging.

Hostility, *n.* A peculiarly sharp and specially applied sense of the earth's over-population. Hostility is classed as active and passive; as (respectively) the feeling of a woman for her female friends, and that which she entertains for all the rest of her sex.

Houri, *n.* A comely female inhabiting the Mohammedan Paradise to make things cheery for the good Mussulman, whose belief in her existence marks a noble discontent with his earthly spouse, whom he denies a soul. By that good lady the Houris are said to be held in deficient esteem.

House, *n.* A hollow edifice erected for the habitation of man, rat, mouse, beetle, cockroach, fly, mosquito, flea, bacillus and microbe. *House of Correction*, a place of reward for political and personal service, and for the detention of offenders and appropriations. *House of God*, a building with a steeple and a mortage on it. *House-dog*, a pestilent beast kept on domestic premises to insult persons passing by and appal the hardy visitor. *House-maid*, a youngerly person of the opposing sex employed to be variously disagreeable and ingeniously unclean in the station in which it has pleased God to place her.

Houseless, *adj.* Having paid all taxes on household goods.

Hovel, *n.* The fruit of a flower called the Palace.

> Twaddle had a hovel,
>   Twiddle had a palace;
> Twaddle said: "I'll grovel
>   Or he'll think I bear him malice"—
> A sentiment as novel
>   As a castor on a chalice.
>
> Down upon the middle
>   Of his legs fell Twaddle
> And astonished Mr. Twiddle
>   Who began to lift his noddle,
>
>   Feed upon the fiddle—
>   Faddle flummery, unswaddle
> A new-born self-sufficiency and think himself a model.
>
> G.J.

Humanity, *n.* The human race, collectively, exclusive of the anthropoid poets.

Humorist, *n.* A plague that would have softened down the hoar austerity of Pharaoh's heart and persuaded him to dismiss Israel with his best wishes, cat-quick.

> Lo! the poor humorist, whose tortured mind
> See jokes in crowds, though still to gloom inclined—
> Whose simple appetite, untaught to stray,
> His brains, renewed by night, consumes by day.
> He thinks, admitted to an equal sty,
> A graceful hog would bear his company.
>
> *Alexander Poke*

Hurricane, *n.* An atmospheric demonstration once very common but now generally abandoned for the tornado and cyclone. The hurricane is still in popular use in the West Indies and is preferred by certain old-fashioned sea-captains. It is also used in the construction of the upper decks of steamboats, but generally speaking, the hurricane's usefulness has outlasted it.

Hurry, *n.* The dispatch of bunglers.

Husband, *n.* One who, having dined, is charged with the care of the plate.

Hybrid, *n.* A pooled issue.

Hydra, *n.* A kind of animal that the ancients catalogued under many heads.

Hyena, *n.* A beast held in reverence by some oriental nations from its habit of frequenting at night the burial-places of the dead. But the medical student does that.

Hypochondriasis, *n.* Depression of one's own spirits.

> Some heaps of trash upon a vacant lot
> Where long the village rubbish had been shot
> Displayed a sign among the stuff and stumps—
> "Hypochondriasis." It meant The Dumps.
> *Bogul S. Purvy*

Hypocrite, *n.* One who, professing virtues that he does not respect, secures the advantage of seeming to be what he despises.

I is the first letter of the alphabet, the first word of the language, the first thought of the mind, the first object of affection. In grammar it is a pronoun of the first person and singular number. Its plural is said to be *We*, but how there can be more than one myself is doubtless clearer to the grammarians than it is to the author of this incomparable dictionary. Conception of two myselves is difficult, but fine. The frank yet graceful use of "I" distinguishes a good writer from a bad; the latter carries it with the manner of a thief trying to cloak his loot.

Ichor, *n*. A fluid that serves the gods and goddesses in place of blood.

> Fair Venus, speared by Diomed,
> Restrained the raging chief and said:
> "Behold, rash mortal, whom you've bled—
> Your soul's stained white with ichorshed!"
>
> *Mary Doke*

Iconoclast, *n*. A breaker of idols, the worshipers whereof are imperfectly gratified by the performance, and most strenuously protest that he unbuildeth but doth not reëdify, that he pulleth down but pileth not up. For the poor things would have other idols in place of those he thwacketh upon the mazzard and dispelleth. But the iconoclast saith: "Ye shall have none at all, for ye need them not; and if the rebuilder fooleth round hereabout, behold I will depress the head of him and sit thereon till he squawk it."

Idiot, *n.* A member of a large and powerful tribe whose influence in human affairs has always been dominant and controlling. The Idiot's activity is not confined to any special field of thought or action, but "pervades and regulates the whole." He has the last word in everything; his decision is unappealable. He sets the fashions of opinion and taste, dictates the limitations of speech and circumscribes conduct with a dead-line.

Idleness, *n.* A model farm where the devil experiments with seeds of new sins and promotes the growth of staple vices.

Ignoramus, *n.* A person unacquainted with certain kinds of knowledge familiar to yourself, and having certain other kinds that you know nothing about.

> Dumble was an ignoramus,
> Mumble was for learning famous.
> Mumble said one day to Dumble:
> "Ignorance should be more humble.
> Not a spark have you of knowledge
> That was got in any college."
> Dumble said to Mumble: "Truly
> You're self-satisfied unduly.
> Of things in college I'm denied
> A knowledge—you of all beside."
>
> *Borelli*

Illuminati, *n.* A sect of Spanish heretics of the latter part of the sixteenth century; so called because they were light weights—*cunctationes illuminati.*

Illustrious, *adj.* Suitably placed for the shafts of malice, envy and detraction.

Imagination, *n.* A warehouse of facts, with poet and liar in joint ownership.

Imbecility, *n.* A kind of divine inspiration, or sacred fire affecting censorious critics of this dictionary.

Immigrant, *n.* An unenlightened person who thinks one country better than another.

Immodest, *adj.* Having a strong sense of one's own merit, coupled with a feeble conception of worth in others.

> There was once a man in Ispahan
>   Ever and ever so long ago,
>
> And he had a head, the phrenologists said,
>   That fitted him for a show.
>
> For his modesty's bump was so large a lump
>   (Nature, they said, had taken a freak)
> That its summit stood far above the wood
>   Of his hair, like a mountain peak.
>
> So modest a man in all Ispahan,
>   Over and over again they swore—
> So humble and meek, you would vainly seek;
>   None ever was found before.
>
> Meantime the hump of that awful bump
>   Into the heavens contrived to get
> To so great a height that they called the wight
>   The man with a minaret.
>
> There wasn't a man in all Ispahan
>   Prouder, or louder in praise of his chump:
> With a tireless tongue and a brazen lung
>   He bragged of that beautiful bump
>
> Till the Shah in a rage sent a trusty page
>   Bearing a sack and a bow-string too,
> And that gentle child explained as he smiled:
>   "A little present for you."
>
> The saddest man in all Ispahan,
>   Sniffed at the gift, yet accepted the same.
> "If I'd lived," said he, "my humility
>   Had given me deathless fame!"
>
> *Sukker Uffro*

Immoral, *adj.* Inexpedient. Whatever in the long run and with regard to the greater number of instances men find to be generally inexpedient comes to be considered wrong, wicked, immoral. If man's notions of right and wrong have any other basis than this of expediency; if they originated, or could have originated, in any other way; if actions have in themselves a moral character apart from and nowise dependent on, their consequences—then all philosophy is a lie and reason a disorder of the mind.

Immortality, *n.*

> A toy which people cry for,
> And on their knees apply for,
> Dispute, contend and lie for,
>   And if allowed
>   Would be right proud
> Eternally to die for.
>
> G.J.

Impale, *v.t.* In popular usage to pierce with any weapon which remains fixed in the wound. This, however, is inaccurate; to impale is, properly, to put to death by thrusting an upright sharp stake into the body, the victim being left in a sitting posture. This was a common mode of punishment among many of the nations of antiquity, and is still in high favor in China and other parts of Asia. Down to the beginning of the fifteenth century it was widely employed in "churching" heretics and schismatics. Wolecraft calls it the "stoole of repentynge," and among the common people it was jocularly known as "riding the one-legged horse." Ludwig Salzmann informs us that in Thibet impalement is considered the most appropriate punishment for crimes against religion; and although in China it is sometimes awarded for secular offences, it is most frequently adjudged in cases of sacrilege. To the person in actual experience of impalement it must be a matter of minor importance by what kind of civil or religious dissent he was made acquainted with its discomforts; but doubtless he would feel a certain satisfaction if able to contemplate himself in the character of a weather-cock on the spire of the True Church.

Impartial, *adj.* Unable to perceive any promise of personal advantage from espousing either side of a controversy or adopting either of two conflicting opinions.

Impenitence, *n.* A state of mind intermediate in point of time between sin and punishment.

Impiety, *n.* Your irreverence toward my deity.

Imposition, *n.* The act of blessing or consecrating by the laying on of hands—a ceremony common to many ecclesiastical systems, but performed with the frankest sincerity by the sect known as Thieves.

> "Lo! by the laying on of hands,"
>   Say parson, priest and dervise,
> "We consecrate your cash and lands
>   To ecclesiastic service.
> No doubt you'll swear till all is blue
> At such an imposition. Do."
>
>   *Pollo Doncas*

Impostor, *n.* A rival aspirant to public honors.

Improbability, *n.*

> His tale he told with a solemn face
> And a tender, melancholy grace.
>   Improbable 'twas, no doubt,
>   When you came to think it out,
>   But the fascinated crowd
>   Their deep surprise avowed
> And all with a single voice averred
> 'Twas the most amazing thing they'd heard—
> All save one who spake never a word,
>   But sat as mum
>   As if deaf and dumb,
> Serene, indifferent and unstirred.
>
> Then all the others turned to him
> And scrutinized him limb from limb—
>   Scanned him alive;
>   But he seemed to thrive
> And tranquiler grow each minute,
> As if there were nothing in it.

> "What! what!" cried one, "are you not amazed
> At what our friend has told?" He raised
> Soberly then his eyes and gazed
>   In a natural way
>   And proceeded to say,
> As he crossed his feet on the mantel-shelf:
> "O no—not at all; I'm a liar myself."

Improvidence, *n.* Provision for the needs of to-day from the revenues of tomorrow.

Impunity, *n.* Wealth.

Inadmissible, *adj.* Not competent to be considered. Said of certain kinds of testimony which juries are supposed to be unfit to be entrusted with, and which judges, therefore, rule out, even of proceedings before themselves alone. Hearsay evidence is inadmissible because the person quoted was unsworn and is not before the court for examination; yet most momentous actions, military, political, commercial and of every other kind, are daily undertaken on hearsay evidence. There is no religion in the world that has any other basis than hearsay evidence. Revelation is hearsay evidence; that the Scriptures are the word of God we have only the testimony of men long dead whose identity is not clearly established and who are not known to have been sworn in any sense. Under the rules of evidence as they now exist in this country, no single assertion in the Bible has in its support any evidence admissible in a court of law. It cannot be proved that the battle of Blenheim ever was fought, that there was such a person as Julius Cæsar, such an empire as Assyria.

But as records of courts of justice are admissible, it can easily be proved that powerful and malevolent magicians once existed and were a scourge to mankind. The evidence (including confession) upon which certain women were convicted of witchcraft and executed was without a flaw; it is still unimpeachable. The judges' decisions based on it were sound in logic and in law. Nothing in any existing court was ever more thoroughly proved than the charges of witchcraft and sorcery for which so many suffered death. If there were no witches, human testimony and human reason are alike destitute of value.

Inauspiciously, *adv.* In an unpromising manner, the auspices being unfavorable. Among the Romans it was customary before undertaking any important action or enterprise to obtain from the augurs, or state prophets, some hint of its probable outcome; and one of their favorite and most trustworthy modes of divination consisted in observing the flight of birds—the omens thence derived being called *auspices.* Newspaper reporters and certain miscreant lexicographers have decided that the word—always in the plural—shall mean "patronage" or "management"; as, "The festivities were under the auspices of the Ancient and Honorable Order of Body-Snatchers"; or, "The hilarities were auspicated by the Knights of Hunger."

> A Roman slave appeared one day
> Before the Augur. "Tell me, pray,
> If—" here the Augur, smiling, made
> A checking gesture and displayed
> His open palm, which plainly itched,
> For visibly its surface twitched.
> A *denarius* (the Latin nickel)
> Successfully allayed the tickle,
> And then the slave proceeded: "Please
> Inform me whether Fate decrees
> Success or failure in what I
> To-night (if it be dark) shall try.
> Its nature? Never mind—I think
> 'Tis writ on this"—and with a wink
> Which darkened half the earth, he drew
> Another denarius to view,
> Its shining face attentive scanned,
> Then slipped it into the good man's hand,
> Who with great gravity said: "Wait
> While I retire to question Fate."
> That holy person then withdrew
> His sacred clay and passing through
> The temple's rearward gate, cried "Shoo!"
> Waving his robe of office. Straight
> Each sacred peacock and its mate
> (Maintained for Juno's favor) fled
> With clamor from the trees o'erhead,
> Where they were perching for the night.

The temple's roof received their flight,
For thither they would always go,
When danger threatened them below.
Back to the slave the Augur went:
"My son, forecasting the event
By flight of birds, I must confess
The auspices deny success."
That slave retired, a sadder man,
Abandoning his secret plan—
Which was (as well the crafty seer
Had from the first divined) to clear
The wall and fraudulently seize
On Juno's poultry in the trees.

G.J.

Income, *n.* The natural and rational gauge and measure of respectability, the commonly accepted standards being artificial, arbitrary and fallacious; for, as "Sir Sycophas Chrysolater" in the play has justly remarked, "the true use and function of property (in whatsoever it consisteth—coins or land, or houses, or merchant-stuff, or anything which may be named as holden of right to one's own subservience) as also of honors, titles, preferments and place, and all favor and acquaintance of persons of quality or ableness, are but to get money. Hence it followeth that all things are truly to be rated as of worth in measure of their serviceableness to that end; and their possessors should take rank in agreement thereto, neither the lord of an unproducing manor, howsoever broad and ancient, nor he who bears an unremunerate dignity, nor yet the pauper favorite of a king, being esteemed of level excellency with him whose riches are of daily accretion; and hardly should they whose wealth is barren claim and rightly take more honor than the poor and unworthy."

Incompatibility, *n.* In matrimony a similarity of tastes, particularly the taste for domination. Incompatibility may, however, consist of a meek-eyed matron living just around the corner. It has even been known to wear a moustache.

Incompossible, *adj.* Unable to exist if something else exists. Two things are incompossible when the world of being has scope enough for one of them, but not enough for both—as Walt Whitman's poetry and God's mercy to man. Incompossibility, it will be seen, is only incompatibility let loose. Instead of such low language as "Go heel yourself—I mean to kill you on sight," the words, "Sir, we are incompossible," would convey an equally significant intimation and in stately courtesy are altogether superior.

Incubus, *n.* One of a race of highly improper demons who, though probably not wholly extinct, may be said to have seen their best nights. For a complete account of *incubi* and *succubi*, including *incubæ*, and *succubæ*, see the *Liber Demonorum* of Protassus (Paris, 1328), which contains much curious information that would be out of place in a dictionary intended as a text-book for the public schools.

Victor Hugo relates that in the Channel Islands Satan himself— tempted more than elsewhere by the beauty of the women, doubtless—sometimes plays at *incubus*, greatly to the inconvenience and alarm of the good dames who wish to be loyal to their marriage vows, generally speaking. A certain lady applied to the parish priest to learn how they might, in the dark, distinguish the hardy intruder from their husbands. The holy man said they must feel his brow for horns; but Hugo is ungallant enough to hint a doubt of the efficacy of the test.

Incumbent, *n.* A person of the liveliest interest to the outcumbents.

Indecision, *n.* The chief element of success; "for whereas," said Sir Thomas Brewbold, "there is but one way to do nothing and divers ways to do something, whereof, to a surety, only one is the right way, it followeth that he who from indecision standeth still hath not so many chances of going astray as he who pusheth forwards"—a most clear and satisfactory exposition of the matter.

"Your prompt decision to attack," said General Grant on a certain occasion to General Gordon Granger, "was admirable; you had but five minutes to make up your mind in."

"Yes, sir," answered the victorious subordinate, "it is a great thing to know exactly what to do in an emergency. When in doubt whether to attack or retreat I never hesitate a moment—I toss up a copper."

"Do you mean to say that's what you did this time?"

"Yes, General; but for Heaven's sake don't reprimand me: I disobeyed the coin."

Indifferent, *adj.* Imperfectly sensible to distinctions among things.

> "You tiresome man!" cried Indolentio's wife,
> "You've grown indifferent to all in life."
> "Indifferent?" he drawled with a slow smile;
> "I would be, dear, but it is not worth while."
>
> *Apuleius M. Gokul*

Indigestion, *n.* A disease which the patient and his friends frequently mistake for deep religious conviction and concern for the salvation of mankind. As the simple Red Man of the western wild put it, with, it must be confessed, a certain force: "Plenty well, no pray; big bellyache, heap God."

Indiscretion, *n.* The guilt of woman.

Inexpedient, *adj.* Not calculated to advance one's interests.

Infancy, *n.* The period of our lives when, according to Wordsworth, "Heaven lies about us." The world begins lying about us pretty soon afterward.

Inferiæ, *n.* (Latin.) Among the Greeks and Romans, sacrifices for propitiation of the *Dii Manes,* or souls of dead heroes; for the pious ancients could not invent enough gods to satisfy their spiritual needs, and had to have a number of makeshift deities, or, as a sailor might say, jury-gods, which they made out of the most unpromising materials. It was while sacrificing a bullock to the spirit of Agamemnon that Laiaides, a priest of Aulis, was favored with an audience of that illustrious warrior's shade, who prophetically recounted to him the birth of Christ and the triumph of Christianity, giving him also a rapid but tolerably complete review of events down to the reign of Saint Louis. The narrative ended abruptly at that point owing to the inconsiderate crowing of a cock, which compelled the ghosted King of Men to scamper back to Hades. There is a fine mediæval flavor to this story, and as it has not been traced back further than Père Brateille, a pious but obscure writer at the court of Saint Louis, we shall probably not err on the side of presumption in considering it apocryphal, though Monsignor Capel's judgment of the matter might be different; and to that I bow—wow.

Infidel, *n.* In New York, one who does not believe in the Christian religion; in Constantinople, one who does. (See GIAOUR.) A kind of scoundrel imperfectly reverent of, and niggardly contributory to, divines, ecclesiastics, popes, parsons, canons, monks, mollahs, voodoos, presbyters, hierophants, prelates, obeah-men, abbés, nuns, missionaries, exhorters, deacons, friars, hadjis, high-priests, muezzins, brahmins, medicine-men, confessors, eminences, elders, primates, prebendaries, pilgrims, prophets, imaums, beneficiaries, clerks, vicars-choral, archbishops, bishops, abbots, priors, preachers, padres, abbotesses, caloyers, palmers, curates, patriarchs, bonezs, santons, beadsmen, canonesses, residentiaries, diocesans, deans, subdeans, rural deans, abdals, charm-sellers, archdeacons, hierarchs, class-leaders, incumbents, capitulars, sheiks, talapoins, postulants, scribes, gooroos, precentors, beadles, fakeers, sextons, reverences, revivalists, cenobites, perpetual curates, chaplains, mudjoes, readers, novices, vicars, pastors, rabbis, ulemas, lamas, sacristans, vergers, dervises, lectors, church wardens, cardinals, prioresses, suffragans, acolytes, rectors, cures, sophis, mutifs and pumpums.

Influence, *n.* In politics, a visionary *quo* given in exchange for a substantial *quid*.

Infralapsarian, *n.* One who ventures to believe that Adam need not have sinned unless he had a mind to—in opposition to the Supralapsarians, who hold that that luckless person's fall was decreed from the beginning. Infralapsarians are sometimes called Sublapsarians without material effect upon the importance and lucidity of their views about Adam.

> Two theologues once, as they wended their way
> To chapel, engaged in colloquial fray—
> An earnest logomachy, bitter as gall,
> Concerning poor Adam and what made him fall.
> "'Twas Predestination," cried one—"for the Lord
> Decreed he should fall of his own accord."
> "Not so—'twas Free will," the other maintained,
> "Which led him to choose what the Lord had ordained."
> So fierce and so fiery grew the debate
> That nothing but bloodshed their dudgeon could sate;

So off flew their cassocks and caps to the ground
And, moved by the spirit, their hands went round.
Ere either had proved his theology right
By winning, or even beginning, the fight,
A gray old professor of Latin came by,
A staff in his hand and a scowl in his eye,
And learning the cause of their quarrel (for still
As they clumsily sparred they disputed with skill
Of foreordinational freedom of will)
Cried: "Sirrahs! this reasonless warfare compose:
Atwixt ye's no difference worthy of blows.
The sects ye belong to—I'm ready to swear
Ye wrongly interpret the names that they bear.
You—Infralapsarian son of a clown!—
Should only contend that Adam slipped down;
While *you*—you Supralapsarian pup!—
Should nothing aver but that Adam slipped up."
It's all the same whether up or down
You slip on a peel of banana brown.
Even Adam analyzed not his blunder,
But thought he had slipped on a peal of thunder!

G.J.

Ingrate, *n.* One who receives a benefit from another, or is otherwise an object of charity.

"All men are ingrates," sneered the cynic. "Nay,"
    The good philanthropist replied;
"I did great service to a man one day
Who never since has cursed me to repay,
    Nor vilified."

"Ho!" cried the cynic, "lead me to him straight—
    With veneration I am overcome,
And fain would have his blessing." "Sad your fate—
He cannot bless you, for I grieve to state
    The man is dumb."

Ariel Selp

Injury, *n.* An offense next in degree of enormity to a slight.

Injustice, *n.* A burden which of all those that we load upon others and carry ourselves is lightest in the hands and heaviest upon the back.

Ink, *n.* A villainous compound of tanno-gallate of iron, gum-arabic and water, chiefly used to facilitate the infection of idiocy and promote intellectual crime. The properties of ink are peculiar and contradictory: it may be used to make reputations and unmake them; to blacken them and to make them white; but it is most generally and acceptably employed as a mortar to bind together the stones in an edifice of fame, and as a whitewash to conceal afterward the rascal quality of the material. There are men called journalists who have established ink baths which some persons pay money to get into, others to get out of. Not infrequently it occurs that a person who has paid to get in pays twice as much to get out.

Innate, *adj.* Natural, inherent—as innate ideas, that is to say, ideas that we are born with, having had them previously imparted to us. The doctrine of innate ideas is one of the most admirable faiths of philosophy, being itself an innate idea and therefore inaccessible to disproof, though Locke foolishly supposed himself to have given it "a black eye." Among innate ideas may be mentioned the belief in one's ability to conduct a newspaper, in the greatness of one's country, in the superiority of one's civilization, in the importance of one's personal affairs and in the interesting nature of one's diseases.

In'ards, *n.* The stomach, heart, soul and other bowels. Many eminent investigators do not class the soul as an in'ard, but that acute observer and renowned authority, Dr. Gunsaulus, is persuaded that the mysterious organ known as the spleen is nothing less than our immortal part. To the contrary, Professor Garrett P. Servis holds that man's soul is that prolongation of his spinal marrow which forms the pith of his no tail; and for demonstration of his faith points confidently to the fact that tailed animals have no souls. Concerning these two theories, it is best to suspend judgment by believing both.

Inscription, *n.* Something written on another thing. Inscriptions are of many kinds, but mostly memorial, intended to commemorate the fame of some illustrious person and hand down to distant ages the record of his services and virtues. To this class of inscriptions belongs the name of John Smith, penciled on the Washington monument. Following are examples of memorial inscriptions on tombstones: (See EPITAPH.)

"In the sky my soul is found,
And my body in the ground.
By and by my body'll rise
To my spirit in the skies,
Soaring up to Heaven's gate.
    1878."

"Sacred to the memory of Jeremiah Tree. Cut down May 9th, 1862, aged 27 yrs. 4 mos. and 12 ds. Indigenous."

"Affliction sore long time she boar,
Phisicians was in vain,
Till Deth released the dear deceased
    And left her a remain.
Gone to join Ananias in the regions of bliss."

"The clay that rests beneath this stone
As Silas Wood was widely known.
Now, lying here, I ask what good
It was to me to be S. Wood.
O Man, let not ambition trouble you,
Is the advice of Silas W."

"Richard Haymon, of Heaven. Fell to Earth Jan. 20, 1807, and had the dust brushed off him Oct. 3, 1874."

Insectivora, *n.*

"See," cries the chorus of admiring preachers,
"How Providence provides for all His creatures!"
"His care," the gnat said, "even the insect follows:
For us He has provided wrens and swallows."

Sempen Railey

Insurance, *n.* An ingenious modern game of chance in which the player is permitted to enjoy the comfortable conviction that he is beating the man who keeps the table.

INSURANCE AGENT: My dear sir, that is a fine house—pray let me insure it.

HOUSE OWNER: With pleasure. Please make the annual premium so low that by the time when, according to the tables of your actuary, it will probably be destroyed by fire I will have paid you considerably less than the face of the policy.

INSURANCE AGENT: O dear, no—we could not afford to do that. We must fix the premium so that you will have paid more.

HOUSE OWNER: How, then, can *I* afford *that*?

INSURANCE AGENT: Why, your house may burn down at any time. There was Smith's house, for example, which—

HOUSE OWNER: Spare me—there were Brown's house, on the contrary, and Jones's house, and Robinson's house, which—

INSURANCE AGENT: Spare *me*!

HOUSE OWNER: Let us understand each other. You want me to pay you money on the supposition that something will occur previously to the time set by yourself for its occurrence. In other words, you expect me to bet that my house will not last so long as you say that it will probably last.

INSURENCE AGENT: But if your house burns without insurance it will be a total loss.

HOUSE OWNER: Beg your pardon—by your own actuary's tables I shall probably have saved, when it burns, all the premiums I would otherwise have paid to you—amounting to more than the face of the policy they would have bought. But suppose it to burn, uninsured, before the time upon which your figures are based. If I could not afford that, how could you if it were insured?

INSURANCE AGENT: O, we should make ourselves whole from our luckier ventures with other clients. Virtually, they pay your loss.

HOUSE OWNER: And virtually, then, don't I help to pay their losses? Are not their houses as likely as mine to burn before they have paid you as much as you must pay them? The case stands this way: you expect to take more money from your clients than you pay to them, do you not?

INSURANCE AGENT: Certainly; if we did not—

HOUSE OWNER: I would not trust you with my money. Very well, then. If it is *certain*, with reference to the whole body of your clients, that they lose money on you it is *probable*, with reference to any one of them, that *he* will. It is these individual probabilities that made the aggregate certainty.

INSURANCE AGENT: I will not deny it—but look at the figures in this pamph—

HOUSE OWNER: Heaven forbid!

INSURANCE AGENT: You spoke of saving the premiums which you would otherwise pay to me. Will you not be more likely to squander them? We offer you an incentive to thrift.

HOUSE OWNER: The willingness of A to take care of B's money is not peculiar to insurance, but as a charitable institution you command esteem. Deign to accept its expression from a Deserving Object.

Insurrection, *n.* An unsuccessful revolution. Disaffection's failure to substitute misrule for bad government.

Intention, *n.* The mind's sense of the prevalence of one set of influences over another set; an effect whose cause is the imminence, immediate or remote, of the performance of an involuntary act.

Interpreter, *n.* One who enables two persons of different languages to understand each other by repeating to each what it would have been to the interpreter's advantage for the other to have said.

Interregnum, *n.* The period during which a monarchical country is governed by a warm spot on the cushion of a throne. The experiment of letting the spot grow cold has commonly been attended by most unhappy results from the zeal of many worthy persons to make it warm again.

Intimacy, *n.* A relation into which fools are providentially drawn for their mutual destruction.

Two Seidlitz powders, one in blue
And one in white, together drew,
And having each a pleasant sense
Of t'other powder's excellence,
Forsook their jackets for the snug
Enjoyment of a common mug.
So close their intimacy grew
One paper would have held the two.
To confidences straight they fell,
Less anxious each to hear than tell;
Then each remorsefully confessed
To all the virtues he possessed,
Acknowledging he had them in
So high degree it was a sin.

The more they said, the more they felt
Their spirits with emotion melt,
Till tears of sentiment expressed
Their feelings. Then they effervesced!
So Nature executes her feats
Of wrath on friends and sympathetes
The good old rule who won't apply,
That you are you and I am I.

Introduction, *n.* A social ceremony invented by the devil for the gratification of his servants and the plaguing of his enemies. The introduction attains its most malevolent development in this country, being, indeed, closely related to our political system. Every American being the equal of every other American, it follows that everybody has the right to know everybody else, which implies the right to introduce without request or permission. The Declaration of Independence should have read thus:

> "We hold these truths to be self-evident: that all men are created equal; that they are endowed by their Creator with certain inalienable rights; that among these are life, and the right to make that of another miserable by thrusting upon him an incalculable quantity of acquaintances; liberty, particularly the liberty to introduce persons to one another without first ascertaining if they are not already acquainted as enemies; and the pursuit of another's happiness with a running pack of strangers."

Inventor, *n.* A person who makes an ingenious arrangement of wheels, levers and springs, and believes it civilization.

Irreligion, *n.* The principal one of the great faiths of the world.

Itch, *n.* The patriotism of a Scotchman.

J is a consonant in English, but some nations use it as a vowel—than which nothing could be more absurd. Its original form, which has been but slightly modified, was that of the tail of a subdued dog, and it was not a letter but a character, standing for a Latin verb, *jacere*, "to throw," because when a stone is thrown at a dog the dog's tail assumes that shape. This is the origin of the letter, as expounded by the renowned Dr. Jocolpus Bumer, of the University of Belgrade, who established his conclusions on the subject in a work of three quarto volumes and committed suicide on being reminded that the j in the Roman alphabet had originally no curl.

Jealous, *adj.* Unduly concerned about the preservation of that which can be lost only if not worth keeping.

Jester, *n.* An officer formerly attached to a king's household, whose business it was to amuse the court by ludicrous actions and utterances, the absurdity being attested by his motley costume. The king himself being attired with dignity, it took the world some centuries to discover that his own conduct and decrees were sufficiently ridiculous for the amusement not only of his court but of all mankind. The jester was commonly called a fool, but the poets and romancers have ever delighted to represent him as a singularly wise and witty person. In the circus of to-day the melancholy ghost of the court fool effects the dejection of humbler audiences with the same jests wherewith in life he gloomed the marble hall,

panged the patrician sense of humor and tapped the tank of royal
tears.

> The widow-queen of Portugal
>   Had an audacious jester
> Who entered the confessional
>   Disguised, and there confessed her.
>
> "Father," she said, "thine ear bend down—
>   My sins are more than scarlet:
> I love my fool—blaspheming clown,
>   And common, base-born varlet."
>
> "Daughter," the mimic priest replied,
>   "That sin, indeed, is awful:
> The church's pardon is denied
>   To love that is unlawful.
>
> "But since thy stubborn heart will be
>   For him forever pleading,
> Thou'dst better make him, by decree,
>   A man of birth and breeding."
>
> She made the fool a duke, in hope
>   With Heaven's taboo to palter;
> Then told a priest, who told the Pope,
>   Who damned her from the altar!

Barel Dort

Jews-harp, *n.* An unmusical instrument, played by holding it fast with
the teeth and trying to brush it away with the finger.

Joss-sticks, *n.* Small sticks burned by the Chinese in their pagan tom-
foolery, in imitation of certain sacred rites of our holy religion.

Justice, *n.* A commodity which in a more or less adulterated condition
the State sells to the citizen as a reward for his allegiance, taxes and
personal service.

K is a consonant that we get from the Greeks, but it can be traced away back beyond them to the Cerathians, a small commercial nation inhabiting the peninsula of Smero. In their tongue it was called *Klatch*, which means "destroyed." The form of the letter was originally precisely that of our H, but the erudite Dr. Snedeker explains that it was altered to its present shape to commemorate the destruction of the great temple of Jarute by an earthquake, *circa* 730 B.C. This building was famous for the two lofty columns of its portico, one of which was broken in half by the catastrophe, the other remaining intact. As the earlier form of the letter is supposed to have been suggested by these pillars, so, it is thought by the great antiquary, its later was adopted as a simple and natural—not to say touching—means of keeping the calamity ever in the national memory. It is not known if the name of the letter was altered as an additional mnemonic, or if the name was always *Klatch* and the destruction one of nature's puns. As each theory seems probable enough, I see no objection to believing both and Dr. Snedeker arrayed himself on that side of the question.

Keep, *v.t.*

> He willed away his whole estate,
>   And then in death he fell asleep,
> Murmuring: "Well, at any rate,
>   My name unblemished I shall keep."

But when upon the tomb 'twas wrought
Whose was it?—for the dead keep naught.

Durang Gophel Arn

Kill, *v.t.* To create a vacancy without nominating a successor.

Kilt, *n.* A costume sometimes worn by Scotchmen in America and Americans in Scotland.

Kindness, *n.* A brief preface to ten volumes of exaction.

King, *n.* A male person commonly known in America as a "crowned head," although he never wears a crown and has usually no head to speak of.

A king, in times long, long gone by,
    Said to his lazy jester:
"If I were you and you were I
My moments merrily would fly—
    No care nor grief to pester."

"The reason, Sire, that you would thrive,"
    The fool said—"if you'll hear it—
Is that of all the fools alive
Who own you for their sovereign, I've
    The most forgiving spirit."

Oogum Bem

King's Evil, *n.* A malady that was formerly cured by the touch of the sovereign, but has now to be treated by the physicians. Thus "the most pious Edward" of England used to lay his royal hand upon his ailing subjects and make them whole—

a crowd of wretched souls
That stay his cure: their malady convinces
The great essay of art; but at his touch,
Such sanctity hath Heaven given his hand,
They presently amend.

as the "Doctor" in *Macbeth* hath it. This useful property of the royal hand could, it appears, be transmitted along with other crown properties; for according to "Malcolm,"

'tis spoken,
To the succeeding royalty he leaves
The healing benediction.

But the gift somewhere dropped out of the line of succession: the later sovereigns of England have not been tactual healers, and the disease once honored with the name "king's evil" now bears the humbler one of "scrofula," from *scrofa,* a sow. The date and author of the following epigram are known only to the author of this dictionary, but it is old enough to show that the jest about Scotland's national disorder is not a thing of yesterday.

Yᵉ Kynge his evill in me laye,
Wh. he of Scottlande charmed awaye.
He layde his hand on mine and sayd:
"Be gone!" Yᵉ ill no longer stayd.
But O yᵉ wofull plyght in wh.
I'm now y-pight: I have yᵉ itche!

The superstition that maladies can be cured by royal taction is dead, but like many a departed conviction it has left a monument of custom to keep its memory green. The practice of forming in line and shaking the President's hand had no other origin, and when that great dignitary bestows his healing salutation on

strangely visited people,
All swoln and ulcerous, pitiful to the eye,
The mere despair of surgery,

he and his patients are handing along an extinguished torch which once was kindled at the altar-fire of a faith long held by all classes of men. It is a beautiful and edifying "survival"—one which brings the sainted past close home to our "business and bosoms."

Kiss, *n.* A word invented by the poets as a rhyme for "bliss." It is supposed to signify, in a general way, some kind of rite or ceremony appertaining to a good understanding; but the manner of its performance is unknown to this lexicographer.

Kleptomaniac, *n.* A rich thief.

Knight, *n.*

> Once a warrior gentle of birth,
> Then a person of civic worth,
> Now a fellow to move our mirth.
> Warrior, person, and fellow—no more:
> We must knight our dogs to get any lower.
> Brave Knights Kennelers then shall be,
> Noble Knights of the Golden Flea,
> Knights of the Order of St. Steboy,
> Knights of St. Gorge and Sir Knights Jawy.
> God speed the day when this knighting fad
> Shall go to the dogs and the dogs go mad.

Koran, *n.* A book which the Mohammedans foolishly believe to have been written by divine inspiration, but which Christians know to be a wicked imposture, contradictory to the Holy Scriptures.

Labor, *n.* One of the processes by which A acquires property for B.

Land, *n.* A part of the earth's surface, considered as property. The theory that land is property subject to private ownership and control is the foundation of modern society, and is eminently worthy of the superstructure. Carried to its logical conclusion, it means that some have the right to prevent others from living; for the right to own implies the right exclusively to occupy; and in fact laws of trespass are enacted wherever property in land is recognized. It follows that if the whole area of *terra firma* is owned by A, B and C, there will be no place for D, E, F and G to be born, or, born as trespassers, to exist.

> A life on the ocean wave,
>   A home on the rolling deep,
> For the spark that nature gave
>   I have there the right to keep.
>
> They give me the cat-o'-nine
>   Whenever I go ashore.
> Then ho! for the flashing brine—
>   I'm a natural commodore!

> *Dodle*

Language, *n.* The music with which we charm the serpents guarding another's treasure.

Laocoon, *n.* A famous piece of antique sculpture representing a priest of that name and his two sons in the folds of two enormous serpents. The skill and diligence with which the old man and lads support the serpents and keep them up to their work have been justly regarded as one of the noblest artistic illustrations of the mastery of human intelligence over brute inertia.

Lap, *n.* One of the most important organs of the female system—an admirable provision of nature for the repose of infancy, but chiefly useful in rural festivities to support plates of cold chicken and heads of adult males. The male of our species has a rudimentary lap, imperfectly developed and in no way contributing to the animal's substantial welfare.

Last, *n.* A shoemaker's implement, named by a frowning Providence as opportunity to the maker of puns.

> Ah, punster, would my lot were cast,
>   Where the cobbler is unknown
> So that I might forget his last
>   And hear your own.
>
> *Gargo Repsky*

Laughter, *n.* An interior convulsion, producing a distortion of the features and accompanied by inarticulate noises. It is infectious and, though intermittent, incurable. Liability to attacks of laughter is one of the characteristics distinguishing man from the animals—these being not only inaccessible to the provocation of his example, but impregnable to the microbes having original jurisdiction in bestowal of the disease. Whether laughter could be imparted to animals by inoculation from the human patient is a question that has not been answered by experimentation. Dr. Meir Witchell holds that the infectious character of laughter is due to instantaneous fermentation of *sputa* diffused in a spray. From this peculiarity he names the disorder *Convulsio spargens*.

Laureate, *adj.* Crowned with leaves of the laurel. In England the Poet Laureate is an officer of the sovereign's court, acting as dancing skeleton at every royal feast and singing—mute at every royal funeral. Of all incumbents of that high office, Robert Southey had the most notable knack at drugging the Samson of public joy and cutting his hair to the quick; and he had an artistic color-sense which enabled him so to blacken a public grief as to give it the aspect of a national crime.

Laurel, *n.* The *laurus*, a vegetable dedicated to Apollo, and formerly defoliated to wreathe the brows of victors and such poets as had influence at court. (*Vide Supra.*)

Law, *n.*

> Once Law was sitting on the bench,
>   And Mercy knelt a-weeping.
> "Clear out!" he cried, "disordered wench!
>   Nor come before me creeping.
> Upon your knees if you appear,
> 'Tis plain you have no standing here."
>
> Then Justice came. His Honor cried:
>   "*Your* status? —devil seize you!"
> "*Amica curiae*," she replied—
>   "Friend of the court, so please you."
> "Begone!" he shouted—"there's the door—
> I never saw your face before!"
>
>   G.J.

Lawful, *adj.* Compatible with the will of a judge having jurisdiction.

Lawyer, *n.* One skilled in circumvention of the law.

Laziness, *n.* Unwarranted repose of manner in a person of low degree.

Lead, *n.* A heavy blue-gray metal much used in giving stability to light lovers—particularly to those who love not wisely but other men's wives. Lead is also of great service as a counterpoise to an argument of such weight that it turns the scale of debate the wrong way. An interesting fact in the chemistry of international controversy is that at the point of contact of two patriotisms lead is precipitated in great quantities.

> Hail, holy Lead!—of human feuds the great
>   And universal arbiter; endowed
>   With penetration to pierce any cloud
> Fogging the field of controversial hate,

And with a swift, inevitable, straight,
Searching precision find the unavowed
But vital point. Thy judgment, when allowed
By the chirurgeon, settles the debate.
O useful metal!—were it not for thee
We'd grapple one another's ears alway:
But when we hear thee buzzing like a bee
We, like old Muhlenberg, "care to stay."
And when the quick have run away like pullets
Jack Satan smelts the dead to make new bullets.

Learning, *n.* The kind of ignorance distinguishing the studious.

Lecturer, *n.* One with his hand in your pocket, his tongue in your ear and his faith in your patience.

Legacy, *n.* A gift from one who is legging it out of this vale of tears.

Leonine, *adj.* Unlike a menagerie lion. Leonine verses are those in which a word in the middle of a line rhymes with a word at the end, as in this famous passage from Bella Peeler Silcox:

The electric light invades the dunnest deep of Hades.
Cries Pluto, 'twixt his snores: "O tempora! O mores!"

It should be explained that Mrs. Silcox does not undertake to teach the pronunciation of the Greek and Latin tongues. Leonine verses are so called in honor of a poet named Leo, whom prosodists appear to find a pleasure in believing to have been the first to discover that a rhyming couplet could be run into a single line.

Lettuce, *n.* An herb of the genus *Lactuca,* "Wherewith," says that pious gastronome, Hengist Pelly, "God has been pleased to reward the good and punish the wicked. For by his inner light the righteous man has discerned a manner of compounding for it a dressing to the appetency whereof a multitude of gustible condiments conspire, being reconciled and ameliorated with profusion of oil, the entire comestible making glad the heart of the godly and causing his face to shine. But the person of spiritual unworth is successfully tempted of the Adversary to eat of lettuce with destitution of oil, mustard, egg, salt and garlic, and with a rascal bath of vinegar polluted with sugar. Wherefore the person of spiritual unworth suffers an intestinal pang of strange complexity and raises the song."

Leviathan, *n.* An enormous aquatic animal mentioned by Job. Some suppose it to have been the whale, but that distinguished ichthyologer, Dr. Jordan, of Stanford University, maintains with considerable heat that it was a species of gigantic Tadpole (*Thaddeus Polandensis*) or Polliwig-*Maria pseudo-hirsuta*. For an exhaustive description and history of the Tadpole consult the famous monograph of Jane Porter, *Thaddeus of Warsaw*.

Lexicographer, *n.* A pestilent fellow who, under the pretense of recording some particular stage in the development of a language, does what he can to arrest its growth, stiffen its flexibility and mechanize its methods. For your lexicographer, having written his dictionary, comes to be considered "as one having authority," whereas his function is only to make a record, not to give a law. The natural servility of the human understanding having invested him with judicial power, surrenders its right of reason and submits itself to a chronicle as if it were a statute. Let the dictionary (for example) mark a good word as "obsolete" or "obsolescent" and few men thereafter venture to use it, whatever their need of it and however desirable its restoration to favor—whereby the process of impoverishment is accelerated and speech decays. On the contrary, the bold and discerning writer who, recognizing the truth that language must grow by innovation if it grow at all, makes new words and uses the old in an unfamiliar sense, has no following and is tartly reminded that "it isn't in the dictionary"—although down to the time of the first lexicographer (Heaven forgive him!) no author ever had used a word that *was* in the dictionary. In the golden prime and high noon of English speech; when from the lips of the great Elizabethans fell words that made their own meaning and carried it in their very sound; when a Shakespeare and a Bacon were possible, and the language now rapidly perishing at one end and slowly renewed at the other was in vigorous growth and hardy preservation—sweeter than honey and stronger than a lion—the lexicographer was a person unknown, the dictionary a creation which his Creator had not created him to create.

God said: "Let Spirit perish into Form,"
And lexicographers arose, a swarm!
Thought fled and left her clothing, which they took,
And catalogued each garment in a book.
Now, from her leafy covert when she cries:
"Give me my clothes and I'll return," they rise
And scan the list, and say without compassion:
"Excuse us—they are mostly out of fashion."

Sigismund Smith

Liar, *n.* A lawyer with a roving commission.

Liberty, *n.* One of Imagination's most precious possessions.

The rising People, hot and out of breath,
Roared round the palace: "Liberty or death!"
"If death will do," the King said, "let me reign;
You'll have, I'm sure, no reason to complain."

Martha Braymance

Lickspittle, *n.* A useful functionary, not infrequently found editing a newspaper. In his character of editor he is closely allied to the blackmailer by the tie of occasional identity; for in truth the lickspittle is only the blackmailer under another aspect, though the latter is frequently found as an independent species. Lickspittling is more detestable than blackmailing, precisely as the business of a confidence man is more detestable than that of a highway robber; and the parallel maintains itself throughout, for whereas few robbers will cheat, every sneak will plunder if he dare.

Life, *n.* A spiritual pickle preserving the body from decay. We live in daily apprehension of its loss; yet when lost it is not missed. The question, "Is life worth living?" has been much discussed; particularly by those who think it is not, many of whom have written at great length in support of their view and by careful observance of the laws of health enjoyed for long terms of years the honors of successful controversy.

"Life's not worth living, and that's the truth,"
Carelessly caroled the golden youth.
In manhood still he maintained that view
And held it more strongly the older he grew.

When kicked by a jackass at eighty-three,
"Go fetch me a surgeon at once!" cried he.

Han Soper

Lighthouse, *n.* A tall building on the seashore in which the government maintains a lamp and the friend of a politician.

Limb, *n.* The branch of a tree or the leg of an American woman.

'Twas a pair of boots that the lady bought,
    And the salesman laced them tight
    To a very remarkable height—
Higher, indeed, than I think he ought—
    Higher than *can* be right.
For the Bible declares—but never mind:
    It is hardly fit
To censure freely and fault to find
With others for sins that I'm not inclined
    Myself to commit.
Each has his weakness, and though my own
Is freedom from every sin,
    It still were unfair to pitch in,
Discharging the first censorious stone.
Besides, the truth compels me to say,
The boots in question were *made* that way.
As he drew the lace she made a grimace,
    And blushingly said to him:
"This boot, I'm sure, is too high to endure,
It hurts me—hurts my—limb."
The salesman smiled in a manner mild,
Like an artless, undesigning child;
Then, checking himself, to his face he gave
A look as sorrowful as the grave,
    Though he didn't care two figs
For her pains and throes,
As he stroked her toes,
Remarking with speech and manner just
Befitting his calling: "Madam, I trust
    That it doesn't hurt your twigs."

B. Percival Dike

Linen, *n.* "A kind of cloth the making of which, when made of hemp, entails a great waste of hemp."—*Calcraft the Hangman*

Litigant, *n.* A person about to give up his skin for the hope of retaining his bones.

Litigation, *n.* A machine which you go into as a pig and come out of as a sausage.

Liver, *n.* A large red organ thoughtfully provided by nature to be bilious with. The sentiments and emotions which every literary anatomist now knows to haunt the heart were anciently believed to infest the liver; and even Gascoygne, speaking of the emotional side of human nature, calls it "our hepaticall parte." It was at one time considered the seat of life; hence its name—liver, the thing we live with. The liver is heaven's best gift to the goose; without it that bird would be unable to supply us with the Strasbourg *pâté*.

LL.D. Letters indicating the degree *Legumptionorum Doctor,* one learned in laws, gifted with legal gumption. Some suspicion is cast upon this derivation by the fact that the title was formerly *££.d.*, and conferred only upon gentlemen distinguished for their wealth. At the date of this writing Columbia University is considering the expediency of making another degree for clergymen, in place of the old D.D.—*Damnator Diaboli.* The new honor will be known as *Sanctorum Custus,* and written *$$c.* The name of the Rev. John Satan has been suggested as a suitable recipient by a lover of consistency, who points out that Professor Harry Thurston Peck has long enjoyed the advantage of a degree.

Lock-and-key, *n.* The distinguishing device of civilization and enlightenment.

Lodger, *n.* A less popular name for the Second Person of that delectable newspaper Trinity, the Roomer, the Bedder and the Mealer.

Logic, *n.* The art of thinking and reasoning in strict accordance with the limitations and incapacities of the human misunderstanding. The basic of logic is the syllogism, consisting of a major and a minor premise and a conclusion—thus:

Major Premise: Sixty men can do a piece of work sixty times as quickly as one man.

Minor Premise: One man can dig a post-hole in sixty seconds; therefore—*Conclusion*: Sixty men can dig a post-hole in one second.

This may be called the syllogism arithmetical, in which, by

combining logic and mathematics, we obtain a double certainty
and are twice blessed.

Logomachy, *n.* A war in which the weapons are words and the wounds
punctures in the swim-bladder of self-esteem—a kind of contest in
which, the vanquished being unconscious of defeat, the victor is
denied the reward of success.

> 'Tis said by divers of the scholar-men
> That poor Salmasius died of Milton's pen.
> Alas! we cannot know if this is true,
> For reading Milton's wit we perish too.

Longanimity, *n.* The disposition to endure injury with meek forbear-
ance while maturing a plan of revenge.

Longevity, *n.* Uncommon extension of the fear of death.

Looking-glass, *n.* A vitreous plane upon which to display a fleeting
show for man's disillusion given.

The King of Manchuria had a magic looking-glass, whereon
whoso looked saw, not his own image, but only that of the king. A
certain courtier who had long enjoyed the king's favor and was
thereby enriched beyond any other subject of the realm, said to
the king: "Give me, I pray, thy wonderful mirror, so that when
absent out of thine august presence I may yet do homage before
thy visible shadow, prostrating myself night and morning in the
glory of thy benign countenance, as which nothing has so divine
splendor, O Noonday Sun of the Universe!"

Pleased with the speech, the king commanded that the mirror
be conveyed to the courtier's palace; but after, having gone thither
without apprisal, he found it in an apartment where was naught
but idle lumber. And the mirror was dimmed with dust and over-
laced with cobwebs. This so angered him that he fisted it hard,
shattering the glass, and was sorely hurt. Enraged all the more by
this mischance, he commanded that the ungrateful courtier be
thrown into prison, and that the glass be repaired and taken back
to his own palace; and this was done. But when the king looked
again on the mirror he saw not his image as before, but only the
figure of a crowned ass, having a bloody bandage on one of its hinder hooves—as the artificers and all who had looked upon it had

before discerned but feared to report. Taught wisdom and charity, the king restored his courtier to liberty, had the mirror set into the back of the throne and reigned many years with justice and humility; and one day when he fell asleep in death while on the throne, the whole court saw in the mirror the luminous figure of an angel, which remains to this day.

Loquacity, *n.* A disorder which renders the sufferer unable to curb his tongue when you wish to talk.

Lord, *n.* In American society, an English tourist above the state of a costermonger, as, Lord 'Aberdasher, Lord Hartisan and so forth. The traveling Briton of lesser degree is addressed as "Sir," as, Sir 'Arry Donkiboi, of 'Amstead 'Eath. The word "Lord" is sometimes used, also, as a title of the Supreme Being; but this is thought to be rather flattery than true reverence.

> Miss Sallie Ann Splurge, of her own accord,
> Wedded a wandering English lord—
> Wedded and took him to dwell with her "paw,"
> A parent who throve by the practice of Draw.
> Lord Cadde I don't hesitate here to declare
> Unworthy the father-in-legal care
> Of that elderly sport, notwithstanding the truth
> That Cadde had renounced all the follies of youth;
> For, sad to relate, he'd arrived at the stage
> Of existence that's marked by the vices of age.
> Among them, cupidity caused him to urge
> Repeated demands on the pocket of Splurge,
> Till, wrecked in his fortune, that gentleman saw
> Inadequate aid in the practice of Draw,
> And took, as a means of augmenting his pelf,
> To the business of being a lord himself.
> His neat-fitting garments he wilfully shed
> And sacked himself strangely in checks instead;
> Denuded his chin, but retained at each ear
> A whisker that looked like a blasted career.
> He painted his neck an incarnadine hue
> Each morning and varnished it all that he knew.
> The moony monocular set in his eye
> Appeared to be scanning the Sweet Bye-and-Bye.
> His head was enroofed with a billycock hat,

And his low-necked shoes were aduncous and flat.
In speech he eschewed his American ways,
Denying his nose to the use of his A's
And dulling their edge till the delicate sense
Of a babe at their temper could take no offence.
His H's—'twas most inexpressibly sweet,
The patter they made as they fell at his feet!
Re-outfitted thus, Mr. Splurge without fear
Began as Lord Splurge his recouping career.
Alas, the Divinity shaping his end
Entertained other views and decided to send
His lordship in horror, despair and dismay
From the land of the nobleman's natural prey.
For, smit with his Old World ways, Lady Cadde
Fell—suffering Cæsar!—in love with her dad!

                                                                    G.J.

Lore, *n.* Learning—particularly that sort which is not derived from a regular course of instruction but comes of the reading of occult books, or by nature. This latter is commonly designated as folk-lore and embraces popularly myths and superstitions. In Baring-Gould's *Curious Myths of the Middle Ages* the reader will find many of these traced backward, through various peoples on converging lines, toward a common origin in remote antiquity. Among these are the fables of "Teddy the Giant Killer," "The Sleeping John Sharp Williams," "Little Red Riding Hood and the Sugar Trust," "Beauty and the Brisbane," "The Seven Aldermen of Ephesus," "Rip Van Fairbanks," and so forth. The fable which Goethe so affectingly relates under the title of "The Erl-King" was known two thousand years ago in Greece as "The Demos and the Infant Industry." One of the most general and ancient of these myths is that Arabian tale of "Ali Baba and the Forty Rockefellers."

Loss, *n.* Privation of that which we had, or had not. Thus, in the latter sense, it is said of a defeated candidate that he "lost his election"; and of that eminent man, the poet Gilder, that he has "lost his mind." It is in the former and more legitimate sense, that the word is used in the famous epitaph:

    Here Huntington's ashes long have lain
    Whose loss is our own eternal gain,

For while he exercised all his powers
Whatever he gained, the loss was ours.

Love, *n.* A temporary insanity curable by marriage or by removal of the patient from the influences under which he incurred the disorder. This disease, like *caries* and many other ailments, is prevalent only among civilized races living under artificial conditions; barbarous nations breathing pure air and eating simple food enjoy immunity from its ravages. It is sometimes fatal, but more frequently to the physician than to the patient.

Low-bred, *adj.* "Raised" instead of brought up.

Luminary, *n.* One who throws light upon a subject; as an editor by not writing about it.

Lunarian, *n.* An inhabitant of the moon, as distinguished from Lunatic, one whom the moon inhabits. The Lunarians have been described by Lucian, Locke and other observers, but without much agreement. For example, Bragellos avers their anatomical identity with Man, but Professor Newcomb says they are more like the hill tribes of Vermont.

Lyre, *n.* An ancient instrument of torture. The word is now used in a figurative sense to denote the poetic faculty, as in the following fiery lines of our great poet, Ella Wheeler Wilcox:

> I sit astride Parnassus with my lyre,
> And pick with care the disobedient wire.
> The stupid shepherd lolling on his crook
> With deaf attention scarcely deigns to look.
> I bide my time, and it shall come at length,
> When, with a Titan's energy and strength,
> I'll grab a fistful of the strings, and O,
> The world shall suffer when I let them go!

Farquharson Harris

Mace, *n.* A staff of office signifying authority. Its form, that of a heavy club, indicates its original purpose and use in dissuading from dissent.

Machination, *n.* The method employed by one's opponents in baffling one's open and honorable efforts to do the right thing.

> So plain the advantages of machination
> It constitutes a moral obligation,
> And honest wolves who think upon't with loathing
> Feel bound to don the sheep's deceptive clothing.
> So prospers still the diplomatic art,
> And Satan bows, with hand upon his heart.
>
> *R.S.K.*

Macrobian, *n.* One forgotten of the gods and living to a great age. History is abundantly supplied with examples, from Methuselah to Old Parr, but some notable instances of longevity are less well known. A Calabrian peasant named Coloni, born in 1753, lived so long that he had what he considered a glimpse of the dawn of universal peace. Scanavius relates that he knew an archbishop who was so old that he could remember a time when he did not deserve hanging. In 1566 a linen draper of Bristol, England, declared that he had lived five hundred years, and that in all that time he had never told a lie. There are instances of longevity *(macrobiosis)* in our own country. Senator Chauncey Depew is old enough to know better. The editor of *The American*, a newspaper in New York City, has a memory that goes back to the time when he was a rascal, but not to the fact. The President of the United States was born so long ago that many of the friends of his youth have risen to high political and military preferment without the assistance of personal merit. The verses following were written by a macrobian:

When I was young the world was fair
　And amiable and sunny.
A brightness was in all the air,
　In all the waters, honey.
　The jokes were fine and funny,
The statesmen honest in their views,
　And in their lives, as well,
And when you heard a bit of news
　'Twas true enough to tell.
Men were not ranting, shouting, reeking,
Nor women "generally speaking."

The Summer then was long indeed:
　It lasted one whole season!
The sparkling Winter gave no heed
　When ordered by Unreason
　To bring the early peas on.
Now, where the dickens is the sense
　In calling that a year
Which does no more than just commence
　Before the end is near?
When I was young the year extended
From month to month until it ended.

I know not why the world has changed
　To something dark and dreary,
And everything is now arranged
　To make a fellow weary.
　The Weather Man—I fear he
Has much to do with it, for, sure,
　The air is not the same:
It chokes you when it is impure,
　When pure it makes you lame.
With windows closed you are asthmatic;
Open, neuralgic or sciatic.

> Well, I suppose this new régime
>   Of dun degeneration
> Seems eviler than it would seem
>   To a better observation,
>   And has for compensation
> Some blessings in a deep disguise
>   Which mortal sight has failed
> To pierce, although to angels' eyes
>   They're visibly unveiled.
> If Age is such a boon, good land!
> He's costumed by a master hand!
>
> *Venable Strigg*

Mad, *adj.* Affected with a high degree of intellectual independence; not conforming to standards of thought, speech and action derived by the conformants from study of themselves; at odds with the majority; in short, unusual. It is noteworthy that persons are pronounced mad by officials destitute of evidence that themselves are sane. For illustration, this present (and illustrious) lexicographer is no firmer in the faith of his own sanity than is any inmate of any madhouse in the land; yet for aught he knows to the contrary, instead of the lofty occupation that seems to him to be engaging his powers he may really be beating his hands against the window bars of an asylum and declaring himself Noah Webster, to the innocent delight of many thoughtless spectators.

Magdalene, *n.* An inhabitant of Magdala. Popularly, a woman found out. This definition of the word has the authority of ignorance, Mary of Magdala being another person than the penitent woman mentioned by St. Luke. It has also the official sanction of the governments of Great Britain and the United States. In England the word is pronounced Maudlin, whence maudlin, adjective, unpleasantly sentimental. With their Maudlin for Magdalen, and their Bedlam for Bethlehem, the English may justly boast themselves the greatest of revisers.

Magic, *n.* An art of converting superstition into coin. There are other arts serving the same high purpose, but the discreet lexicographer does not name them.

Magnet, *n.* Something acted upon by magnetism.

Magnetism, *n.* Something acting upon a magnet.

The two definitions immediately foregoing are condensed from the works of one thousand eminent scientists, who have illuminated the subject with a great white light, to the inexpressible advancement of human knowledge.

Magnificent, *adj.* Having a grandeur or splendor superior to that to which the spectator is accustomed, as the ears of an ass, to a rabbit, or the glory of a glow-worm, to a maggot.

Magnitude, *n.* Size. Magnitude being purely relative, nothing is large and nothing small. If everything in the universe were increased in bulk one thousand diameters nothing would be any larger than it was before, but if one thing remained unchanged all the others would be larger than they had been. To an understanding familiar with the relativity of magnitude and distance the spaces and masses of the astronomer would be no more impressive than those of the microscopist. For anything we know to the contrary, the visible universe may be a small part of an atom, with its component ions, floating in the life-fluid (luminiferous ether) of some animal. Possibly the wee creatures peopling the corpuscles of our own blood are overcome with the proper emotion when contemplating the unthinkable distance from one of these to another.

Magpie, *n.* A bird whose thievish disposition suggested to some one that it might be taught to talk.

Maiden, *n.* A young person of the unfair sex addicted to clewless conduct and views that madden to crime. The genus has a wide geographical distribution, being found wherever sought and deplored wherever found. The maiden is not altogether unpleasing to the eye, nor (without her piano and her views) insupportable to the ear, though in respect to comeliness distinctly inferior to the rainbow, and, with regard to the part of her that is audible, beaten out of the field by the canary—which, also, is more portable.

> A lovelorn maiden she sat and sang—
> This quaint, sweet song sang she:
> "It's O for a youth with a football bang
> And a muscle fair to see!

The Captain he
Of a team to be!
On the gridiron he shall shine,
A monarch by right divine,
    And never to roast on it—me!"

Opoline Jones

Majesty, *n.* The state and title of a king. Regarded with a just contempt by the Most Eminent Grand Masters, Grand Chancellors, Great Incohonees and Imperial Potentates of the ancient and honorable orders of republican America.

Male, *n.* A member of the unconsidered, or negligible sex. The male of the human race is commonly known (to the female) as Mere Man. The genus has two varieties: good providers and bad providers.

Malefactor, *n.* The chief factor in the progress of the human race.

Malthusian, *adj.* Pertaining to Malthus and his doctrines. Malthus believed in artificially limiting population, but found that it could not be done by talking. One of the most practical exponents of the Malthusian idea was Herod of Judea, though all the famous soldiers have been of the same way of thinking.

Mammalia, *n. pl.* A family of vertebrate animals whose females in a state of nature suckle their young, but when civilized and enlightened put them out to nurse, or use the bottle.

Mammon, *n.* The god of the world's leading religion. His chief temple is in the holy city of New York.

He swore that all other religions were gammon,
And wore out his knees in the worship of Mammon.

Jared Oopf

Man, *n.* An animal so lost in rapturous contemplation of what he thinks he is as to overlook what he indubitably ought to be. His chief occupation is extermination of other animals and his own species, which, however, multiplies with such insistent rapidity as to infest the whole habitable earth and Canada.

When the world was young and Man was new,
    And everything was pleasant,
Distinctions Nature never drew

'Mongst king and priest and peasant.
We're not that way at present,
Save here in this Republic, where
We have that old régime,
For all are kings, however bare
Their backs, howe'er extreme
Their hunger. And, indeed, each has a voice
To accept the tyrant of his party's choice.

A citizen who would not vote,
And, therefore, was detested,
Was one day with a tarry coat
(With feathers backed and breasted)
By patriots invested.
"It is your duty," cried the crowd,
"Your ballot true to cast
For the man o' your choice." He humbly bowed,
And explained his wicked past:
"That's what I very gladly would have done,
Dear patriots, but he has never run."

Apperton Duke

Manes, *n.* The immortal parts of dead Greeks and Romans. They were in a state of dull discomfort until the bodies from which they had exhaled were buried and burned; and they seem not to have been particularly happy afterward.

Manicheism, *n.* The ancient Persian doctrine of an incessant warfare between Good and Evil. When Good gave up the fight the Persians joined the victorious Opposition.

Manna, *n.* A food miraculously given to the Israelites in the wilderness. When it was no longer supplied to them they settled down and tilled the soil, fertilizing it, as a rule, with the bodies of the original occupants.

Marriage, *n.* The state or condition of a community consisting of a master, a mistress and two slaves, making in all, two.

Martyr, *n.* One who moves along the line of least reluctance to a desired death.

Material, *adj.* Having an actual existence, as distinguished from an imaginary one. Important.

> Material things I know, or feel, or see;
> All else is immaterial to me.
>
> *Jamarach Holobom*

Mausoleum, *n.* The final and funniest folly of the rich.

Mayonnaise, *n.* One of the sauces which serve the French in place of a state religion.

Me, *pro.* The objectionable case of I. The personal pronoun in English has three cases, the dominative, the objectionable and the oppressive. Each is all three.

Meander, *n.* To proceed sinuously and aimlessly. The word is the ancient name of a river about one hundred and fifty miles south of Troy, which turned and twisted in the effort to get out of hearing when the Greeks and Trojans boasted of their prowess.

Medal, *n.* A small metal disk given as a reward for virtues, attainments or services more or less authentic.

It is related of Bismark, who had been awarded a medal for gallantly rescuing a drowning person, that, being asked the meaning of the medal, he replied: "I save lives sometimes." And sometimes he didn't.

Medicine, *n.* A stone flung down the Bowery to kill a dog in Broadway.

Meekness, *n.* Uncommon patience in planning a revenge that is worth while.

> M is for Moses,
>   Who slew the Egyptian.
> As sweet as a rose is
> The meekness of Moses.
> No monument shows his
>   Post-mortem inscription,
> But M is for Moses,
>   Who slew the Egyptian.
>
> *The Biographical Alphabet*

Meerschaum, *n.* (Literally, seafoam, and by many erroneously supposed to be made of it.) A fine white clay, which for convenience in colouring it brown is made into tobacco pipes and smoked by the workmen engaged in that industry. The purpose of coloring it has not been disclosed by the manufacturers.

> There was a youth (you've heard before,
>   This woful tale, may be),
> Who bought a meerschaum pipe and swore
>   That colour it would be!
>
> He shut himself from the world away,
>   Nor any soul he saw.
> He smoked by night, he smoked by day,
>   As hard as he could draw.
>
> His dog died moaning in the wrath
>   Of winds that blew aloof;
> The weeds were in the gravel path,
>   The owl was on the roof.
>
> "He's gone afar, he'll come no more,"
>   The neighbors sadly say.
> And so they batter in the door
>   To take his goods away.
>
> Dead, pipe in mouth, the youngster lay,
>   Nut-brown in face and limb.
> "That pipe's a lovely white," they say,
>   "But it has colored him!"
>
> The moral there's small need to sing—
>   'Tis plain as day to you:
> Don't play your game on any thing
>   That is a gamester too.
>
> *Martin Bulstrode*

Mendacious, *adj.* Addicted to rhetoric.

Merchant, *n.* One engaged in a commercial pursuit. A commercial pursuit is one in which the thing pursued is a dollar.

Mercy, *n.* An attribute beloved of detected offenders.

Mesmerism, *n.* Hypnotism before it wore good clothes, kept a carriage and asked Incredulity to dinner.

Metropolis, *n.* A stronghold of provincialism.

Millennium, *n.* The period of a thousand years when the lid is to be screwed down, with all reformers on the under side.

Mind, *n.* A mysterious form of matter secreted by the brain. Its chief activity consists in the endeavor to ascertain its own nature, the futility of the attempt being due to the fact that it has nothing but itself to know itself with. From the Latin *mens,* a fact unknown to that honest shoe-seller, who, observing that his learned competitor over the way had displayed the motto *"Mens conscia recti,"* emblazoned his own shop front with the words "Men's, women's and children's conscia recti."

Mine, *adj.* Belonging to me if I can hold or seize it.

Minister, *n.* An agent of a higher power with a lower responsibility. In diplomacy an officer sent into a foreign country as the visible embodiment of his sovereign's hostility. His principle qualification is a degree of plausible inveracity next below that of an ambassador.

Minor, *adj.* Less objectionable.

Minstrel, *adj.* Formerly a poet, singer or musician; now a nigger with a color less than skin deep and a humor more than flesh and blood can bear.

Miracle, *n.* An act or event out of the order of nature and unaccountable, as beating a normal hand of four kings and an ace with four aces and a king.

Miscreant, *n.* A person of the highest degree of unworth. Etymologically, the word means unbeliever, and its present signification may be regarded as theology's noblest contribution to the development of our language.

Misdemeanor, *n.* An infraction of the law having less dignity than a felony and constituting no claim to admittance into the best criminal society.

> By misdemeanors he essayed to climb
> Into the aristocracy of crime.

O, woe was him!—with manner chill and grand
"Captains of industry" refused his hand,
"Kings of finance" denied him recognition
And "railway magnates" jeered his low condition.
He robbed a bank to make himself respected.
They still rebuffed him, for he was detected.

S. V. Hanipur

Misericorde, *n.* A dagger which in mediæval warfare was used by the foot soldier to remind an unhorsed knight that he was mortal.

Misfortune, *n.* The kind of fortune that never misses.

Miss, *n.* A title with which we brand unmarried women to indicate that they are in the market. Miss, Missis (Mrs.) and Mister (Mr.) are the three most distinctly disagreeable words in the language, in sound and sense. Two are corruptions of Mistress, the other of Master. In the general abolition of social titles in this our country they miraculously escaped to plague us. If we must have them let us be consistent and give one to the unmarried man. I venture to suggest Mush, abbreviated to Mh.

Molecule, *n.* The ultimate, indivisible unit of matter. It is distinguished from the corpuscle, also the ultimate, indivisible unit of matter, by a closer resemblance to the atom, also the ultimate, indivisible unit of matter. Three great scientific theories of the structure of the universe are the molecular, the corpuscular and the atomic. A fourth affirms, with Haeckel, the condensation or precipitation of matter from ether—whose existence is proved by the condensation or precipitation. The present trend of scientific thought is toward the theory of ions. The ion differs from the molecule, the corpuscle and the atom in that it is an ion. A fifth theory is held by idiots, but it is doubtful if they know any more about the matter than the others.

Monad, *n.* The ultimate, indivisible unit of matter. (See *Molecule.*) According to Leibnitz, as nearly as he seems willing to be understood, the monad has body without bulk, and mind without manifestation—Leibnitz knows him by the innate power of considering. He has founded upon him a theory of the universe, which the creature bears without resentment, for the monad is a gentleman. Small as he is, the monad contains all the powers and possibilities needful to his evolution into a German philosopher of the first class—altogether a very capable little fellow. He is not to be confounded with the microbe, or bacillus; by its inability to discern him, a good microscope shows him to be of an entirely distinct species.

Monarch, *n.* A person engaged in reigning. Formerly the monarch ruled, as the derivation of the word attests, and as many subjects have had occasion to learn. In Russia and the Orient the monarch has still a considerable influence in public affairs and in the disposition of the human head, but in western Europe political administration is mostly entrusted to his ministers, he being somewhat preoccupied with reflections relating to the status of his own head.

Monarchical Government, *n.* Government.

Monday, *n.* In Christian countries, the day after the baseball game.

Money, *n.* A blessing that is of no advantage to us excepting when we part with it. An evidence of culture and a passport to polite society. Supportable property.

Monkey, *n.* An arboreal animal which makes itself at home in genealogical trees.

Monosyllabic, *adj.* Composed of words of one syllable, for literary babes who never tire of testifying their delight in the vapid compound by appropriate googoogling. The words are commonly Saxon—that is to say, words of a barbarous people destitute of ideas and incapable of any but the most elementary sentiments and emotions.

> The man who writes in Saxon
> Is the man to use an ax on.
>
> *Judibras*

Monsignor, *n.* A high ecclesiastical title, of which the Founder of our religion overlooked the advantages.

Monument, *n.* A structure intended to commemorate something which either needs no commemoration or cannot be commemorated.

> The bones of Agememnon are a show
> And ruined is his royal monument.

but Agamemnon's fame suffers no diminution in consequence. The monument custom has its *reductiones ad absurdum* in monuments "to the unknown dead"—that is to say, monuments to perpetuate the memory of those who have left no memory.

Moral, *adj.* Conforming to a local and mutable standard of right. Having the quality of general expediency.

> It is sayd there be a raunge of mountaynes in the Easte, on one syde of the which certayn conducts are immorall, yet on the other syde they are holden in good esteeme; wherebye the mountayneer is much conveenyenced, for it is given to him to goe downe eyther way and act as it shall suite his moode, withouten offence.—*Gooke's Meditations.*

More, *adj.* The comparative degree of too much.

Mouse, *n.* An animal which strews its path with fainting women. As in Rome Christians were thrown to the lions, so centuries earlier in Otumwee, the most ancient and famous city of the world, female heretics were thrown to the mice. Jakak-Zotp, the historian, the only Otumwump whose writings have descended to us, says that these martyrs met their death with little dignity and much exertion. He even attempts to exculpate the mice (such is the malice of bigotry) by declaring that the unfortunate women perished, some from exhaustion, some of broken necks from falling over their own feet, and some from lack of restoratives. The mice, he avers, enjoyed the pleasures of the chase with composure. But if "Roman history is nine-tenths lying," we can hardly expect a smaller proportion of that rhetorical figure in the annals of a people capable of so incredible cruelty to lovely woman; for a hard heart has a false tongue.

Mousquetaire, *n.* A long glove covering a part of the arm. Worn in New Jersey. But "mousquetaire" is a mighty poor way to spell muskeeter.

Mouth, *n.* In man, the gateway to the soul; in woman, the outlet of the heart.

Mugwump, *n.* In politics one afflicted with self-respect and addicted to the vice of independence. A term of contempt.

Mulatto, *n.* A child of two races, ashamed of both.

Multitude, *n.* A crowd; the source of political wisdom and virtue. In a republic, the object of the statesman's adoration. "In a multitude of counsellors there is wisdom," saith the proverb. If many men of equal individual wisdom are wiser than any one of them, it must be that they acquire the excess of wisdom by the mere act of getting together. Whence comes it? Obviously from nowhere—as well say that a range of mountains is higher than the single mountains composing it. A multitude is as wise as its wisest member if it obey him; if not, it is no wiser than its most foolish.

Mummy, *n.* An ancient Egyptian, formerly in universal use among modern civilized nations as medicine, and now engaged in supplying art with an excellent pigment. He is handy, too, in museums in gratifying the vulgar curiosity that serves to distinguish man from the lower animals.

> By means of the Mummy, mankind, it is said,
> Attests to the gods its respect for the dead.
> We plunder his tomb, be he sinner or saint,
> Distil him for physic and grind him for paint,
> Exhibit for money his poor, shrunken frame,
> And with levity flock to the scene of the shame.
> O, tell me, ye gods, for the use of my rhyme:
> For respecting the dead what's the limit of time?
>
> *Scopas Brune*

Mustang, *n.* An indocile horse of the western plains. In English society, the American wife of an English nobleman.

Myrmidon, *n.* A follower of Achilles—particularly when he didn't lead.

Mythology, *n.* The body of a primitive people's beliefs concerning its origin, early history, heroes, deities and so forth, as distinguished from the true accounts which it invents later.

Nectar, *n.* A drink served at banquets of the Olympian deities. The secret of its preparation is lost, but the modern Kentuckians believe that they come pretty near to a knowledge of its chief ingredient.

> Juno drank a cup of nectar,
> But the draught did not affect her.
> Juno drank a cup of rye—
> Then she bade herself good-bye.

J.G.

Negro, *n.* The *pièce de résistance* in the American political problem. Representing him by the letter *n*, the Republicans begin to build their equation thus: "Let *n* = the white man." This, however, appears to give an unsatisfactory solution.

Neighbor, *n.* One whom we are commanded to love as ourselves, and who does all he knows how to make us disobedient.

Nepotism, *n.* Appointing your grandmother to office for the good of the party.

Newtonian, *adj.* Pertaining to a philosophy of the universe, invented by Newton, who discovered that an apple will fall to the ground, but was unable to say why. His successors and disciples have advanced so far as to be able to say when.

Nihilist, *n.* A Russian who denies the existence of anything but Tolstoi. The leader of the school is Tolstoi.

Nirvana, *n.* In the Buddhist religion, a state of pleasurable annihilation awarded to the wise, particularly to those wise enough to understand it.

Nobleman, *n.* Nature's provision for wealthy American maids ambitious to incur social distinction and suffer high life.

Noise, *n.* A stench in the ear. Undomesticated music. The chief product and authenticating sign of civilization.

Nominate, *v.* To designate for the heaviest political assessment. To put forward a suitable person to incur the mudgobbing and deadcatting of the opposition.

Nominee, *n.* A modest gentleman shrinking from the distinction of private life and diligently seeking the honorable obscurity of public office.

Non-Combatant, *n.* A dead Quaker.

Nonsense, *n.* The objections that are urged against this excellent dictionary.

Nose, *n.* The extreme outpost of the face. From the circumstance that great conquerors have great noses, Getius, whose writings antedate the age of humor, calls the nose the organ of quell. It has been observed that one's nose is never so happy as when thrust into the affairs of another, from which some physiologists have drawn the inference that the nose is devoid of the sense of smell.

> There's a man with a Nose,
> And wherever he goes
> The people run from him and shout:
> "No cotton have we
> For our ears if so be
> He blows that interminous snout!"

> So the lawyers applied
> For injunction. "Denied,"
> Said the Judge: "the defendant prefixion,

Whate'er it portend,
Appears to transcend
The bounds of this court's jurisdiction."

Arpad Singiny

Notoriety, *n.* The fame of one's competitor for public honors. The kind of renown most accessible and acceptable to mediocrity. A Jacob's-ladder leading to the vaudeville stage, with angels ascending and descending.

Noumenon, *n.* That which exists, as distinguished from that which merely seems to exist, the latter being a phenomenon. The noumenon is a bit difficult to locate; it can be apprehended only by a process of reasoning—which is a phenomenon. Nevertheless, the discovery and exposition of noumena offer a rich field for what Lewes calls "the endless variety and excitement of philosophic thought." Hurrah (therefore) for the noumenon!

Novel, *n.* A short story padded. A species of composition bearing the same relation to literature that the panorama bears to art. As it is too long to be read at a sitting the impressions made by its successive parts are successively effaced, as in the panorama. Unity, totality of effect, is impossible; for besides the few pages last read all that is carried in mind is the mere plot of what has gone before. To the romance the novel is what photography is to painting. Its distinguishing principle, probability, corresponds to the literal actuality of the photograph and puts it distinctly into the category of reporting; whereas the free wing of the romancer enables him to mount to such altitudes of imagination as he may be fitted to attain; and the first three essentials of the literary art are imagination, imagination and imagination. The art of writing novels, such as it was, is long dead everywhere except in Russia, where it is new. Peace to its ashes—some of which have a large sale.

November, *n.* The eleventh twelfth of a weariness.

Oath, *n.* In law, a solemn appeal to the Deity, made binding upon the conscience by a penalty for perjury.

Oblivion, *n.* The state or condition in which the wicked cease from struggling and the dreary are at rest. Fame's eternal dumping ground. Cold storage for high hopes. A place where ambitious authors meet their works without pride and their betters without envy. A dormitory without an alarm clock.

Observatory, *n.* A place where astronomers conjecture away the guesses of their predecessors.

Obsessed, *pp.* Vexed by an evil spirit, like the Gadarene swine and other critics. Obsession was once more common than it is now. Arasthus tells of a peasant who was occupied by a different devil for every day in the week, and on Sundays by two. They were frequently seen, always walking in his shadow, when he had one, but were finally driven away by the village notary, a holy man; but they took the peasant with them, for he vanished utterly. A devil thrown out of a woman by the Archbishop of Rheims ran through the streets, pursued by a hundred persons, until the open country was reached, where by a leap higher than a church spire he escaped into a bird. A chaplain in Cromwell's army exorcised a soldier's devil by throwing the soldier into the water, when the devil came to the surface. The soldier, unfortunately, did not.

Obsolete, *adj.* No longer used by the timid. Said chiefly of words. A word which some lexicographer has marked obsolete is ever thereafter an object of dread and loathing to the fool writer, but if it is a good word and has no exact modern equivalent equally good, it is good enough for the good writer. Indeed, a writer's attitude toward "obsolete" words is as true a measure of his literary ability as anything except the character of his work. A dictionary of obsolete and obsolescent words would not only be singularly rich in strong and sweet parts of speech; it would add large possessions to the vocabulary of every competent writer who might not happen to be a competent reader.

Obstinate, *adj.* Inaccessible to the truth as it is manifest in the splendor and stress of our advocacy.

   The popular type and exponent of obstinacy is the mule, a most intelligent animal.

Occasional, *adj.* Afflicting us with greater or less frequency. That, however, is not the sense in which the word is used in the phrase "occasional verses," which are verses written for an "occasion," such as an anniversary, a celebration or other event. True, they afflict us a little worse than other sorts of verse, but their name has no reference to irregular recurrence.

Occident, *n.* The part of the world lying west (or east) of the Orient. It is largely inhabited by Christians, a powerful sub-tribe of the Hypocrites, whose principal industries are murder and cheating, which they are pleased to call "war" and "commerce." These, also, are the principal industries of the Orient.

Ocean, *n.* A body of water occupying about two-thirds of a world made for man—who has no gills.

Offensive, *adj.* Generating disagreeable emotions or sensations, as the advance of an army against its enemy.

   "Were the enemy's tactics offensive?" the king asked. "I should say so!" replied the unsuccessful general. "The blackguard wouldn't come out of his works!"

Old, *adj.* In that stage of usefulness which is not inconsistent with general inefficiency, as an *old man*. Discredited by lapse of time and offensive to the popular taste, as an *old* book.

"Old books? The devil take them!" Goby said.
"Fresh every day must be my books and bread."
Nature herself approves the Goby rule
And gives us every moment a fresh fool.

                                                        Harley Shum

Oleaginous, *adj.* Oily, smooth, sleek.
    Disraeli once described the manner of Bishop Wilberforce as
"unctuous, oleaginous, saponaceous." And the good prelate was
ever afterward known as Soapy Sam. For every man there is something in the vocabulary that would stick to him like a second skin.
His enemies have only to find it.

Olympian, *adj.* Relating to a mountain in Thessaly, once inhabited by
    gods, now a repository of yellowing newspapers, beer bottles and
    mutilated sardine cans, attesting the presence of the tourist and his
    appetite.

        His name the smirking tourist scrawls
        Upon Minerva's temple walls,
        Where thundered once Olympian Zeus,
        And marks his appetite's abuse.

                                                        Averil Joop

Omen, *n.* A sign that something will happen if nothing happens.

Once, *adv.* Enough.

Opera, *n.* A play representing life in another world, whose inhabitants
    have no speech but song, no motions but gestures and no postures
    but attitudes. All acting is simulation, and the word *simulation* is
    from *simia,* an ape; but in opera the actor takes for his model *Simia
    audibilis* (or *Pithecanthropos stentor*)—the ape that howls.

        The actor apes a man—at least in shape;
        The opera performer apes an ape.

Opiate, *n.* An unlocked door in the prison of Identity. It leads into the
    jail yard.

Opportunity, *n.* A favorable occasion for grasping a disappointment.

Oppose, *v.* To assist with obstructions and objections.

How lonely he who thinks to vex
With badinage the Solemn Sex!
Of levity, Mere Man, beware;
None but the Grave deserve the Unfair.

Percy P. Orminder

Opposition, *n.* In politics the party that prevents the Government from running amuck by hamstringing it.

The King of Ghargaroo, who had been abroad to study the science of government, appointed one hundred of his fattest subjects as members of a parliament to make laws for the collection of revenue. Forty of these he named the Party of Opposition and had his Prime Minister carefully instruct them in their duty of opposing every royal measure. Nevertheless, the first one that was submitted passed unanimously. Greatly displeased, the King vetoed it, informing the Opposition that if they did that again they would pay for their obstinacy with their heads. The entire forty promptly disemboweled themselves.

"What shall we do now?" the King asked. "Liberal institutions cannot be maintained without a party of Opposition."

"Splendor of the universe," replied the Prime Minister, "it is true these dogs of darkness have no longer their credentials, but all is not lost. Leave the matter to this worm of the dust."

So the Minister had the bodies of his Majesty's Opposition embalmed and stuffed with straw, put back into the seats of power and nailed there. Forty votes were recorded against every bill and the nation prospered. But one day a bill imposing a tax on warts was defeated—the members of the Government party had not been nailed to their seats! This so enraged the King that the Prime Minister was put to death, the parliament was dissolved with a battery of artillery, and government of the people, by the people, for the people perished from Ghargaroo.

Optimism, *n.* The doctrine, or belief that everything is beautiful, including what is ugly, everything good, especially the bad, and everything right that is wrong. It is held with greatest tenacity by those most accustomed to the mischance of falling into adversity, and is most acceptably expounded with the grin that apes a smile. Being a blind faith, it is inaccessible to the light of disproof—an intellectual disorder, yielding to no treatment but death. It is hereditary, but fortunately not contagious.

Optimist, *n.* A proponent of the doctrine that black is white.

A pessimist applied to God for relief.

"Ah, you wish me to restore your hope and cheerfulness," said God.

"No," replied the petitioner, "I wish you to create something that would justify them."

"The world is all created," said God, "but you have overlooked something—the mortality of the optimist."

Oratory, *n.* A conspiracy between speech and action to cheat the understanding. A tyranny tempered by stenography.

Orphan, *n.* A living person whom death has deprived of the power of filial ingratitude—a privation appealing with a particular eloquence to all that is sympathetic in human nature. When young the orphan is commonly sent to an asylum, where by careful cultivation of its rudimentary sense of locality it is taught to know its place. It is then instructed in the arts of dependence and servitude and eventually turned loose to prey upon the world as a bootblack or scullery maid.

Orthodox, *n.* An ox wearing the popular religious yoke.

Orthography, *n.* The science of spelling by the eye instead of the ear. Advocated with more heat than light by the outmates of every asylum for the insane. They have had to concede a few things since the time of Chaucer, but are none the less hot in defence of those to be conceded hereafter.

> A spelling reformer indicted
> For fudge was before the court cicted.
>   The judge said: "Enough—
>   His candle we'll snough,
> And his sepulchre shall not be whicted."

Ostrich, *n.* A large bird to which (for its sins, doubtless) nature has denied that hinder toe in which so many pious naturalists have seen a conspicuous evidence of design. The absence of a good working pair of wings is no defect, for, as has been ingeniously pointed out, the ostrich does not fly.

Otherwise, *adv.* No better.

Outcome, *n.* A particular type of disappointment. By the kind of intelligence that sees in an exception a proof of the rule the wisdom of an act is judged by the outcome, the result. This is immortal nonsense; the wisdom of an act is to be judged by the light that the doer had when he performed it.

Outdo, *v.t.* To make an enemy.

Out-of-Doors, *n.* That part of one's environment upon which no government has been able to collect taxes. Chiefly useful to inspire poets.

> I climbed to the top of a mountain one day
>   To see the sun setting in glory,
> And I thought, as I looked at his vanishing ray,
>   Of a perfectly splendid story.
>
> 'Twas about an old man and the ass he bestrode
>   Till the strength of the beast was o'ertested;
> Then the man would carry him miles on the road
>   Till Neddy was pretty well rested.
>
> The moon rising solemnly over the crest
>   Of the hills to the east of my station
> Displayed her broad disk to the darkening west
>   Like a visible new creation.
>
> And I thought of a joke (and I laughed till I cried)
>   Of an idle young woman who tarried
> About a church-door for a look at the bride,
>   Although 'twas herself that was married.
>
> To poets all Nature is pregnant with grand
>   Ideas—with thought and emotion.
> I pity the dunces who don't understand
>   The speech of earth, heaven and ocean.
>
> *Stromboli Smith*

Ovation, *n.* In ancient Rome, a definite, formal pageant in honor of one who had been disserviceable to the enemies of the nation. A lesser "triumph." In modern English the word is improperly used to signify any loose and spontaneous expression of popular homage to the hero of the hour and place.

"I had an ovation!" the actor man said,
    But I thought it uncommonly queer,
That people and critics by him had been led
    By the ear.

The Latin lexicon makes his absurd
    Assertion as plain as a peg;
In "ovum" we find the true root of the word.
    It means egg.

Dudley Spink

Overeat, *v.* To dine.

Hail, Gastronome, Apostle of Excess,
Well skilled to overeat without distress!
Thy great invention, the unfatal feast,
Shows Man's superiority to Beast.

John Boop

Overwork, *n.* A dangerous disorder affecting high public functionaries who want to go fishing.

Owe, *v.* To have (and to hold) a debt. The word formerly signified not indebtedness, but possession; meant "own," and in the minds of debtors there is still a good deal of confusion between assets and liabilities.

Oyster, *n.* A slimy, gobby shellfish which civilization gives men the hardihood to eat without removing its entrails! The shells are sometimes given to the poor.

Pain, *n.* An uncomfortable frame of mind that may have a physical basis in something that is being done to the body, or may be purely mental, caused by the good fortune of another.

Painting, *n.* The art of protecting flat surfaces from the weather and exposing them to the critic.

Formerly, painting and sculpture were combined in the same work: the ancients painted their statues. The only present alliance between the two arts is that the modern painter chisels his patrons.

Palace, *n.* A fine and costly residence, particularly that of a great official. The residence of a high dignitary of the Christian Church is called a palace; that of the Founder of his religion was known as a field, or wayside. There is progress.

Palm, *n.* A species of tree having several varieties, of which the familiar "itching palm" (*Palma hominis*) is most widely distributed and sedulously cultivated. This noble vegetable exudes a kind of invisible gum, which may be detected by applying to the bark a piece of gold or silver. The metal will adhere with remarkable tenacity. The fruit of the itching palm is so bitter and unsatisfying that a considerable percentage of it is sometimes given away in what are known as "benefactions."

Palmistry, *n.* The 947th method (according to Mimbleshaw's classification) of obtaining money by false pretences. It consists in "reading character" in the wrinkles made by closing the hand. The pretence is not altogether false; character can really be read very accurately in this way, for the wrinkles in every hand submitted plainly spell the word "dupe." The imposture consists in not reading it aloud.

Pandemonium, *n.* Literally, the Place of All the Demons. Most of them have escaped into politics and finance, and the place is now used as a lecture hall by the Audible Reformer. When disturbed by his voice the ancient echoes clamor appropriate responses most gratifying to his pride of distinction.

Pantaloons, *n.* A nether habiliment of the adult civilized male. The garment is tubular and unprovided with hinges at the points of flexion. Supposed to have been invented by a humorist. Called "trousers" by the enlightened and "pants" by the unworthy.

Pantheism, *n.* The doctrine that everything is God, in contradistinction to the doctrine that God is everything.

Pantomime, *n.* A play in which the story is told without violence to the language. The least disagreeable form of dramatic action.

Pardon, *v.* To remit a penalty and restore to a life of crime. To add to the lure of crime the temptation of ingratitude.

Passport, *n.* A document treacherously inflicted upon a citizen going abroad, exposing him as an alien and pointing him out for special reprobation and outrage.

Past, *n.* That part of Eternity with some small fraction of which we have a slight and regrettable acquaintance. A moving line called the Present parts it from an imaginary period known as the Future. These two grand divisions of Eternity, of which the one is continually effacing the other, are entirely unlike. The one is dark with sorrow and disappointment, the other, bright with prosperity and joy. The Past is the region of sobs, the Future is the realm of song. In one crouches Memory, clad in sackcloth and ashes, mumbling penitential prayer; in the sunshine of the other Hope flies with a free wing, beckoning to temples of success and bowers of ease. Yet the Past is the Future of yesterday, the Future is the Past of tomorrow. They are one—the knowledge and the dream.

Pastime, *n.* A device for promoting dejection. Gentle exercise for intellectual debility.

Patience, *n.* A minor form of despair, disguised as a virtue.

Patriot, *n.* One to whom the interests of a part seem superior to those of the whole. The dupe of statesmen and the tool of conquerors.

Patriotism, *n.* Combustible rubbish ready to the torch of any one ambitious to illuminate his name.

In Dr. Johnson's famous dictionary patriotism is defined as the last resort of a scoundrel. With all due respect to an enlightened but inferior lexicographer I beg to submit that it is the first.

Peace, *n.* In international affairs, a period of cheating between two periods of fighting.

> O, what's the loud uproar assailing
>   Mine ears without cease?
> 'Tis the voice of the hopeful, all-hailing
>   The horrors of peace.
>
> Ah, Peace Universal; they woo it—
>   Would marry it, too.
> If only they knew how to do it
>   'Twere easy to do.
>
> They're working by night and by day
>   On their problem, like moles.
> Have mercy, O Heaven, I pray,
>   On their meddlesome souls!
>
>   *Ro Amil*

Pedestrian, *n.* The variable (and audible) part of the roadway for an automobile.

Pedigree, *n.* The known part of the route from an arboreal ancestor with a swim bladder to an urban descendant with a cigarette.

Penitent, *adj.* Undergoing or awaiting punishment.

Perfection, *n.* An imaginary state or quality distinguished from the actual by an element known as excellence; an attribute of the critic.

The editor of an English magazine having received a letter pointing out the erroneous nature of his views and style, and signed "Perfection," promptly wrote at the foot of the letter: "I don't agree with you," and mailed it to Matthew Arnold.

Peripatetic, *adj.* Walking about. Relating to the philosophy of Aristotle, who, while expounding it, moved from place to place in order to avoid his pupil's objections. A needless precaution—they knew no more of the matter than he.

Peroration, *n.* The explosion of an oratorical rocket. It dazzles, but to an observer having the wrong kind of nose its most conspicuous peculiarity is the smell of the several kinds of powder used in preparing it.

Perseverance, *n.* A lowly virtue whereby mediocrity achieves an inglorious success.

> "Persevere, persevere!" cry the homilists all,
> Themselves, day and night, persevering to bawl.
> "Remember the fable of tortoise and hare—
> The one at the goal while the other is—where?"
> Why, back there in Dreamland, renewing his lease
> Of life, all his muscles preserving the peace,
>
> The goal and the rival forgotten alike,
> And the long fatigue of the needless hike.
> His spirit a-squat in the grass and the dew
> Of the dogless Land beyond the Stew,
> He sleeps, like a saint in a holy place,
> A winner of all that is good in a race.
>
> *Sukker Uffro*

Pessimism, *n.* A philosophy forced upon the convictions of the observer by the disheartening prevalence of the optimist with his scarecrow hope and his unsightly smile.

Philanthropist, *n.* A rich (and usually bald) old gentleman who has trained himself to grin while his conscience is picking his pocket.

Philistine, *n.* One whose mind is the creature of its environment, following the fashion in thought, feeling and sentiment. He is sometimes learned, frequently prosperous, commonly clean and always solemn.

Philosophy, *n.* A route of many roads leading from nowhere to nothing.

Phœnix, *n.* The classical prototype of the modern "small hot bird."

Phonograph, *n.* An irritating toy that restores life to dead noises.

Photograph, *n.* A picture painted by the sun without instruction in art.

It is a little better than the work of an Apache, but not quite so good as that of a Cheyenne.

Phrenology, *n.* The science of picking the pocket through the scalp. It consists in locating and exploiting the organ that one is a dupe with.

Physician, *n.* One upon whom we set our hopes when ill and our dogs when well.

Physiognomy, *n.* The art of determining the character of another by the resemblances and differences between his face and our own, which is the standard of excellence.

> "There is no art," says Shakespeare, foolish man,
>   "To read the mind's construction in the face."
> The physiognomists his portrait scan,
>   And say: "How little wisdom here we trace!
> He knew his face disclosed his mind and heart,
> So, in his own defence, denied our art."
>
> *Lavatar Shunk*

Piano, *n.* A parlor utensil for subduing the impenitent visitor. It is operated by depressing the keys of the machine and the spirits of the audience.

Pickaninny, *n.* The young of the *Procyanthropos*, or *Americanus dominans*. It is small, black and charged with political fatalities.

Picture, *n.* A representation in two dimensions of something wearisome in three.

> "Behold great Daubert's picture here on view—
> Taken from Life." If that description's true,
> Grant, heavenly Powers, that I be taken, too.
>
> *Jali Hane*

Pie, *n.* An advance agent of the reaper whose name is Indigestion.

> Cold pie was highly esteemed by the remains.—*The Rev. Dr. Mucker, in a Funeral Sermon Over a British Nobleman.*

> Cold pie is a detestable
> American comestible.
> That's why I'm done—or undone—
> So far from that dear London.
>   —*From the Headstone of a British Nobleman, in Kalamazoo.*

Piety, *n.* Reverence for the Supreme Being, based upon His supposed resemblance to man.

> The pig is taught by sermons and epistles
> To think the God of Swine has snout and bristles.
>
> *Judibras*

Pig, *n.* An animal (*Porcus omnivorus*) closely allied to the human race by the splendor and vivacity of its appetite, which, however, is inferior in scope, for it sticks at pig.

Pigmy, *n.* One of a tribe of very small men found by ancient travelers in many parts of the world, but by modern in Central Africa only. The Pigmies are so called to distinguish them from the bulkier Caucasians—who are Hogmies.

Pilgrim, *n.* A traveler that is taken seriously. A Pilgrim Father was one who, leaving Europe in 1620 because not permitted to sing psalms through his nose, followed it to Massachusetts, where he could personate God according to the dictates of his conscience.

Pillory, *n.* A mechanical device for inflicting personal distinction— prototype of the modern newspaper conducted by persons of austere virtues and blameless lives.

Piracy, *n.* Commerce without its folly-swaddles, just as God made it.

Pitiful, *adj.* The state of an enemy or opponent after an imaginary encounter with oneself.

Pity, *n.* A failing sense of exemption, inspired by contrast.

Plagiarism, *n.* A literary coincidence compounded of a discreditable priority and an honorable subsequence.

Plagiarize, *v.* To take the thought or style of another writer whom one has never, never read.

Plague, *n.* In ancient times a general punishment of the innocent for admonition of their ruler, as in the familiar instance of Pharaoh the Immune. The plague as we of to-day have the happiness to know it is merely Nature's fortuitous manifestation of her purposeless objectionableness.

Plan, *v.t.* To bother about the best method of accomplishing an accidental result.

Platitude, *n.* The fundamental element and special glory of popular literature. A thought that snores in words that smoke. The wisdom of a million fools in the diction of a dullard. A fossil sentiment in artificial rock. A moral without the fable. All that is mortal of a departed truth. A demi-tasse of milk-and-morality. The Pope's-nose of a featherless peacock. A jelly-fish withering on the shore of the sea of thought. The cackle surviving the egg. A desiccated epigram.

Platonic, *adj.* Pertaining to the philosophy of Socrates. Platonic Love is a fool's name for the affection between a disability and a frost.

Plaudits, *n.* Coins with which the populace pays those who tickle and devour it.

Please, *v.* To lay the foundation for a superstructure of imposition.

Pleasure, *n.* The least hateful form of dejection.

Plebeian, *n.* An ancient Roman who in the blood of his country stained nothing but his hands. Distinguished from the Patrician, who was a saturated solution.

Plebiscite, *n.* A popular vote to ascertain the will of the sovereign.

Plenipotentiary, *adj.* Having full power. A Minister Plenipotentiary is a diplomatist possessing absolute authority on condition that he never exert it.

Pleonasm, *n.* An army of words escorting a corporal of thought.

Plow, *n.* An implement that cries aloud for hands accustomed to the pen.

Plunder, *v.* To take the property of another without observing the decent and customary reticences of theft. To effect a change of ownership with the candid concomitance of a brass band. To wrest the wealth of A from B and leave C lamenting a vanished opportunity.

Pocket, *n.* The cradle of motive and the grave of conscience. In woman this organ is lacking; so she acts without motive, and her conscience, denied burial, remains ever alive, confessing the sins of others.

Poetry, *n.* A form of expression peculiar to the Land beyond the Magazines.

Poker, *n.* A game said to be played with cards for some purpose to this lexicographer unknown.

Police, *n.* An armed force for protection and participation.

Politeness, *n.* The most acceptable hypocrisy.

Politics, *n.* A strife of interests masquerading as a contest of principles. The conduct of public affairs for private advantage.

Politician, *n.* An eel in the fundamental mud upon which the superstructure of organized society is reared. When he wriggles he mistakes the agitation of his tail for the trembling of the edifice. As compared with the statesman, he suffers the disadvantage of being alive.

Polygamy, *n.* A house of atonement, or expiatory chapel, fitted with several stools of repentance, as distinguished from monogamy, which has but one.

Populist, *n.* A fossil patriot of the early agricultural period, found in the old red soapstone underlying Kansas; characterized by an uncommon spread of ear, which some naturalists contend gave him the power of flight, though Professors Morse and Whitney, pursuing independent lines of thought, have ingeniously pointed out that had he possessed it he would have gone elsewhere. In the picturesque speech of his period, some fragments of which have come down to us, he was known as "The Matter with Kansas."

Portable, *adj.* Exposed to a mutable ownership through vicissitudes of possession.

> His light estate, if neither he did make it
> Nor yet its former guardian forsake it,
> Is portable improperty, I take it.
>
> *Worgum Slupsky*

Portuguese, *n. pl.* A species of geese indigenous to Portugal. They are mostly without feathers and imperfectly edible, even when stuffed with garlic.

Positive, *adj.* Mistaken at the top of one's voice.

Positivism, *n.* A philosophy that denies our knowledge of the Real and affirms our ignorance of the Apparent. Its longest exponent is Comte, its broadest Mill and its thickest Spencer.

Posterity, *n* An appellate court which reverses the judgment of a popular author's contemporaries, the appellant being his obscure competitor.

Potable, *n.* Suitable for drinking. Water is said to be potable; indeed, some declare it our natural beverage, although even they find it palatable only when suffering from the recurrent disorder known as thirst, for which it is a medicine. Upon nothing has so great and diligent ingenuity been brought to bear in all ages and in all countries, except the most uncivilized, as upon the invention of substitutes for water. To hold that this general aversion to that liquid has no basis in the preservative instinct of the race is to be unscientific—and without science we are as the snakes and toads.

Poverty, *n.* A file provided for the teeth of the rats of reform. The number of plans for its abolition equals that of the reformers who suffer from it, plus that of the philosophers who know nothing about it. Its victims are distinguished by possession of all the virtues and by their faith in leaders seeking to conduct them into a prosperity where they believe these to be unknown.

Pray, *v.* To ask that the laws of the universe be annulled in behalf of a single petitioner confessedly unworthy.

Pre-Adamite, *n.* One of an experimental and apparently unsatisfactory race that ante-dated Creation and lived under conditions not easily conceived. Melsius believed them to have inhabited "the Void" and to have been something intermediate between fishes and birds. Little is known of them beyond the fact that they supplied Cain with a wife and theologians with a controversy.

Precedent, *n.* In Law, a previous decision, rule or practice which, in the absence of a definite statute, has whatever force and authority a Judge may choose to give it, thereby greatly simplifying his task of doing as he pleases. As there are precedents for everything, he has only to ignore those that make against his interest and accentuate those in the line of his desire. Invention of the precedent elevates the trial-at-law from the low estate of a fortuitous ordeal to the noble attitude of a dirigible arbitrament.

Precipitate, *adj.* Anteprandial.

> Precipitate in all, this sinner
> Took action first, and then his dinner.
>
> *Judibras*

Predestination, *n.* The doctrine that all things occur according to programme. This doctrine should not be confused with that of foreordination, which means that all things are programmed, but does not affirm their occurrence, that being only an implication from other doctrines by which this is entailed. The difference is great enough to have deluged Christendom with ink, to say nothing of the gore. With the distinction of the two doctrines kept well in mind, and a reverent belief in both, one may hope to escape perdition if spared.

Predicament, *n.* The wage of consistency.

Predilection, *n.* The preparatory stage of disillusion.

Pre-existence, *n.* An unnoted factor in creation.

Preference, *n.* A sentiment, or frame of mind, induced by the erroneous belief that one thing is better than another.

> An ancient philosopher, expounding his conviction that life is no better than death, was asked by a disciple why, then, he did not die. "Because," he replied, "death is no better than life."
>
> It is longer.

Prehistoric, *adj.* Belonging to an early period and a museum. Antedating the art and practice of perpetuating falsehood.

> He lived in a period prehistoric,
> When all was absurd and phantasmagoric.
> Born later, when Clio, celestial recorder,
> Set down great events in succession and order,
> He surely had seen nothing droll or fortuitous
> In anything here but the lies that she threw at us.
>
> *Orpheus Bowen*

Prejudice, *n.* A vagrant opinion without visible means of support.

Prelate, *n.* A church officer having a superior degree of holiness and a fat preferment. One of Heaven's aristocracy. A gentleman of God.

Prerogative *n.* A sovereign's right to do wrong.

Presbyterian, *n.* One who holds the conviction that the governing authorities of the Church should be called presbyters.

Prescription, *n.* A physician's guess at what will best prolong the situation with least harm to the patient.

Present, *n.* That part of eternity dividing the domain of disappointment from the realm of hope.

Presentable, *adj.* Hideously appareled after the manner of the time and place.

    In Boorioboola-Gha a man is presentable on occasions of ceremony if he have his abdomen painted a bright blue and wear a cow's tail; in New York he may, if it please him, omit the paint, but after sunset he must wear two tails made of the wool of a sheep and dyed black.

Preside, *v.* To guide the action of a deliberative body to a desirable result. In Journalese, to perform upon a musical instrument; as, "He presided at the piccolo."

> The Headliner, holding the copy in hand,
>   Read with a solemn face:
> "The music was very uncommonly grand—
>   The best that was ever provided,
>   For our townsman Brown presided
>   At the organ with skill and grace."
> The Headliner discontinued to read,
>   And, spreading the paper down
> On the desk, he dashed in at the top of the screed:
>   "Great playing by President Brown."
>
>   *Orpheus Bowen*

Presidency, *n.* The greased pig in the field game of American politics.

President, *n.* The leading figure in a small group of men of whom— and of whom only it is positively known that immense numbers of their countrymen did not want any of them for President.

> If that's an honor surely 'tis a greater
> To have been a simple and undamned spectator.
> Behold in me a man of mark and note
> Whom no elector e'er denied a vote!—

An undiscredited, unhooted gent
Who might, for all we know, be President
By acclamation. Cheer, ye varlets, cheer—
I'm passing with a wide and open ear!

Jonathan Fomry

Prevaricator, *n.* A liar in the caterpillar state.

Price, *n.* Value, plus a reasonable sum for the wear and tear of conscience in demanding it.

Primate, *n.* The head of a church, especially a State church supported by involuntary contributions. The Primate of England is the Archbishop of Canterbury, an amiable old gentleman, who occupies Lambeth Palace when living and Westminster Abbey when dead. He is commonly dead.

Prison, *n.* A place of punishments and rewards. The poet assures us that

. "Stone walls do not a prison make,"

but a combination of the stone wall, the political parasite and the moral instructor is no garden of sweets.

Private, *n.* A military gentleman with a field-marshal's baton in his knapsack and an impediment in his hope.

Proboscis, *n.* The rudimentary organ of an elephant which serves him in place of the knife-and-fork that Evolution has as yet denied him. For purposes of humor it is popularly called a trunk.

Asked how he knew that an elephant was going on a journey, the illustrious Jo. Miller cast a reproachful look upon his tormentor, and answered, absently: "When it is ajar," and threw himself from a high promontory into the sea. Thus perished in his pride the most famous humorist of antiquity, leaving to mankind a heritage of woe! No successor worthy of the title has appeared, though Mr. Edward Bok, of *The Ladies' Home Journal,* is much respected for the purity and sweetness of his personal character.

Projectile, *n.* The final arbiter in international disputes. Formerly these disputes were settled by physical contact of the disputants, with such simple arguments as the rudimentary logic of the times could supply the sword, the spear, and so forth. With the growth of prudence in military affairs the projectile came more and more into favor, and is now held in high esteem by the most courageous. Its capital defect is that it requires personal attendance at the point of propulsion.

Proof, *n.* Evidence having a shade more of plausibility than of unlikelihood. The testimony of two credible witnesses as opposed to that of only one.

Proof-reader, *n.* A malefactor who atones for making your writing nonsense by permitting the compositor to make it unintelligible.

Property, *n.* Any material thing, having no particular value, that may be held by A against the cupidity of B. Whatever gratifies the passion for possession in one and disappoints it in all the others. The object of man's brief rapacity and long indifference.

Prophecy, *n.* The art and practice of selling one's credibility for future delivery.

Prospect, *n.* An outlook, usually forbidding. An expectation, usually forbidden.

> Blow, blow, ye spicy breezes—
> O'er Ceylon blow your breath,
> Where every prospect pleases,
> Save only that of death.
>
> *Bishop Sheber*

Providential, *adj.* Unexpectedly and conspicuously beneficial to the person so describing it.

Prude, *n.* A bawd hiding behind the back of her demeanor.

Publish, *v.* In literary affairs, to become the fundamental element in a cone of critics.

Push, *n.* One of the two things mainly conducive to success, especially in politics. The other is Pull.

Pyrrhonism, *n.* An ancient philosophy, named for its inventor. It consisted of an absolute disbelief in everything but Pyrrhonism. Its modern professors have added that.

Queen, *n.* A woman by whom the realm is ruled when there is a king, and through whom it is ruled when there is not.

Quill, *n.* An implement of torture yielded by a goose and commonly wielded by an ass. This use of the quill is now obsolete, but its modern equivalent, the steel pen, is wielded by the same everlasting Presence.

Quiver, *n.* A portable sheath in which the ancient statesman and the aboriginal lawyer carried their lighter arguments.

> He extracted from his quiver,
>   Did this controversial Roman,
> An argument well fitted
> To the question as submitted,
> Then addressed it to the liver,
>   Of the unpersuaded foeman.

Oglum P. Boomp

Quixotic, *adj.* Absurdly chivalric, like Don Quixote. An insight into the beauty and excellence of this incomparable adjective is unhappily denied to him who has the misfortune to know that the gentleman's name is pronounced Ke-ho-tay.

> When ignorance from out our lives can banish
> Philology, 'tis folly to know Spanish.

Juan Smith

Quorum, *n.* A sufficient number of members of a deliberative body to have their own way and their own way of having it. In the United States Senate a quorum consists of the chairman of the Committee on Finance and a messenger from the White House; in the House of Representatives, of the Speaker and the devil.

Quotation, *n.* The act of repeating erroneously the words of another. The words erroneously repeated.

> Intent on making his quotation truer,
> He sought the page infallible of Brewer,
> Then made a solemn vow that he would be
> Condemned eternally. Ah, me, ah, me!
>
> *Stumpo Gaker*

Quotient, *n.* A number showing how many times a sum of money belonging to one person is contained in the pocket of another— usually about as many times as it can be got there.

Rabble, *n.* In a republic, those who exercise a supreme authority tempered by fraudulent elections. The rabble is like the sacred Simurgh, of Arabian fable—omnipotent on condition that it do nothing. (The word is Aristocratese, and has no exact equivalent in our tongue, but means, as nearly as may be, "soaring swine.")

Rack, *n.* An argumentative implement formerly much used in persuading devotees of a false faith to embrace the living truth. As a call to the unconverted the rack never had any particular efficacy, and is now held in light popular esteem.

Radicalism, *n.* The conservatism of to-morrow injected into the affairs of to-day.

Radium, *n.* A mineral that gives off heat and stimulates the organ that a scientist is a fool with.

Railroad, *n.* The chief of many mechanical devices enabling us to get away from where we are to where we are no better off. For this purpose the railroad is held in highest favor by the optimist, for it permits him to make the transit with great expedition.

Ramshackle, *adj.* Pertaining to a certain order of architecture, otherwise known as the Normal American. Most of the public buildings of the United States are of the Ramshackle order, though some of our earlier architects preferred the Ironic. Recent additions to the White House in Washington are Theo-Doric, the ecclesiastic order of the Dorians. They are exceedingly fine and cost one hundred dollars a brick.

Rank, *n.* Relative elevation in the scale of human worth.

> He held at court a rank so high
> That other noblemen asked why.
> "Because," 'twas answered, "others lack
> His skill to scratch the royal back."
>
> *Aramis Jukes*

Ransom, *n.* The purchase of that which neither belongs to the seller, nor can belong to the buyer. The most unprofitable of investments.

Rapacity, *n.* Providence without industry. The thrift of power.

Rarebit, *n.* A Welsh rabbit, in the speech of the humorless, who point out that it is not a rabbit. To whom it may be solemnly explained that the comestible known as toad-in-the-hole is really not a toad, and that *riz-de-veau à la financière* is not the smile of a calf prepared after the recipe of a she banker.

Rascal, *n.* A fool considered under another aspect.

Rascality, *n.* Stupidity militant. The activity of a clouded intellect.

Rash, *adj.* Insensible to the value of our advice.

> "Now lay your bet with mine, nor let
>   These gamblers take your cash."
> "Nay, this child makes no bet." "Great snakes!
>   How can you be so rash?"
>
> *Bootle P. Gish*

Rational, *adj.* Devoid of all delusions save those of observation, experience and reflection.

Rattlesnake, *n.* Our prostrate brother, *Homo ventrambulans.*

Razor, *n.* An instrument used by the Caucasian to enhance his beauty, by the Mongolian to make a guy of himself, and by the Afro-American to affirm his worth.

Reach, *n.* The radius of action of the human hand. The area within which it is possible (and customary) to gratify directly the propensity to provide.

> This is a truth, as old as the hills,
>   That life and experience teach:
> The poor man suffers that keenest of ills,
>   An impediment in his reach.

G.J.

Reading, *n.* The general body of what one reads. In our country it consists, as a rule, of Indiana novels, short stories in "dialect" and humor in slang.

> We know by one's reading
> His learning and breeding;
> By what draws his laughter
> We know his Hereafter.
> Read nothing, laugh never—
> The Sphinx was less clever!

Jupiter Muke

Realism, *n.* The art of depicting nature as it is seen by toads. The charm suffusing a landscape painted by a mole, or a story written by a measuring-worm.

Reality, *n.* The dream of a mad philosopher. That which would remain in the cupel if one should assay a phantom. The nucleus of a vacuum.

Really, *adv.* Apparently.

Rear, *n.* In American military matters, that exposed part of the army that is nearest to Congress.

Reason, *v.i.* To weigh probabilities in the scales of desire.

Reason, *n.* Propensitate of prejudice.

Reasonable, *adj.* Accessible to the infection of our own opinions. Hospitable to persuasion, dissuasion and evasion.

Rebel, *n.* A proponent of a new misrule who has failed to establish it.

Recollect, *v.* To recall with additions something not previously known.

Reconciliation, *n.* A suspension of hostilities. An armed truce for the purpose of digging up the dead.

Reconsider, *v.* To seek a justification for a decision already made.

Recount, *n.* In American politics, another throw of the dice, accorded to the player against whom they are loaded.

Recreation, *n.* A particular kind of dejection to relieve a general fatigue.

Recruit, *n.* A person distinguishable from a civilian by his uniform and from a soldier by his gait.

> Fresh from the farm or factory or street,
> His marching, in pursuit or in retreat,
> Were an impressive martial spectacle
> Except for two impediments—his feet.
>
> *Thompson Johnson*

Rector, *n.* In the Church of England, the Third Person of the parochial Trinity, the Curate and the Vicar being the other two.

Redemption, *n.* Deliverance of sinners from the penalty of their sin, through their murder of the deity against whom they sinned. The doctrine of Redemption is the fundamental mystery of our holy religion, and whoso believeth in it shall not perish, but have everlasting life in which to try to understand it.

> We must awake Man's spirit from its sin,
> And take some special measure for redeeming it;
> Though hard indeed the task to get it in
> Among the angels any way but teaming it,
> Or purify it otherwise than steaming it.
> I'm awkward at Redemption—a beginner:
> My method is to crucify the sinner.
>
> *Golgo Brone*

Redress, *n.* Reparation without satisfaction.

Among the Anglo-Saxons a subject conceiving himself wronged by the king was permitted, on proving his injury, to beat a brazen image of the royal offender with a switch that was afterward applied to his own naked back. The latter rite was performed by the public hangman, and it assured moderation in the plaintiff's choice of a switch.

Red-skin, *n.* A North American Indian, whose skin is not red—at least not on the outside.

Redundant, *adj.* Superfluous; needless; *de trop.*

> The Sultan said: "There's evidence abundant
> To prove this unbelieving dog redundant."
> To whom the Grand Vizier, with mien impressive,
> Replied: "His head, at least, appears excessive."
> *Habeed Suleiman*

> Mr. Debs is a redundant citizen.—*Theodore Roosevelt*

Referendum, *n.* A law for submission of proposed legislation to a popular vote to learn the nonsensus of public opinion.

Reflection, *n.* An action of the mind whereby we obtain a clearer view of our relation to the things of yesterday and are able to avoid the perils that we shall not again encounter.

Reform, *n.* A thing that mostly satisfies reformers opposed to reformation.

Refuge, *n.* Anything assuring protection to one in peril. Moses and Joshua provided six cities of refuge—Bezer, Golan, Ramoth, Kadesh, Schekem and Hebron—to which one who had taken life inadvertently could flee when hunted by relatives of the deceased. This admirable expedient supplied him with wholesome exercise and enabled them to enjoy the pleasures of the chase; whereby the soul of the dead man was appropriately honored by observances akin to the funeral games of early Greece.

Refusal, *n.* Denial of something desired; as an elderly maiden's hand in marriage, to a rich and handsome suitor; a valuable franchise to a rich corporation, by an alderman; absolution to an impenitent king, by a priest, and so forth. Refusals are graded in a descending scale of finality thus: the refusal absolute, the refusal conditional, the refusal tentative and the refusal feminine. The last is called by some casuists the refusal assentive.

Regalia, *n.* Distinguishing insignia, jewels and costume of such ancient

and honorable orders as Knights of Adam; Visionaries of
Delectable Bosh; the Ancient Order of Modern Troglodytes; the
League of Holy Humbug; the Golden Phalanx of Phalangers; the
Genteel Society of Expurgated Hoodlums; the Mystic Alliance of
Gorgeous Regalians; Knights and Ladies of the Yellow Dog; the
Oriental Order of Sons of the West; the Blatherhood of
Insufferable Stuff; Warriors of the Long Bow; Guardians of the
Great Horn Spoon; the Band of Brutes; the Impenitent Order of
Wife-Beaters; the Sublime Legion of Flamboyant Conspicuants;
Worshipers at the Electroplated Shrine; Shining Inaccessibles; Fee-
Faw-Fummers of the Inimitable Grip; Jannissaries of the Broad-
Blown Peacock; Plumed Increscencies of the Magic Temple; the
Grand Cabal of Able-Bodied Sedentarians; Associated Deities of
the Butter Trade; the Garden of Galoots; the Affectionate
Fraternity of Men Similarly Warted; the Flashing Astonishers;
Ladies of Horror; Coöperative Association for Breaking into the
Spotlight; Dukes of Eden; Disciples Militant of the Hidden Faith;
Knights-Champions of the Domestic Dog; the Holy Gregarians;
the Resolute Optimists; the Ancient Sodality of Inhospitable Hogs;
Associated Sovereigns of Mendacity; Dukes-Guardian of the
Mystic Cesspool; the Society for Prevention of Prevalence; Kings
of Drink; Polite Federation of Gents-Consequential; the
Mysterious Order of the Undecipherable Scroll; Uniformed Rank
of Lousy Cats; Monarchs of Worth and Hunger; Sons of the South
Star; Prelates of the Tub-and-Sword.

Religion, *n.* A daughter of Hope and Fear, explaining to Ignorance the
nature of the Unknowable.

"What is your religion, my son?" inquired the Archbishop of
Rheims.

"Pardon, monseigneur," replied Rochebriant; "I am ashamed of
it."

"Then why do you not become an atheist?"

"Impossible! I should be ashamed of atheism."

"In that case, monsieur, you should join the Protestants."

Reliquary, *n.* A receptacle for such sacred objects as pieces of the true
cross, short-ribs of saints, the ears of Balaam's ass, the lung of the
cock that called Peter to repentance and so forth. Reliquaries are
commonly of metal, and provided with a lock to prevent the con-

tents from coming out and performing miracles at unseasonable times. A feather from the wing of the Angel of the Annunciation once escaped during a sermon in Saint Peter's and so tickled the noses of the congregation that they woke and sneezed with great vehemence three times each. It is related in the "Gesta Sanctorum" that a sacristan in the Canterbury cathedral surprised the head of Saint Dennis in the library. Reprimanded by its stern custodian, it explained that it was seeking a body of doctrine. This unseemly levity so enraged the diocesan that the offender was publicly anathematized, thrown into the Stour and replaced by another head of Saint Dennis, brought from Rome.

Renown, *n.* A degree of distinction between notoriety and fame—a little more supportable than the one and a little more intolerable than the other. Sometimes it is conferred by an unfriendly and inconsiderate hand.

> I touched the harp in every key,
>   But found no heeding ear;
> And then Ithuriel touched me
>   With a revealing spear.
>
> Not all my genius, great as 'tis,
>   Could urge me out of night.
> I felt the faint appulse of his,
>   And leapt into the light!
>
> *W.J. Candleton*

Reparation, *n.* Satisfaction that is made for a wrong and deducted from the satisfaction felt in committing it.

Repartee, *n.* Prudent insult in retort. Practiced by gentlemen with a constitutional aversion to violence, but a strong disposition to offend. In a war of words, the tactics of the North American Indian.

Repentance, *n.* The faithful attendant and follower of Punishment. It is usually manifest in a degree of reformation that is not inconsistent with continuity of sin.

> Desirous to avoid the pains of Hell,
> You will repent and join the Church, Parnell?

How needless!—Nick will keep you off the coals
And add you to the woes of other souls.

Jomater Abemy

Replica, *n.* A reproduction of a work of art, by the artist that made the original. It is so called to distinguish it from a "copy," which is made by another artist. When the two are made with equal skill the replica is the more valuable, for it is supposed to be more beautiful than it looks.

Reporter, *n.* A writer who guesses his way to the truth and dispels it with a tempest of words.

"More dear than all my bosom knows, O thou
Whose 'lips are sealed' and will not disavow!"
So sang the blithe reporter-man as grew
Beneath his hand the leg-long "interview."

Barson Maith

Repose, *v.i.* To cease from troubling.

Representative, *n.* In national politics, a member of the Lower House in this world, and without discernible hope of promotion in the next.

Reprobation, *n.* In theology, the state of a luckless mortal prenatally damned. The doctrine of reprobation was taught by Calvin, whose joy in it was somewhat marred by the sad sincerity of his conviction that although some are foredoomed to perdition, others are predestined to salvation.

Republic, *n.* A nation in which, the thing governing and the thing governed being the same, there is only a permitted authority to enforce an optional obedience. In a republic the foundation of public order is the ever lessening habit of submission inherited from ancestors who, being truly governed, submitted because they had to. There are as many kinds of republics as there are gradations between the despotism whence they came and the anarchy whither they lead.

Requiem, *n.* A mass for the dead which the minor poets assure us the winds sing o'er the graves of their favorites. Sometimes, by way of providing a varied entertainment, they sing a dirge.

Resident, *adj.* Unable to leave.

Resign, *v.t.* To renounce an honor for an advantage. To renounce an advantage for a greater advantage.

> 'Twas rumored Leonard Wood had signed
>   A true renunciation
> Of title, rank and every kind
>   Of military station—
>   Each honorable station.
>
> By his example fired—inclined
>   To noble emulation,
> The country humbly was resigned
>   To Leonard's resignation—
>   His Christian resignation.
>
> *Politian Greame*

Resolute, *adj.* Obstinate in a course that we approve.

Respectability, *n.* The offspring of a *liaison* between a bald head and a bank account.

Respirator, *n.* An apparatus fitted over the nose and mouth of an inhabitant of London, whereby to filter the visible universe in its passage to the lungs.

Respite, *n.* A suspension of hostilities against a sentenced assassin, to enable the Executive to determine whether the murder may not have been done by the prosecuting attorney. Any break in the continuity of a disagreeable expectation.

> Altgeld upon his incandescent bed
> Lay, an attendant demon at his head.
>
> "O cruel cook, pray grant me some relief—
> Some respite from the roast, however brief.
>
> "Remember how on earth I pardoned all
> Your friends in Illinois when held in thrall."
>
> "Unhappy soul! for that alone you squirm
> O'er fire unquenched, a never-dying worm.
> "Yet, for I pity your uneasy state,

Your doom I'll mollify and pains abate.

"Naught, for a season, shall your comfort mar,
Not even the memory of who you are."

Throughout eternal space dread silence fell;
Heaven trembled as Compassion entered Hell.

"As long, sweet demon, let my respite be
As, governing down here, I'd respite thee."

"As long, poor soul, as any of the pack
You thrust from jail consumed in getting back."

A genial chill affected Altgeld's hide
While they were turning him on t'other side.

                                          Joel Spate Woop

Resplendent, *adj.* Like a simple American citizen beduking himself in his lodge, or affirming his consequence in the Scheme of Things as an elemental unit of a parade.

> The Knights of Dominion were so resplendent in their velvet-and-gold that their masters would hardly have known them.
> —"Chronicles of the Classes."

Respond, *v.i.* To make answer, or disclose otherwise a consciousness of having inspired an interest in what Herbert Spencer calls "external coexistences," as Satan "squat like a toad" at the ear of Eve, responded to the touch of the angel's spear. To respond in damages is to contribute to the maintenance of the plaintiff's attorney and, incidentally, to the gratification of the plaintiff.

Responsibility, *n.* A detachable burden easily shifted to the shoulders of God, Fate, Fortune, Luck or one's neighbor. In the days of astrology it was customary to unload it upon a star.

> Alas, things ain't what we should see
> If Eve had let that apple be;
> And many a feller which had ought
> To set with monarchses of thought,
> Or play some rosy little game

With battle-chaps on fields of fame,
Is downed by his unlucky star
And hollers: "Peanuts!—here you are!"

"The Sturdy Beggar"

Restitution, *n.* The founding or endowing of universities and public libraries by gift or bequest.

Restitutor, *n.* Benefactor; philanthropist.

Retaliation, *n.* The natural rock upon which is reared the Temple of Law.

Retribution, *n.* A rain of fire-and-brimstone that falls alike upon the just and such of the unjust as have not procured shelter by evicting them.

In the lines following, addressed to an Emperor in exile by Father Gassalasca Jape, the reverend poet appears to hint his sense of the imprudence of turning about to face Retribution when it is taking exercise:

What, what! Dom Pedro, you desire to go
    Back to Brazil to end your days in quiet?
Why, what assurance have you 'twould be so?
    'Tis not so long since you were in a riot,
And your dear subjects showed a will to fly at
Your throat and shake you like a rat. You know
That empires are ungrateful; are you certain
Republics are less handy to get hurt in?

Reveille, *n* A signal to sleeping soldiers to dream of battlefields no more, but get up and have their blue noses counted. In the American army it is ingeniously called "rev-e-lee," and to that pronunciation our countrymen have pledged their lives, their misfortunes and their sacred dishonour.

Revelation, *n.* A famous book in which St. John the Divine concealed all that he knew. The revealing is done by the commentators, who know nothing.

Reverence, *n.* The spiritual attitude of a man to a god and a dog to a man.

Review, *v.t.*

> To set your wisdom (holding not a doubt of it,
>   Although in truth there's neither bone nor skin to it)
> At work upon a book, and so read out of it
> The qualities that you have first read into it.

Revolution, *n.* In politics, an abrupt change in the form of misgovernment. Specifically, in American history, the substitution of the rule of an Administration for that of a Ministry, whereby the welfare and happiness of the people were advanced a full half-inch. Revolutions are usually accompanied by a considerable effusion of blood, but are accounted worth it—this appraisement being made by beneficiaries whose blood had not the mischance to be shed. The French revolution is of incalculable value to the Socialist of to-day; when he pulls the string actuating its bones its gestures are inexpressibly terrifying to gory tyrants suspected of fomenting law and order.

Rhadomancer, *n.* One who uses a divining-rod in prospecting for precious metals in the pocket of a fool.

Ribaldry, *n.* Censorious language by another concerning oneself.

Ribroaster, *n.* Censorious language by oneself concerning another. The word is of classical refinement, and is even said to have been used in a fable by Georgius Coadjutor, one of the most fastidious writers of the fifteenth century—commonly, indeed, regarded as the founder of the Fastidiotic School.

Rice-water, *n.* A mystic beverage secretly used by our most popular novelists and poets to regulate the imagination and narcotize the conscience. It is said to be rich in both obtundite and lethargine, and is brewed in a midnight fog by a fat witch of the Dismal Swamp.

Rich, *adj.* Holding in trust and subject to an accounting the property of the indolent, the incompetent, the unthrifty, the envious and the luckless. That is the view that prevails in the underworld, where the Brotherhood of Man finds its most logical development and candid advocacy. To denizens of the midworld the word means good and wise.

Riches, *n.*

> A gift from Heaven signifying, "This is my beloved son, in whom I am well pleased."—*John D. Rockefeller*

> The reward of toil and virtue.—*J.P. Morgan*

> The savings of many in the hands of one.—*Eugene Debs*

To these excellent definitions the inspired lexicographer feels that he can add nothing of value.

Ridicule, *n.* Words designed to show that the person of whom they are uttered is devoid of the dignity of character distinguishing him who utters them. It may be graphic, mimetic or merely rident. Shaftesbury is quoted as having pronounced it the test of truth—a ridiculous assertion, for many a solemn fallacy has undergone centuries of ridicule with no abatement of its popular acceptance. What, for example has been more valorously derided than the doctrine of Infant Respectability?

Right, *n.* Legitimate authority to be, to do or to have; as the right to be a king, the right to do one's neighbor, the right to have measles, and the like. The first of these rights was once universally believed to be derived directly from the will of God; and this is still sometimes affirmed in *partibus infidelium* outside the enlightened realms of Democracy; as the well-known lines of Sir Abednego Bink, following:

> By what right, then, do royal rulers rule?
>   Whose is the sanction of their state and pow'r?
> He surely were as stubborn as a mule
>   Who, God unwilling, could maintain an hour
> His uninvited session on the throne, or air
> His pride securely in the Presidential chair.

>   Whatever is is so by Right Divine;
>   Whate'er occurs, God wills it so. Good land!
>   It were a wondrous thing if His design
>   A fool could baffle or a rogue withstand!
> If so, then God, I say (intending no offence)
> Is guilty of contributory negligence.

Righteousness, *n.* A sturdy virtue that was once found among the Pantidoodles inhabiting the lower part of the peninsula of Oque. Some feeble attempts were made by returned missionaries to introduce it into several European countries, but it appears to have been imperfectly expounded. An example of this faulty exposition is found in the only extant sermon of the pious Bishop Rowley, a characteristic passage from which is here given:

> "Now righteousness consisteth not merely in a holy state of mind, nor yet in performance of religious rites and obedience to the letter of the law. It is not enough that one be pious and just: one must see to it that others also are in the same state; and to this end compulsion is a proper means. Forasmuch as my injustice may work ill to another, so by his injustice may evil be wrought upon still another, the which it is as manifestly my duty to estop as to forestall mine own tort. Wherefore if I would be righteous I am bound to restrain my neighbor, by force if needful, in all those injurious enterprises from which, through a better disposition and by the help of Heaven, I do myself refrain."

Rime, *n.* Agreeing sounds in the terminals of verse, mostly bad. The verses themselves, as distinguished from prose, mostly dull. Usually (and wickedly) spelled "rhyme."

Rimer, *n.* A poet regarded with indifference or disesteem.

> The rimer quenches his unheeded fires,
> The sound surceases and the sense expires.
> Then the domestic dog, to east and west,
> Expounds the passions burning in his breast.
> The rising moon o'er that enchanted land
> Pauses to hear and yearns to understand.
>
> *Mowbray Myles*

Riot, *n.* A popular entertainment given to the military by innocent bystanders.

R.I.P. A careless abbreviation of *requiescat in pace*, attesting an indolent goodwill to the dead. According to the learned Dr. Drigge, however, the letters originally meant nothing more than *reductus in pulvis*.

Rite, *n.* A religious or semi-religious ceremony fixed by law, precept or custom, with the essential oil of sincerity carefully squeezed out of it.

Ritualism, *n.* A Dutch Garden of God where He may walk in rectilinear freedom, keeping off the grass.

Road, *n.* A strip of land along which one may pass from where it is too tiresome to be to where it is futile to go.

> All roads, howsoe'er they diverge, lead to Rome,
> Whence, thank the good Lord, at least one leads back
> home.
>
> *Borey the Bald*

Robber, *n.* A candid man of affairs.
It is related of Voltaire that one night he and some traveling companions lodged at a wayside inn. The surroundings were suggestive, and after supper they agreed to tell robber stories in turn. When Voltaire's turn came he said: "Once there was a Farmer-General of the Revenues." Saying nothing more, he was encouraged to continue. "That," he said, "is the story."

Romance, *n.* Fiction that owes no allegiance to the God of Things as They Are. In the novel the writer's thought is tethered to probability, as a domestic horse to the hitching-post, but in romance it ranges at will over the entire region of the imagination—free, lawless, immune to bit and rein. Your novelist is a poor creature, as Carlyle might say—a mere reporter. He may invent his characters and plot, but he must not imagine anything taking place that might not occur, albeit his entire narrative is candidly a lie. Why he imposes this hard condition on himself, and "drags at each remove a lengthening chain" of his own forging he can explain in ten thick volumes without illuminating by so much as a candle's ray the black profound of his own ignorance of the matter. There are great novels, for great writers have "laid waste their powers" to write them, but it remains true that far and away the most fascinating fiction that we have is "The Thousand and One Nights."

Rope, *n.* An obsolescent appliance for reminding assassins that they too are mortal. It is put about the neck and remains in place one's whole life long. It has been largely superseded by a more complex electrical device worn upon another part of the person; and this is rapidly giving place to an apparatus known as the preachment.

Rostrum, *n.* In Latin, the beak of a bird or the prow of a ship. In

American, a place from which a candidate for office energetically expounds the wisdom, virtue and power of the rabble.

Roundhead, *n.* A member of the Parliamentary party in the English civil war—so called from his habit of wearing his hair short, whereas his enemy, the Cavalier, wore his long. There were other points of difference between them, but the fashion in hair was the fundamental cause of quarrel. The Cavaliers were royalists because the king, an indolent fellow, found it more convenient to let his hair grow than to wash his neck. This the Roundheads, who were mostly barbers and soap-boilers, deemed an injury to trade, and the royal neck was therefore the object of their particular indignation. Descendants of the belligerents now wear their hair all alike, but the fires of animosity enkindled in that ancient strife smoulder to this day beneath the snows of British civility.

Rubbish, *n.* Worthless matter, such as the religions, philosophies, literatures, arts and sciences of the tribes infesting the regions lying due south from Boreaplas.

Ruin, *v.* To destroy. Specifically, to destroy a maid's belief in the virtue of maids.

Rum, *n.* Generically, fiery liquors that produce madness in total abstainers.

Rumor, *n.* A favorite weapon of the assassins of character.

> Sharp, irresistible by mail or shield,
>   By guard unparried as by flight unstayed,
> O serviceable Rumor, let me wield
>   Against my enemy no other blade.
> His be the terror of a foe unseen,
>   His the inutile hand upon the hilt,
> And mine the deadly tongue, long, slender, keen,
>   Hinting a rumor of some ancient guilt.
> So shall I slay the wretch without a blow,
> Spare me to celebrate his overthrow,
> And nurse my valor for another foe.
>
> *Joel Buxter*

Russian, *n.* A person with a Caucasian body and a Mongolian soul. A Tartar Emetic.

Sabbath, *n.* A weekly festival having its origin in the fact that God made the world in six days and was arrested on the seventh. Among the Jews observance of the day was enforced by a Commandment of which this is the Christian version: "Remember the seventh day to make thy neighbor keep it wholly." To the Creator it seemed fit and expedient that the Sabbath should be the last day of the week, but the Early Fathers of the Church held other views. So great is the sanctity of the day that even where the Lord holds a doubtful and precarious jurisdiction over those who go down to (and down into) the sea it is reverently recognized, as is manifest in the following deep-water version of the Fourth Commandment:

> Six days shalt thou labor and do all thou art able,
> And on the seventh holystone the deck and scrape the cable.

Decks are no longer holystoned, but the cable still supplies the captain with opportunity to attest a pious respect for the divine ordinance.

Sacerdotalist, *n.* One who holds the belief that a clergyman is a priest. Denial of this momentous doctrine is the hardiest challenge that is now flung into the teeth of the Episcopolian church by the Neo-Dictionarians.

Sacrament, *n.* A solemn religious ceremony to which several degrees of authority and significance are attached. Rome has seven sacraments, but the Protestant churches, being less prosperous, feel that they can afford only two, and these of inferior sanctity. Some of the smaller sects have no sacraments at all—for which mean economy they will indubitably be damned.

Sacred, *adj.* Dedicated to some religious purpose; having a divine character; inspiring solemn thoughts or emotions; as, the Dalai Lama of Thibet; the Moogum of M'bwango; the temple of Apes in Ceylon; the Cow in India; the Crocodile, the Cat and the Onion of ancient Egypt; the Mufti of Moosh; the hair of the dog that bit Noah, etc.

> All things are either sacred or profane.
> The former to ecclesiasts bring gain;
> The latter to the devil appertain.
>
> Dumbo Omohundro

Sandlotter, *n.* A vertebrate mammal holding the political views of Denis Kearney, a notorious demagogue of San Francisco, whose audiences gathered in the open spaces (sandlots) of the town. True to the traditions of his species, this leader of the proletariat was finally bought off by his law-and-order enemies, living prosperously silent and dying impenitently rich. But before his treason he imposed upon California a constitution that was a confection of sin in a diction of solecisms. The similarity between the words "sandlotter" and "sansculotte" is problematically significant, but indubitably suggestive.

Safety-Clutch, *n.* A mechanical device acting automatically to prevent the fall of an elevator, or cage, in case of an accident to the hoisting apparatus.

> Once I seen a human ruin
> In a elevator-well,
> And his members was bestrewin'
> All the place where he had fell.
>
> And I says, apostrophisin'
> That uncommon woful wreck:
> "Your position's so surprisin'
> That I tremble for your neck!"

Then that ruin, smilin' sadly
   And impressive, up and spoke:
"Well, I wouldn't tremble badly,
   For it's been a fortnight broke."

Then, for further comprehension
   Of his attitude, he begs
I will focus my attention
   On his various arms and legs—

How they all are contumacious;
   Where they each, respective, lie;
How one trotter proves ungracious,
   T'other one an *alibi*.

These particulars is mentioned
   For to show his dismal state,
Which I wasn't first intentioned
   To specifical relate.

None is worser to be dreaded
   That I ever have heard tell
Than the gent's who there was spreaded
   In that elevator-well.

Now this tale is allegoric—
   It is figurative all,
For the well is metaphoric
   And the feller didn't fall.

I opine it isn't moral
   For a writer-man to cheat,
And despise to wear a laurel
   As was gotten by deceit.

For 'tis Politics intended
   By the elevator, mind,
It will boost a person splendid
   If his talent is the kind.

Col. Bryan had the talent
   (For the busted man is him)

And it shot him up right gallant
  Till his head begun to swim.

Then the rope it broke above him
  And he painful came to earth
Where there's nobody to love him
  For his detrimented worth.

Though he's living' none would know him,
  Or at leastwise not as such.
Moral of this woful poem:
  Frequent oil your safety-clutch.

Porfer Poog

Saint, *n.* A dead sinner revised and edited.
  The Duchess of Orleans relates that the irreverent old calumni-
ator, Marshal Villeroi, who in his youth had known St. Francis de
Sales, said, on hearing him called saint: "I am delighted to hear that
Monsieur de Sales is a saint. He was fond of saying indelicate
things, and used to cheat at cards. In other respects he was a perfect gentleman, though a fool."

Salacity, *n.* A certain literary quality frequently observed in popular
  novels, especially in those written by women and young girls, who
  give it another name and think that in introducing it they are
  occupying a neglected field of letters and reaping an overlooked
  harvest. If they have the misfortune to live long enough they are
  tormented with a desire to burn their sheaves.

Salamander, *n.* Originally a reptile inhabiting fire; later, an anthropo-
  morphous immortal, but still a pyrophile. Salamanders are now
  believed to be extinct, the last one of which we have an account
  having been seen in Carcassonne by the Abbe Belloc, who exorcised it with a bucket of holy water.

Sarcophagus, *n.* Among the Greeks a coffin which being made of a certain kind of carnivorous stone, had the peculiar property of
  devouring the body placed in it. The sarcophagus known to modern obsequiographers is commonly a product of the carpenter's
  art.

Satan, *n.* One of the Creator's lamentable mistakes, repented in sashcloth and axes. Being instated as an archangel, Satan made himself multifariously objectionable and was finally expelled from Heaven. Halfway in his descent he paused, bent his head in thought a moment and at last went back. "There is one favor that I should like to ask," said he.

"Name it."

"Man, I understand, is about to be created. He will need laws."

"What, wretch! you his appointed adversary, charged from the dawn of eternity with hatred of his soul—you ask for the right to make his laws?"

"Pardon; what I have to ask is that he be permitted to make them himself."

It was so ordered.

Satiety, *n.* The feeling that one has for the plate after he has eaten its contents, madam.

Satire, *n.* An obsolete kind of literary composition in which the vices and follies of the author's enemies were expounded with imperfect tenderness. In this country satire never had more than a sickly and uncertain existence, for the soul of it is wit, wherein we are dolefully deficient, the humor that we mistake for it, like all humor, being tolerant and sympathetic. Moreover, although Americans are "endowed by their Creator" with abundant vice and folly, it is not generally known that these are reprehensible qualities, wherefore the satirist is popularly regarded as a sour-spirited knave, and his every victim's outcry for codefendants evokes a national assent.

> Hail Satire! be thy praises ever sung
> In the dead language of a mummy's tongue,
> For thou thyself art dead, and damned as well—
> Thy spirit (usefully employed) in Hell.
> Had it been such as consecrates the Bible
> Thou hadst not perished by the law of libel.
>
> *Barney Stims*

Satyr, *n.* One of the few characters of the Grecian mythology accorded recognition in the Hebrew (Leviticus, xvii, 7.) The satyr was at first a member of the dissolute community acknowledging a loose allegiance to Dionysius, but underwent many transformations and improvements. Not infrequently he is confounded with the faun, a later and decenter creation of the Romans, who was less like a man and more like a goat.

Sauce, *n.* The one infallible sign of civilization and enlightenment. A people with no sauces has one thousand vices; a people with one sauce has only nine hundred and ninety-nine. For every sauce invented and accepted a vice is renounced and forgiven.

Saw, *n.* A trite popular saying, or proverb. (Figurative and colloquial.) So called because it makes its way into a wooden head. Following are examples of old saws fitted with new teeth.

A penny saved is a penny to squander.

A man is known by the company that he organizes.

A bad workman quarrels with the man who calls him that.

A bird in the hand is worth what it will bring.

Better late than before anybody has invited you.

Example is better than following it.

Half a loaf is better than a whole one if there is much else.

Think twice before you speak to a friend in need.

What is worth doing is worth the trouble of asking somebody to do it.

Least said is soonest disavowed.

He laughs best who laughs least.

Speak of the Devil and he will hear about it.

Of two evils choose to be the least.

Strike while your employer has a big contract.

Where there's a will there's a won't.

Scarabæus, *n.* The sacred beetle of the ancient Egyptians, allied to our familiar "tumble-bug." It was supposed to symbolize immortality, the fact that God knew why giving it its peculiar sanctity. Its habit of incubating its eggs in a ball of ordure may also have commended it to the favor of the priesthood, and may some day assure it an equal reverence among ourselves. True, the American beetle is an inferior beetle, but the American priest is an inferior priest.

Scarabee, *n.* The same as scarabæus.

> He fell by his own hand
> > Beneath the great oak tree.
> > > He'd traveled in a foreign land.
> > > He tried to make her understand
> > > The dance that's called the Saraband,
> > > > But he called it Scarabee.
> He had called it so through an afternoon,
> > And she, the light of his harem if so might be,
> > Had smiled and said naught. O the body was fair to see,
> All frosted there in the shine o' the moon—
> > > Dead for a Scarabee
> And a recollection that came too late.
> > > O Fate!
> > > They buried him where he lay,
> > > He sleeps awaiting the Day,
> > > > In state,
> And two Possible Puns, moon-eyed and wan,
> Gloom over the grave and then move on.
> > > Dead for a Scarabee!

> > > > > > > *Fernando Tapple*

Scarification, *n.* A form of penance practiced by the mediæval pious. The rite was performed, sometimes with a knife, sometimes with a hot iron, but always, says Arsenius Asceticus, acceptably if the penitent spared himself no pain nor harmless disfigurement. Scarification, with other crude penances, has now been superseded by benefaction. The founding of a library or endowment of a university is said to yield to the penitent a sharper and more lasting pain than is conferred by the knife or iron, and is therefore a surer means of grace. There are, however, two grave objections to it as a penitential method: the good that it does and the taint of justice.

Scepter, *n.* A king's staff of office, the sign and symbol of his authority. It was originally a mace with which the sovereign admonished his jester and vetoed ministerial measures by breaking the bones of their proponents.

Scimetar, *n.* A curved sword of exceeding keenness, in the conduct of which certain Orientals attain a surprising proficiency, as the incident here related will serve to show. The account is translated from the Japanese of Shusi Itama, a famous writer of the thirteenth century.

When the great Gichi-Kuktai was Mikado he condemned to decapitation Jijiji Ri, a high officer of the Court. Soon after the hour appointed for performance of the rite what was his Majesty's surprise to see calmly approaching the throne the man who should have been at that time ten minutes dead!

"Seventeen hundred impossible dragons!" shouted the enraged monarch. "Did I not sentence you to stand in the market-place and have your head struck off by the public executioner at three o'clock? And is it not now 3:10?"

"Son of a thousand illustrious deities," answered the condemned minister, "all that you say is so true that the truth is a lie in comparison. But your heavenly Majesty's sunny and vitalizing wishes have been pestilently disregarded. With joy I ran and placed my unworthy body in the market-place. The executioner appeared with his bare scimetar, ostentatiously whirled it in the air, and then, tapping me lightly upon the neck, strode away, pelted by the populace, with whom I was ever a favorite. I am come to pray for justice upon his own dishonorable and treasonous head."

"To what regiment of executioners does the black-boweled caitiff belong?" asked the Mikado.

"To the gallant Ninety-eight Hundred and Thirty-seventh—I know the man. His name is Sakko-Samshi."

"Let him be brought before me," said the Mikado to an attendant, and a half-hour later the culprit stood in the Presence.

"Thou bastard son of a three-legged hunchback without thumbs!" roared the sovereign—"why didst thou but lightly tap the neck that it should have been thy pleasure to sever?"

"Lord of Cranes and Cherry Blooms," replied the executioner, unmoved, "command him to blow his nose with his fingers."

Being commanded, Jijiji Ri laid hold of his nose and

trumpeted like an elephant, all expecting to see the severed
head flung violently from him. Nothing occurred: the performance prospered peacefully to the close, without incident.

All eyes were now turned on the executioner, who had
grown as white as the snows on the summit of Fujiama. His
legs trembled and his breath came in gasps of terror.

"Several kinds of spike-tailed brass lions!" he cried; "I am a
ruined and disgraced swordsman! I struck the villain feebly
because in flourishing the scimetar I had accidentally passed it
through my own neck! Father of the Moon, I resign my
office."

So saying, he grasped his top-knot, lifted off his head, and
advancing to the throne laid it humbly at the Mikado's feet.

Scrap-Book, *n.* A book that is commonly edited by a fool. Many persons of some small distinction compile scrap-books containing
whatever they happen to read about themselves or employ others
to collect. One of these egotists was addressed in the lines following, by Agamemnon Melancthon Peters:

> Dear Frank, that scrap-book where you boast
>   You keep a record true
> Of every kind of peppered roast
>   That's made of you;
>
> Wherein you paste the printed gibes
>   That revel round your name,
> Thinking the laughter of the scribes
>   Attests your fame;
>
> Where all the pictures you arrange
>   That comic pencils trace—
> Your funny figure and your strange
>   Semitic face—
>
> Pray lend it me. Wit I have not,
>   Nor art, but there I'll list
> The daily drubbings you'd have got
>   Had God a fist.

Scribbler, *n.* A professional writer whose views are antagonistic to one's
own.

Scriptures, *n.* The sacred books of our holy religion, as distinguished from the false and profane writings on which all other faiths are based.

Seal, *n.* A mark impressed upon certain kinds of documents to attest their authenticity and authority. Sometimes it is stamped upon wax, and attached to the paper, sometimes into the paper itself. Sealing, in this sense, is a survival of an ancient custom of inscribing important papers with cabalistic words or signs to give them a magical efficacy independent of the authority that they represent. In the British Museum are preserved many ancient papers, mostly of a sacerdotal character, validated by necromantic pentagrams and other devices, frequently initial letters of words to conjure with; and in many instances these are attached in the same way that seals are appended now. As nearly every reasonless and apparently meaningless custom, rite or observance of modern times had origin in some remote utility, it is pleasing to note an example of ancient nonsense evolving in the process of ages into something really useful. Our word "sincere" is derived from *sine cero*, without wax, but the learned are not in agreement as to whether this refers to the absence of the cabalistic signs, or to that of the wax with which letters were formerly closed from public scrutiny. Either view of the matter will serve one in immediate need of an hypothesis. The initials L. S., commonly appended to signatures of legal documents, mean *locum sigillis*, the place of the seal, although the seal is no longer used—an admirable example of conservatism distinguishing Man from the beasts that perish. The words *locum sigillis* are humbly suggested as a suitable motto for the Pribyloff Islands whenever they shall take their place as a sovereign State of the American Union.

Seine, *n.* A kind of net for effecting an involuntary change of environment. For fish it is made strong and coarse, but women are more easily taken with a singularly delicate fabric weighted with small, cut stones.

> The devil casting a seine of lace,
>   (With precious stones 'twas weighted)
> Drew it into the landing place
>   And its contents calculated.

All souls of women were in that sack—
A draft miraculous, precious!
But ere he could throw it across his back
They'd all escaped through the meshes.

Baruch de Loppis

Self-esteem, *n.* An erroneous appraisement.

Self-evident, *adj.* Evident to one's self and to nobody else.

Selfish, *adj.* Devoid of consideration for the selfishness of others.

Senate, *n.* A body of elderly gentlemen charged with high duties and misdemeanors.

Serial, *n.* A literary work, usually a story that is not true, creeping through several issues of a newspaper or magazine. Frequently appended to each instalment is a "synopsis of preceding chapters" for those who have not read them, but a direr need is a synopsis of succeeding chapters for those who do not intend to read *them.* A synopsis of the entire work would be still better.

   The late James F. Bowman was writing a serial tale for a weekly paper in collaboration with a genius whose name has not come down to us. They wrote, not jointly but alternately, Bowman supplying the instalment for one week, his friend for the next, and so on, world without end, they hoped. Unfortunately they quarreled, and one Monday morning when Bowman read the paper to prepare himself for his task, he found his work cut out for him in a way to surprise and pain him. His collaborator had embarked every character of the narrative on a ship and sunk them all in the deepest part of the Atlantic.

Severalty, *n.* Separateness, as, lands in severalty, i.e., lands held individually, not in joint ownership. Certain tribes of Indians are believed now to be sufficiently civilized to have in severalty the lands that they have hitherto held as tribal organizations, and could not sell to the Whites for waxen beads and potato whiskey.

   Lo! the poor Indian whose unsuited mind
   Saw death before, hell and the grave behind;
   Whom thrifty settlers ne'er besought to stay—
   His small belongings their appointed prey;

Whom Dispossession, with alluring wile,
Persuaded elsewhere every little while!
His fire unquenched and his undying worm
By "land in severalty" (charming term!)
Are cooled and killed, respectively, at last,
And he to his new holding anchored fast!

Sheriff, *n.* In America the chief executive officer of a county, whose most characteristic duties, in some of the Western and Southern States, are the catching and hanging of rogues.

John Elmer Pettibone Cajee
(I write of him with little glee)
Was just as bad as he could be.

'Twas frequently remarked: "I swon!
The sun has never looked upon
So bad a man as Neighbor John."

A sinner through and through, he had
This added fault: it made him mad
To know another man was bad.

In such a case he thought it right
To rise at any hour of night
And quench that wicked person's light.

Despite the town's entreaties, he
Would hale him to the nearest tree
And leave him swinging wide and free.

Or sometimes, if the humor came,
A luckless wight's reluctant frame
Was given to the cheerful flame.

While it was turning nice and brown,
All unconcerned John met the frown
Of that austere and righteous town.

"How sad," his neighbors said, "that he
So scornful of the law should be—
An anar c, h, i, s, t."

(That is the way that they preferred
To utter the abhorrent word,
So strong the aversion that it stirred.)

"Resolved," they said, continuing,
"That Badman John must cease this thing
Of having his unlawful fling.

"Now, by these sacred relics"—here
Each man had out a souvenir
Got at a lynching yesteryear—

"By these we swear he shall forsake
His ways, nor cause our hearts to ache
By sins of rope and torch and stake.

"We'll tie his red right hand until
He'll have small freedom to fulfil
The mandates of his lawless will."

So, in convention then and there,
They named him Sheriff. The affair
Was opened, it is said, with prayer.

J. Milton Sloluck

Siren, *n.* One of several musical prodigies famous for a vain attempt to dissuade Odysseus from a life on the ocean wave. Figuratively, any lady of splendid promise, dissembled purpose and disappointing performance.

Slang, *n.* The grunt of the human hog (*Pignoramus intolerabilis*) with an audible memory. The speech of one who utters with his tongue what he thinks with his ear, and feels the pride of a creator in accomplishing the feat of a parrot. A means (under Providence) of setting up as a wit without a capital of sense.

Smithareen, *n.* A fragment, a decomponent part, a remain. The word is used variously, but in the following verses on a noted female reformer who opposed bicycle-riding by women because it "led them to the devil" it is seen at its best:

The wheels go round without a sound—
  The maidens hold high revel;

In sinful mood, insanely gay,
True spinsters spin adown the way
   From duty to the devil!
They laugh, they sing, and—ting-a-ling!
  Their bells go all the morning;
Their lanterns bright bestar the night
   Pedestrians a-warning.
With lifted hands Miss Charlotte stands,
  Good-Lording and O-mying,
Her rheumatism forgotten quite,
   Her fat with anger frying.
She blocks the path that leads to wrath,
  Jack Satan's power defying.
The wheels go round without a sound
  The lights burn red and blue and green.
What's this that's found upon the ground?
  Poor Charlotte Smith's a smithareen!

John William Yope

Sophistry, *n.* The controversial method of an opponent, distinguished from one's own by superior insincerity and fooling. This method is that of the later Sophists, a Grecian sect of philosophers who began by teaching wisdom, prudence, science, art and, in brief, whatever men ought to know, but lost themselves in a maze of quibbles and a fog of words.

His bad opponent's "facts" he sweeps away,
And drags his sophistry to light of day;
Then swears they're pushed to madness who resort
To falsehood of so desperate a sort.
Not so; like sods upon a dead man's breast,
He lies most lightly who the least is pressed.

Polydore Smith

Sorcery, *n.* The ancient prototype and forerunner of political influence. It was, however, deemed less respectable and sometimes was punished by torture and death. Augustine Nicholas relates that a poor peasant who had been accused of sorcery was put to the torture to compel a confession. After enduring a few gentle agonies the suffering simpleton admitted his guilt, but naively asked his tormentors if it were not possible to be a sorcerer without knowing it.

Soul, *n.* A spiritual entity concerning which there hath been brave disputation. Plato held that those souls which in a previous state of existence (antedating Athens) had obtained the clearest glimpses of eternal truth entered into the bodies of persons who became philosophers. Plato was himself a philosopher. The souls that had least contemplated divine truth animated the bodies of usurpers and despots. Dionysius I, who had threatened to decapitate the broadbrowed philosopher, was a usurper and despot. Plato, doubtless, was not the first to construct a system of philosophy that could be quoted against his enemies; certainly he was not the last.

"Concerning the nature of the soul," saith the renowned author of *Diversiones Sanctorum*, "there hath been hardly more argument than that of its place in the body. Mine own belief is that the soul hath her seat in the abdomen—in which faith we may discern and interpret a truth hitherto unintelligible, namely that the glutton is of all men most devout. He is said in the Scripture to 'make a god of his belly'—why, then, should he not be pious, having ever his Deity with him to freshen his faith? Who so well as he can know the might and majesty that he shrines? Truly and soberly, the soul and the stomach are one Divine Entity; and such was the belief of Promasius, who nevertheless erred in denying it immortality. He had observed that its visible and material substance failed and decayed with the rest of the body after death, but of its immaterial essence he knew nothing. This is what we call the Appetite, and it survives the wreck and reek of mortality, to be rewarded or punished in another world, according to what it hath demanded in the flesh. The Appetite whose coarse clamoring was for the unwholesome viands of the general market and the public refectory shall be cast into eternal famine, whilst that which firmly though civilly insisted on ortolans, caviare, terrapin, anchovies, *pâtés de foie gras* and all such Christian comestibles shall flesh its spiritual tooth in the souls of them forever and ever, and wreak its divine thirst upon the immortal parts of the rarest and richest wines ever quaffed here below. Such is my religious faith, though I grieve to confess that neither His Holiness the Pope nor His Grace the Archbishop of Canterbury (whom I equally and profoundly revere) will assent to its dissemination."

Spooker, *n.* A writer whose imagination concerns itself with supernatural phenomena, especially the doings of spooks. One of the most illustrious spookers of our time is Mr. William D. Howells, who introduces a well-credentialed reader to as respectable and mannerly a company of spooks as one could wish to meet. To the terror that invests the chairman of a district school board, the Howells ghost adds something of the mystery enveloping a farmer from another township.

Story, *n.* A narrative, commonly untrue. The truth of the stories here following has, however, not been successfully impeached.

One evening Mr. Rudolph Block, of New York, found himself seated at dinner alongside Mr. Percival Pollard, the distinguished critic.

"Mr. Pollard," said he, "my book, *The Biography of a Dead Cow*, is published anonymously, but you can hardly be ignorant of its authorship. Yet in reviewing it you speak of it as the work of the Idiot of the Century. Do you think that fair criticism?"

"I am very sorry, sir," replied the critic, amiably, "but it did not occur to me that you really might not wish the public to know who wrote it."

Mr. W.C. Morrow, who used to live in San Jose, California, was addicted to writing ghost stories which made the reader feel as if a stream of lizards, fresh from the ice, were streaking it up his back and hiding in his hair. San Jose was at that time believed to be haunted by the visible spirit of a noted bandit named Vasquez, who had been hanged there. The town was not very well lighted, and it is putting it mildly to say that San Jose was reluctant to be out o' nights. One particularly dark night two gentlemen were abroad in the loneliest spot within the city limits, talking loudly to keep up their courage, when they came upon Mr. J.J. Owen, a well-known journalist.

"Why, Owen," said one, "what brings you here on such a night as this? You told me that this is one of Vasquez' favorite haunts! And you are a believer. Aren't you afraid to be out?"

"My dear fellow," the journalist replied with a drear autumnal cadence in his speech, like the moan of a leaf-laden wind, "I'm afraid to be in. I have one of Will Morrow's stories in my pocket and I don't dare to go where there is light enough to read it."

Rear-Admiral Schley and Representative Charles F. Joy were standing near the Peace Monument, in Washington, discussing the question, Is success a failure? Mr. Joy suddenly broke off in the middle of an eloquent sentence, exclaiming: "Hello! I've heard that band before. Santlemann's, I think."

"I don't hear any band," said Schley.

"Come to think, I don't either," said Joy; "but I see General Miles coming down the avenue, and that pageant always affects me in the same way as a brass band. One has to scrutinize one's impressions pretty closely, or one will mistake their origin."

While the Admiral was digesting this hasty meal of philosophy General Miles passed in view, a spectacle of impressive dignity. When the tail of the seeming procession had passed and the two observers had recovered from the transient blindness caused by its effulgence——

"He seems to be enjoying himself," said the Admiral.

"There is nothing," assented Joy, thoughtfully, "that he enjoys one-half so well."

The illustrious statesman, Champ Clark once lived about a mile from the village of Jebigue, in Missouri. One day he rode into town on a favorite mule, and, hitching the beast on the sunny side of a street, in front of a saloon, he went inside in his character of tee-totaler, to apprise the barkeeper that wine is a mocker. It was a dreadfully hot day. Pretty soon a neighbor came in and seeing Clark, said:

"Champ, it is not right to leave that mule out there in the sun. He'll roast, sure!—he was smoking as I passed him."

"O, he's all right," said Clark, lightly: "he's an inveterate smoker."

The neighbor took a lemonade, but shook his head and repeated that it was not right.

He was a conspirator. There had been a fire the night before: a stable just around the corner had burned and a number of horses had put on their immortality, among them a young colt, which was roasted to a rich nut-brown. Some of the boys had turned Mr. Clark's mule loose and substituted the mortal part of the colt. Presently another man entered the saloon.

"For mercy's sake!" he said, taking it with sugar, "do remove that mule, barkeeper: it smells."

"Yes," interposed Clark, "that animal has the best nose in Missouri. But if he doesn't mind, you shouldn't."

In the course of human events Mr. Clark went out, and there, apparently, lay the incinerated and shrunken remains of his charger. The boys did not have any fun out of Mr. Clark, who looked at the body and, with the non-committal expression to which he owes so much of his political preferment, went away. But walking home late that night he saw his mule standing silent and solemn by the wayside in the misty moonlight. Mentioning the name of Helen Blazes with uncommon emphasis, Mr. Clark took the back track as hard as ever he could hook it, and passed the night in town.

General H.H. Wotherspoon, president of the Army War College, has a pet rib-nosed baboon, an animal of uncommon intelligence but imperfectly beautiful. Returning to his apartment one evening, the General was surprised and pained to find Adam (for so the creature is named, the general being a Darwinian) sitting up for him and wearing its master's best uniform coat, epaulettes and all.

"You confounded remote ancestor!" thundered the great strategist, "what do you mean by being out of bed after taps?—and with my coat on!"

Adam rose and with a reproachful look got down on all fours in the manner of his kind and, scuffling across the room to a table, returned with a visiting-card: General Barry had called and, judging by an empty champagne bottle and several cigar-stumps, had been hospitably entertained while waiting. The general apologized to his faithful progenitor and retired. The next day he met General Barry, who said:

"Spoon, old man, when leaving you last evening I forgot to ask you about those excellent cigars. Where do you get them?"

General Wotherspoon did not deign to reply, but walked away.

"Pardon me, please," said Barry, moving after him; "I was joking of course. Why, I knew it was not you before I had been in the room fifteen minutes."

Success, *n.* The one unpardonable sin against one's fellows. In literature, and particularly in poetry, the elements of success are exceedingly simple, and are admirably set forth in the following lines by the reverend Father Gassilasca Jape, entitled, for some mysterious reason, "John A. Joyce."

> The bard who would prosper must carry a book,
>   Do his thinking in prose and wear
> A crimson cravat, a far-away look
>   And a head of hexameter hair.
> Be thin in your thought and your body'll be fat;
> If you wear your hair long you needn't your hat.

Suffrage, *n.* Expression of opinion by means of a ballot. The right of suffrage (which is held to be both a privilege and a duty) means, as commonly interpreted, the right to vote for the man of another man's choice, and is highly prized. Refusal to do so has the bad name of "incivism." The incivilian, however, cannot be properly arraigned for his crime, for there is no legitimate accuser. If the accuser is himself guilty he has no standing in the court of opinion; if not, he profits by the crime, for A's abstention from voting gives greater weight to the vote of B. By female suffrage is meant the right of a woman to vote as some man tells her to. It is based on female responsibility, which is somewhat limited. The woman most eager to jump out of her petticoat to assert her rights is first to jump back into it when threatened with a switching for misusing them.

Sycophant, *n.* One who approaches Greatness on his belly so that he may not be commanded to turn and be kicked. He is sometimes an editor.

> As the lean leech, its victim found, is pleased
> To fix itself upon a part diseased
> Till, its black hide distended with bad blood,
> It drops to die of surfeit in the mud,
> So the base sycophant with joy descries
> His neighbor's weak spot and his mouth applies,
> Gorges and prospers like the leech, although,
> Unlike that reptile, he will not let go.
> Gelasma, if it paid you to devote
> Your talent to the service of a goat,
> Showing by forceful logic that its beard
> Is more than Aaron's fit to be revered;

If to the task of honoring its smell
Profit had prompted you, and love as well,
The world would benefit at last by you
And wealthy malefactors weep anew—
Your favor for a moment's space denied
And to the nobler object turned aside.
Isn't not enough that thrifty millionaires
Who loot in freight and spoliate in fares,
Or, cursed with consciences that bid them fly
To safer villainies of darker dye,
Forswearing robbery and fain, instead,
To steal (they call it "cornering") our bread
May see you groveling their boots to lick
And begging for the favor of a kick?
Still must you follow to the bitter end
Your sycophantic disposition's trend,
And in your eagerness to please the rich
Hunt hungry inners to their final ditch?
In Morgan's praise you smite the sounding wire,
And sing hosannas to great Havemeyer!
What's Satan done that him you should eschew?
He too is reeking rich—deducting *you*.

Syllogism, *n.* A logical formula consisting of a major and a minor assumption and an inconsequent. (See LOGIC.)

Sylph, *n.* An immaterial but visible being that inhabited the air when the air was an element and before it was fatally polluted by factory smoke, sewer gas and similar products of civilization. Sylphs were allied to gnomes, nymphs and salamanders, which dwelt, respectively, in earth, water and fire, all now insalubrious. Sylphs, like fowls of the air, were male and female, to no purpose, apparently, for if they had progeny they must have nested in inaccessible places, none of the chicks having ever been seen.

Symbol, *n.* Something that is supposed to typify or stand for something else. Many symbols are mere "survivals"—things which having no longer any utility continue to exist because we have inherited the tendency to make them; as funereal urns carved on memorial monuments. They were once real urns holding the ashes of the dead. We cannot stop making them, but we can give them a name that conceals our helplessness.

Symbolic, *adj.* Pertaining to symbols and the use and interpretation of
symbols.

> They say 'tis conscience feels compunction;
> I hold that that's the stomach's function,
> For of the sinner I have noted
> That when he's sinned he's somewhat bloated,
> Or ill some other ghastly fashion
> Within that bowel of compassion.
> True, I believe the only sinner
> Is he that eats a shabby dinner.
> You know how Adam with good reason,
> For eating apples out of season,
> Was "cursed." But that is all symbolic:
> The truth is, Adam had the colic.
>
> *G.J.*

T, the twentieth letter of the English alphabet, was by the Greeks absurdly called *tau*. In the alphabet whence ours comes it had the form of the rude corkscrew of the period, and when it stood alone (which was more than the Phœnicians could always do) signified *Tallegal*, translated by the learned Dr. Brownrigg, "tangle-foot."

Table d' Hôte, *n*. A caterer's thrifty concession to the universal passion for irresponsibility.

> Old Paunchinello, freshly wed,
>   Took Madame P. to table,
> And there deliriously fed
>   As fast as he was able.
>
> "I dote upon good grub," he cried,
>   Intent upon its throatage.
> "Ah, yes," said the neglected bride,
>   "You're in your *table d'hôtage*."
>
> *Associated Poets*

Tail, *n*. The part of an animal's spine that has transcended its natural limitations to set up an independent existence in a world of its own. Excepting in his fœtal state, Man is without a tail, a privation of which he attests an hereditary and uneasy consciousness by the coat-skirt of the male and the train of the female, and by a marked tendency to ornament that part of his attire where the tail should be, and indubitably once was. This tendency is most observable in the female of the species, in whom the ancestral sense is strong and persistent. The tailed men described by Lord Monboddo are now generally regarded as a product of an imagination unusually susceptible to influences generated in the golden age of our pithecan past.

Take, *v.t.* To acquire, frequently by force but preferably by stealth.

Talk, *v.t.* To commit an indiscretion without temptation, from an impulse without purpose.

Tariff, *n.* A scale of taxes on imports, designed to protect the domestic producer against the greed of his consumer.

> The Enemy of Human Souls
> Sat grieving at the cost of coals;
> For Hell had been annexed of late,
> And was a sovereign Southern State.
>
> "It were no more than right," said he,
> "That I should get my fuel free.
> The duty, neither just nor wise,
> Compels me to economize—
> Whereby my broilers, every one,
> Are execrably underdone.
> What would they have?—although I yearn
> To do them nicely to a turn,
> I can't afford an honest heat.
> This tariff makes even devils cheat!
> I'm ruined, and my humble trade
> All rascals may at will invade:
> Beneath my nose the public press
> Outdoes me in sulphureousness;
> The bar ingeniously applies
> To my undoing my own lies;
> My medicines the doctors use
> (Albeit vainly) to refuse
> To me my fair and rightful prey
> And keep their own in shape to pay;
> The preachers by example teach
> What, scorning to perform, I preach;

And statesman, aping me, all make
More promises than they can break.
Against such competition I
Lift up a disregarded cry.
Since all ignore my just complaint,
By Hokey-Pokey! I'll turn saint!"
Now, the Republicans, who all
Are saints, began at once to bawl
Against *his* competition; so
There was a devil of a go!
They locked horns with him, tête-à-tête
In acrimonious debate,
Till Democrats, forlorn and lone,
Had hopes of coming by their own.
That evil to avert, in haste
The two belligerents embraced;
But since 'twere wicked to relax
A tittle of the Sacred Tax,
'Twas finally agreed to grant
The bold Insurgent-protestant
A bounty on each soul that fell
Into his ineffectual Hell.

Edam Smith

Technicality, *n.* In an English court a man named Home was tried for slander in having accused a neighbor of murder. His exact words were: "Sir Thomas Holt hath taken a cleaver and stricken his cook upon the head, so that one side of the head fell upon one shoulder and the other side upon the other shoulder." The defendant was acquitted by instruction of the court, the learned judges holding that the words did not charge murder, for they did not affirm the death of the cook, that being only an inference.

Tedium, *n.* Ennui, the state or condition of one that is bored. Many fanciful derivations of the word have been affirmed, but so high an authority as Father Jape says that it comes from a very obvious source—the first words of the ancient Latin hymn *Te Deum Laudamus.* In this apparently natural derivation there is something that saddens.

Teetotaler, *n.* One who abstains from strong drink, sometimes totally, sometimes tolerably totally.

Telephone, *n.* An invention of the devil which abrogates some of the advantages of making a disagreeable person keep his distance.

Telescope, *n.* A device having a relation to the eye similar to that of the telephone to the ear, enabling distant objects to plague us with a multitude of needless details. Luckily it is unprovided with a bell summoning us to the sacrifice.

Tenacity, *n.* A certain quality of the human hand in its relation to the coin of the realm. It attains its highest development in the hand of authority and is considered a serviceable equipment for a career in politics. The following illustrative lines were written of a Californian gentleman in high political preferment, who has passed to his accounting:

> Of such tenacity his grip
> That nothing from his hand can slip.
> Well-buttered eels you may o'erwhelm
> In tubs of liquid slippery-elm
> In vain—from his detaining pinch
> They cannot struggle half an inch!
> 'Tis lucky that he so is planned
> That breath he draws not with his hand,
> For if he did, so great his greed
> He'd draw his last with eager speed.
> Nay, that were well, you say. Not so
> He'd draw but never let it go!

Theosophy, *n.* An ancient faith having all the certitude of religion and all the mystery of science. The modern Theosophist holds, with the Buddhists, that we live an incalculable number of times on this earth, in as many several bodies, because one life is not long enough for our complete spiritual development; that is, a single lifetime does not suffice for us to become as wise and good as we choose to become. To be absolutely wise and good—that is perfection; and the Theosophist is so keen-sighted as to have observed that everything desirous of improvement eventually attains perfection. Less competent observers are disposed to except cats, which seem neither wiser nor better than they were last year. The greatest and fattest of recent Theosophists was the late Madame Blavatsky, who had no cat.

Tights, *n.* An habiliment of the stage designed to reinforce the general acclamation of the press agent with a particular publicity. Public attention was once somewhat diverted from this garment to Miss Lillian Russell's refusal to wear it, and many were the conjectures as to her motive, the guess of Miss Pauline Hall showing a high order of ingenuity and sustained reflection. It was Miss Hall's belief that nature had not endowed Miss Russell with beautiful legs. This theory was impossible of acceptance by the male under-standing, but the conception of a faulty female leg was of so prodigious originality as to rank among the most brilliant feats of philosophical speculation! It is strange that in all the controversy regarding Miss Russell's aversion to tights no one seems to have thought to ascribe it to what was known among the ancients as "modesty." The nature of that sentiment is now imperfectly under-stood, and possibly incapable of exposition with the vocabulary that remains to us. The study of lost arts has, however, been recently revived and some of the arts themselves recovered. This is an epoch of *renaissances*, and there is ground for hope that the primitive "blush" may be dragged from its hiding-place amongst the tombs of antiquity and hissed on to the stage.

Tomb, *n.* The House of Indifference. Tombs are now by common con-sent invested with a certain sanctity, but when they have been long tenanted it is considered no sin to break them open and rifle them, the famous Egyptologist, Dr. Huggyns, explaining that a tomb may be innocently "glened" as soon as its occupant is done "smellynge," the soul being then all exhaled. This reasonable view is now generally accepted by archæologists, whereby the noble sci-ence of Curiosity has been greatly dignified.

Tope, *v.* To tipple, booze, swill, soak, guzzle, lush, bib, or swig. In the individual, toping is regarded with disesteem, but toping nations are in the forefront of civilization and power. When pitted against the hard-drinking Christians the abstemious Mahometans go down like grass before the scythe. In India one hundred thousand beef-eating and brandy-and-soda guzzling Britons hold in subjec-tion two hundred and fifty million vegetarian abstainers of the same Aryan race. With what an easy grace the whisky-loving American pushed the temperate Spaniard out of his possessions! From the time when the Berserkers ravaged all the coasts of west-

ern Europe and lay drunk in every conquered port it has been the
same way: everywhere the nations that drink too much are
observed to fight rather well and not too righteously. Wherefore
the estimable old ladies who abolished the canteen from the
American army may justly boast of having materially augmented
the nation's military power.

Tortoise, *n.* A creature thoughtfully created to supply occasion for the
following lines by the illustrious Ambat Delaso:

TO MY PET TORTOISE

My friend, you are not graceful—not at all;
Your gait's between a stagger and a sprawl.

Nor are you beautiful: your head's a snake's
To look at, and I do not doubt it aches.

As to your feet, they'd make an angel weep.
'Tis true you take them in whene'er you sleep.

No, you're not pretty, but you have, I own,
A certain firmness—mostly you're backbone.

Firmness and strength (you have a giant's thews)
Are virtues that the great know how to use—

I wish that they did not; yet, on the whole,
You lack—excuse my mentioning it—Soul.

So, to be candid, unreserved and true,
I'd rather you were I than I were you.

Perhaps, however, in a time to be,
When Man's extinct, a better world may see

Your progeny in power and control,
Due to the genesis and growth of Soul.

So I salute you as a reptile grand
Predestined to regenerate the land.

Father of Possibilities, O deign
To accept the homage of a dying reign!

In the far region of the unforeknown
I dream a tortoise upon every throne.

I see an Emperor his head withdraw
Into his carapace for fear of Law;

A King who carries something else than fat,
Howe'er acceptably he carries that;

A President not strenuously bent
On punishment of audible dissent—

Who never shot (it were a vain attack)
An armed or unarmed tortoise in the back;

Subjects and citizens that feel no need
To make the March of Mind a wild stampede;

All progress slow, contemplative, sedate,
And "Take your time" the word, in Church and State.

O Tortoise, 'tis a happy, happy dream,
My glorious testudinous régime!

I wish in Eden you'd brought this about
By slouching in and chasing Adam out.

Tree, *n.* A tall vegetable intended by nature to serve as a penal apparatus, though through a miscarriage of justice most trees bear only
a negligible fruit, or none at all. When naturally fruited, the tree is
a beneficent agency of civilization and an important factor in public morals. In the stern West and the sensitive South its fruit (white
and black respectively) though not eaten, is agreeable to the public
taste and, though not exported, profitable to the general welfare.
That the legitimate relation of the tree to justice was no discovery
of Judge Lynch (who, indeed, conceded it no primacy over the
lamp-post and the bridge-girder) is made plain by the following
passage from Morryster, who antedated him by two centuries:

While in y^t londe I was carryed to see ye Ghogo tree, whereof I had hearde moch talk; but sayynge y^t I saw naught
remarkabyll in it, ye hed manne of ye villayge where it grewe
made answer as followeth:

"Y^e tree is not nowe in fruite, but in his seasonne you
shall see dependynge fr. his braunches all soch as have
affroynted ye King his Majesty."

And I was furder tolde y^t ye worde "Ghogo" sygnifyeth in
y^r tong ye same as "rapscal" in our owne.—*Trauvells in y^e
Easte.*

Trial, *n*. A formal inquiry designed to prove and put upon record the
blameless characters of judges, advocates and jurors. In order to
effect this purpose it is necessary to supply a contrast in the person
of one who is called the defendant, the prisoner, or the accused. If
the contrast is made sufficiently clear this person is made to under-
go such an affliction as will give the virtuous gentlemen a comfortable sense of their immunity, added to that of their worth. In
our day the accused is usually a human being, or a socialist, but in
mediæval times, animals, fishes, reptiles and insects were brought
to trial. A beast that had taken human life, or practiced sorcery, was
duly arrested, tried and, if condemned, put to death by the public
executioner. Insects ravaging grain fields, orchards or vineyards
were cited to appeal by counsel before a civil tribunal, and after testimony, argument and condemnation, if they continued *in contu-
maciam* the matter was taken to a high ecclesiastical court, where
they were solemnly excommunicated and anathematized. In a
street of Toledo, some pigs that had wickedly run between the
viceroy's legs, upsetting him, were arrested on a warrant, tried and
punished. In Naples an ass was condemned to be burned at the
stake, but the sentence appears not to have been executed.
D'Addosio relates from the court records many trials of pigs, bulls,
horses, cocks, dogs, goats, etc., greatly, it is believed, to the better-
ment of their conduct and morals. In 1451 a suit was brought
against the leeches infesting some ponds about Berne, and the
Bishop of Lausanne, instructed by the faculty of Heidelberg
University, directed that some of "the aquatic worms" be brought
before the local magistracy. This was done and the leeches, both
present and absent, were ordered to leave the places that they had
infested within three days on pain of incurring "the malediction of

God." In the voluminous records of this *cause celebre* nothing is found to show whether the offenders braved the punishment, or departed forthwith out of that inhospitable jursidiction.

Trichinosis, *n.* The pig's reply to proponents of porcophagy.

Moses Mendlessohn having fallen ill sent for a Christian physician, who at once diagnosed the philosopher's disorder as trichinosis, but tactfully gave it another name. "You need an immediate change of diet," he said; "you must eat six ounces of pork every other day."

"Pork?" shrieked the patient—"pork? Nothing shall induce me to touch it!"

"Do you mean that?" the doctor gravely asked.

"I swear it!"

"Good! —then I will undertake to cure you."

Trinity, *n* In the multiplex theism of certain Christian churches, three entirely distinct deities consistent with only one. Subordinate deities of the polytheistic faith, such as devils and angels, are not dowered with the power of combination, and must urge individually their claims to adoration and propitiation. The Trinity is one of the most sublime mysteries of our holy religion. In rejecting it because it is incomprehensible, Unitarians betray their inadequate sense of theological fundamentals. In religion we believe only what we do not understand, except in the instance of an intelligible doctrine that contradicts an incomprehensible one. In that case we believe the former as a part of the latter.

Troglodyte, *n.* Specifically, a cave-dweller of the paleolithic period, after the Tree and before the Flat. A famous community of troglodytes dwelt with David in the Cave of Adullam. The colony consisted of "every one that was in distress, and every one that was in debt, and every one that was discontented"—in brief, all the Socialists of Judah.

Truce, *n.* Friendship.

Truth, *n.* An ingenious compound of desirability and appearance. Discovery of truth is the sole purpose of philosophy, which is the most ancient occupation of the human mind and has a fair prospect of existing with increasing activity to the end of time.

Truthful, *adj.* Dumb and illiterate.

Trust, *n.* In American politics, a large corporation composed in greater part of thrifty working men, widows of small means, orphans in the care of guardians and the courts, with many similar malefactors and public enemies.

Turkey, *n.* A large bird whose flesh when eaten on certain religious anniversaries has the peculiar property of attesting piety and gratitude. Incidentally, it is pretty good eating.

Twice, *adv.* Once too often.

Type, *n.* Pestilent bits of metal suspected of destroying civilization and enlightenment, despite their obvious agency in this incomparable dictionary.

Tzetze, (or Tsetse) Fly, *n.* An African insect (*Glossina morsitans*) whose bite is commonly regarded as nature's most efficacious remedy for insomnia, though some patients prefer that of the American novelist (*Mendax interminabilis.*)

Ubiquity, *n.* The gift or power of being in all places at one time, but not in all places at all times, which is omnipresence, an attribute of God and the luminiferous ether only. This important distinction between ubiquity and omnipresence was not clear to the mediæval Church and there was much bloodshed about it. Certain Lutherans, who affirmed the presence everywhere of Christ's body were known as Ubiquitarians. For this error they were doubtless damned, for Christ's body is present only in the eucharist, though that sacrament may be performed in more than one place simultaneously. In recent times ubiquity has not always been understood—not even by Sir Boyle Roche, for example, who held that a man cannot be in two places at once unless he is a bird.

Ugliness, *n.* A gift of the gods to certain women, entailing virtue without humility.

Ultimatum, *n.* In diplomacy, a last demand before resorting to concessions.

Having received an ultimatum from Austria, the Turkish Ministry met to consider it.

"O servant of the Prophet," said the Sheik of the Imperial Chibouk to the Mamoosh of the Invincible Army, "how many unconquerable soldiers have we in arms?"

"Upholder of the Faith," that dignitary replied after examining his memoranda, "they are in numbers as the leaves of the forest!"

"And how many impenetrable battleships strike terror to the hearts of all Christian swine?" he asked the Imaum of the Ever Victorious Navy.

"Uncle of the Full Moon," was the reply, "deign to know that they are as the waves of the ocean, the sands of the desert and the stars of Heaven!"

For eight hours the broad brow of the Sheik of the Imperial Chibouk was corrugated with evidences of deep thought: he was calculating the chances of war. Then, "Sons of angels," he said, "the die is cast! I shall suggest to the Ulema of the Imperial Ear that he advise inaction. In the name of Allah, the council is adjourned."

Un-American, *adj.* Wicked, intolerable, heathenish.

Unction, *n.* An oiling, or greasing. The rite of extreme unction consists in touching with oil consecrated by a bishop several parts of the body of one engaged in dying. Marbury relates that after the rite had been administered to a certain wicked English nobleman it was discovered that the oil had not been properly consecrated and no other could be obtained. When informed of this the sick man said in anger: "Then I'll be damned if I die!"

"My son," said the priest, "that is what we fear."

Understanding, *n.* A cerebral secretion that enables one having it to know a house from a horse by the roof on the house. Its nature and laws have been exhaustively expounded by Locke, who rode a house, and Kant, who lived in a horse.

> His understanding was so keen
> That all things which he'd felt, heard, seen,
> He could interpret without fail
> If he was in or out of jail.
> He wrote at Inspiration's call
> Deep disquisitions on them all,
> Then, pent at last in an asylum,
> Performed the service to compile 'em.
> So great a writer, all men swore,
> They never had not read before.
>
> *Jorrock Wormley*

Unitarian, *n.* One who denies the divinity of a Trinitarian.

Universalist, *n.* One who foregoes the advantage of a Hell for persons of another faith.

Urbanity, *n.* The kind of civility that urban observers ascribe to dwellers in all cities but New York. Its commonest expression is heard in the words, "I beg your pardon," and it is not inconsistent with disregard of the rights of others.

> The owner of a powder mill
> Was musing on a distant hill—
>   Something his mind foreboded—
> When from the cloudless sky there fell
> A deviled human kidney! Well,
>   The man's mill had exploded.
> His hat he lifted from his head;
> "I beg your pardon, sir," he said;
> "I didn't know 'twas loaded."
>
> *Swatkin*

Usage, *n.* The First Person of the literary Trinity, the Second and Third being Custom and Conventionality. Imbued with a decent reverence for this Holy Triad an industrious writer may hope to produce books that will live as long as the fashion.

Uxoriousness, *n.* A perverted affection that has strayed to one's own wife.

Valor, *n.* A soldierly compound of vanity, duty and the gambler's hope.

"Why have you halted?" roared the commander of a division at Chickamauga, who had ordered a charge; "move forward, sir, at once."

"General," said the commander of the delinquent brigade, "I am persuaded that any further display of valor by my troops will bring them into collision with the enemy."

Vanity, *n.* The tribute of a fool to the worth of the nearest ass.

> They say that hens do cackle loudest when
>   There's nothing vital in the eggs they've laid;
>   And there are hens, professing to have made
> A study of mankind, who say that men
> Whose business 'tis to drive the tongue or pen
>   Make the most clamorous fanfaronade
>   O'er their most worthless work; and I'm afraid
> They're not entirely different from the hen.
> Lo! the drum-major in his coat of gold,
>   His blazing breeches and high-towering cap—
> Imperiously pompous, grandly bold,
>   Grim, resolute, an awe-inspiring chap!
> Who'd think this gorgeous creature's only virtue
> Is that in battle he will never hurt you?

Hannibal Hunsiker

Virtues, *n. pl.* Certain abstentions.

Vituperation, *n.* Satire, as understood by dunces and all such as suffer from an impediment in their wit.

Vote, *n.* The instrument and symbol of a freeman's power to make a fool of himself and a wreck of his country.

W (double U) has, of all the letters in our alphabet, the only cumbrous name, the names of the others being monosyllabic. This advantage of the Roman alphabet over the Grecian is the more valued after audibly spelling out some simple Greek word, like ἐπιχοριαμβικός. Still, it is now thought by the learned that other agencies than the difference of the two alphabets may have been concerned in the decline of "the glory that was Greece" and the rise of "the grandeur that was Rome." There can be no doubt, however, that by simplifying the name of W (calling it "wow," for example) our civilization could be, if not promoted, at least better endured.

Wall Street, *n.* A symbol of sin for every devil to rebuke. That Wall Street is a den of thieves is a belief that serves every unsuccessful thief in place of a hope in Heaven. Even the great and good Andrew Carnegie has made his profession of faith in the matter.

> Carnegie the dauntless has uttered his call
> To battle: "The brokers are parasites all!"
> Carnegie, Carnegie, you'll never prevail;
> Keep the wind of your slogan to belly your sail,
> Go back to your isle of perpetual brume,
> Silence your pibroch, doff tartan and plume:
> Ben Lomond is calling his son from the fray—
> Fly, fly from the region of Wall Street away!
> While still you're possessed of a single baubee

(I wish it were pledged to endowment of me)
'Twere wise to retreat from the wars of finance
Lest its value decline ere your credit advance.
For a man 'twixt a king of finance and the sea,
Carnegie, Carnegie, your tongue is too free!

Anonymous Bink

War, *n.* A by-product of the arts of peace. The most menacing political condition is a period of international amity. The student of history who has not been taught to expect the unexpected may justly boast himself inaccessible to the light. "In time of peace prepare for war" has a deeper meaning than is commonly discerned; it means, not merely that all things earthly have an end—that change is the one immutable and eternal law—but that the soil of peace is thickly sown with seeds of war and singularly suited to their germination and growth. It was when Kubla Khan had decreed his "stately pleasure dome"—when, that is to say, there were peace and fat feasting in Xanadu—that he

heard from far
Ancestral voices prophesying war.

One of the greatest of poets, Coleridge was one of the wisest of men, and it was not for nothing that he read us this parable. Let us have a little less of "hands across the sea," and a little more of that elemental distrust that is the security of nations. War loves to come like a thief in the night; professions of eternal amity provide the night.

Washingtonian, *n.* A Potomac tribesman who exchanged the privilege of governing himself for the advantage of good government. In justice to him it should be said that he did not want to.

They took away his vote and gave instead
The right, when he had earned, to *eat* his bread.
In vain—he clamors for his "boss," poor soul,
To come again and part him from his roll.

Offenbach Stutz

Weaknesses, *n. pl.* Certain primal powers of Tyrant Woman wherewith she holds dominion over the male of her species, binding him to the service of her will and paralyzing his rebellious energies.

Weather, *n.* The climate of an hour. A permanent topic of conversation among persons whom it does not interest, but who have inherited the tendency to chatter about it from naked arboreal ancestors whom it keenly concerned. The setting up of official weather bureaus and their maintenance in mendacity prove that even governments are accessible to suasion by the rude forefathers of the jungle.

> Once I dipt into the future far as human eye could see,
> And I saw the Chief Forecaster, dead as any one can be—
> Dead and damned and shut in Hades as a liar from his birth,
> With a record of unreason seldom paralleled on earth.
> While I looked he reared him solemnly, that incandescent youth,
> From the coals that he'd preferred to the advantages of truth.
> He cast his eyes about him and above him; then he wrote
> On a slab of thin asbestos what I venture here to quote—
> For I read it in the rose-light of the everlasting glow:
> "Cloudy; variable winds, with local showers; cooler; snow."
>
> *Halcyon Jones*

Wedding, *n.* A ceremony at which two persons undertake to become one, one undertakes to become nothing, and nothing undertakes to become supportable.

Werewolf, *n.* A wolf that was once, or is sometimes, a man. All werewolves are of evil disposition, having assumed a bestial form to gratify a bestial appetite, but some, transformed by sorcery, are as humane as is consistent with an acquired taste for human flesh.

Some Bavarian peasants having caught a wolf one evening, tied it to a post by the tail and went to bed. The next morning nothing was there! Greatly perplexed, they consulted the local priest, who told them that their captive was undoubtedly a werewolf and had resumed its human form during the night. "The next time that you take a wolf," the good man said, "see that you chain it by the leg, and in the morning you will find a Lutheran."

Whangdepootenawah, *n.* In the Ojibwa tongue, disaster; an unexpected affliction that strikes hard.

> Should you ask me whence this laughter,
> Whence this audible big-smiling,

With its labial extension,
With its maxillar distortion
And its diaphragmic rhythmus
Like the billowing of ocean,
Like the shaking of a carpet,
I should answer, I should tell you:
From the great deeps of the spirit,
From the unplummeted abysmus
Of the soul this laughter welleth
As the fountain, the gug-guggle,
Like the river from the cañon,
To entoken and give warning
That my present mood is sunny.
Should you ask me further question—
Why the great deeps of the spirit,
Why the unplummeted abysmus
Of the soul extrudes this laughter,
This all audible big-smiling,
I should answer, I should tell you
With a white heart, tumpitumpy,
With a true tongue, honest Injun:
William Bryan, he has Caught It,
Caught the Whangdepootenawah!

Is't the sandhill crane, the shankank,
Standing in the marsh, the kneedeep,
Standing silent in the kneedeep
With his wing-tips crossed behind him
And his neck close-reefed before him,
With his bill, his william buried
In the down upon his bosom,
With his head retracted inly,
While his shoulders overlook it?
Does the sandhill crane, the shankank,
Shiver grayly in the north wind,
Wishing he had died when little,
As the sparrow, the chipchip, does?
No 'tis not the Shankank standing,
Standing in the gray and dismal
Marsh, the gray and dismal kneedeep.
No, 'tis peerless William Bryan
Realizing that he's Caught It,
Caught the Whangdepootenawah!

Wheat, *n.* A cereal from which a tolerably good whiskey can with some difficulty be made, and which is used also for bread. The French are said to eat more bread per capita of population than any other people, which is natural, for only they know how to make the stuff palatable.

White, *adj.* and *n.* Black.

Widow, *n.* A pathetic figure that the Christian world has agreed to take humorously, although Christ's tenderness towards widows was one of the most marked features of his character.

Wine, *n.* Fermented grape-juice known to the Women's Christian Union as "liquor," sometimes as "rum." Wine, madame is God's next best gift to man.

Wit, *n.* The salt with which the American humorist spoils his intellectual cookery by leaving it out.

Witch, *n.* (1) An ugly and repulsive old woman, in a wicked league with the devil. (2) A beautiful and attractive young woman, in wickedness a league beyond the devil.

Witticism, *n.* A sharp and clever remark, usually quoted, and seldom noted; what the Philistine is pleased to call a "joke."

Woman, *n.* An animal usually living in the vicinity of Man, and having a rudimentary susceptibility to domestication. It is credited by many of the elder zoölogists with a certain vestigial docility acquired in a former state of seclusion, but naturalists of the post-susananthony period, having no knowledge of the seclusion, deny the virtue and declare that such as creation's dawn beheld, it roareth now. The species is the most widely distributed of all beasts of prey, infesting all habitable parts of the globe, from Greenland's spicy mountains to India's moral strand. The popular name (wolf-man) is incorrect, for the creature is of the cat kind. The woman is lithe and graceful in its movements, especially the American variety (*Felis pugnans*), is omnivorous and can be taught not to talk. —*Balthasar Pober*

Worms'-meat, *n.* The finished product of which we are the raw material. The contents of the Taj Mahal, the Tombeau Napoleon and the Grantarium. Worms'-meat is usually outlasted by the structure that houses it, but "this too must pass away." Probably the silliest

work in which a human being can engage is construction of a
tomb for himself. The solemn purpose cannot dignify, but only
accentuates by contrast the foreknown futility.

> Ambitious fool! so mad to be a show!
> How profitless the labor you bestow
>   Upon a dwelling whose magnificence
> The tenant neither can admire nor know.
>
> Build deep, build high, build massive as you can,
> The wanton grass-roots will defeat the plan
>   By shouldering asunder all the stones
> In what to you would be a moment's span.
>
> Time to the dead so all unreckoned flies
> That when your marble all is dust, arise,
>   If wakened, stretch your limbs and yawn—
> You'll think you scarcely can have closed your eyes.
>
> What though of all man's works your tomb alone
> Should stand till Time himself be overthrown?
>   Would it advantage you to dwell therein
> Forever as a stain upon a stone?
>
> *Joel Huck*

Worship, *n.* Homo Creator's testimony to the sound construction and
fine finish of Deus Creatus. A popular form of abjection, having
an element of pride.

Wrath, *n.* Anger of a superior quality and degree, appropriate to exalt-
ed characters and momentous occasions; as, "the wrath of God,"
"the day of wrath," etc. Amongst the ancients the wrath of kings
was deemed sacred, for it could usually command the agency of
some god for its fit manifestation, as could also that of a priest.
The Greeks before Troy were so harried by Apollo that they
jumped out of the frying-pan of the wrath of Chryses into the fire
of the wrath of Achilles, though Agamemnon, the sole offender,
was neither fried nor roasted. A similar noted immunity was that
of David when he incurred the wrath of Yahveh by numbering his
people, seventy thousand of whom paid the penalty with their
lives. God is now Love, and a director of the census performs his
work without apprehension of disaster.

X in our alphabet being a needless letter has an added invincibility to the attacks of the spelling reformers, and like them, will doubtless last as long as the language. X is the sacred symbol of ten dollars, and in such words as Xmas, Xn, etc., stands for Christ, not, as is popularly supposed, because it represents a cross, but because the corresponding letter in the Greek alphabet is the initial of His name—Χριστός. If it represented a cross it would stand for St. Andrew, who "testified" upon one of that shape. In the algebra of psychology x stands for Woman's mind. Words beginning with X are Grecian and will not be defined in this standard English dictionary.

Yankee, *n.* In Europe, an American. In the Northern States of our Union, a New Englander. In the Southern States the word is unknown. (See DAMYANK.)

Year, *n.* A period of three hundred and sixty-five disappointments.

Yesterday, *n.* The infancy of youth, the youth of manhood, the entire past of age.

> But yesterday I should have thought me blest
>   To stand high-pinnacled upon the peak
>   Of middle life and look adown the bleak
> And unfamiliar foreslope to the West,
> Where solemn shadows all the land invest
>   And stilly voices, half-remembered, speak
>   Unfinished prophecy, and witch-fires freak
> The haunted twilight of the Dark of Rest.
> Yea, yesterday my soul was all aflame
>   To stay the shadow on the dial's face
> At manhood's noonmark! Now, in God His name
>   I chide aloud the little interspace
> Disparting me from Certitude, and fain
> Would know the dream and vision ne'er again.
>
> *Baruch Arnegriff*

It is said that in his last illness the poet Arnegriff was attended at different times by seven doctors.

Zany, *n.* A popular character in old Italian plays, who imitated with ludicrous incompetence the *buffone*, or clown, and was therefore the ape of an ape; for the clown himself imitated the serious characters of the play. The zany was progenitor to the specialist in humor, as we to-day have the unhappiness to know him. In the zany we see an example of creation; in the humorist, of transmission. Another excellent specimen of the modern zany is the curate, who apes the rector, who apes the bishop, who apes the archbishop, who apes the devil.

Zanzibari, *n.* An inhabitant of the Sultanate of Zanzibar, off the eastern coast of Africa. The Zanzibaris, a warlike people, are best known in this country through a threatening diplomatic incident that occurred a few years ago. The American consul at the capital occupied a dwelling that faced the sea, with a sandy beach between. Greatly to the scandal of this official's family, and against repeated remonstrances of the official himself, the people of the city persisted in using the beach for bathing. One day a woman came down to the edge of the water and was stooping to remove her attire (a pair of sandals) when the consul, incensed beyond restraint, fired a charge of bird-shot into the most conspicuous part of her person. Unfortunately for the existing *entente cordiale* between two great nations, she was the Sultana.

Zeal, *n.* A certain nervous disorder afflicting the young and inexperienced. A passion that goeth before a sprawl.

When Zeal sought Gratitude for his reward
He went away exclaiming: "O my Lord!"
"What do you want?" the Lord asked, bending down.
"An ointment for my cracked and bleeding crown."

Jum Coople

Zenith, *n.* A point in the heavens directly overhead to a standing man
or a growing cabbage. A man in bed or a cabbage in the pot is not
considered as having a zenith, though from this view of the matter there was once a considerable dissent among the learned, some
holding that the posture of the body was immaterial. These were
called Horizontalists, their opponents, Verticalists. The
Horizontalist heresy was finally extinguished by Xanobus, the
philosopher-king of Abara, a zealous Verticalist. Entering an
assembly of philosophers who were debating the matter, he cast a
severed human head at the feet of his opponents and asked them
to determine its zenith, explaining that its body was hanging by
the heels outside. Observing that it was the head of their leader,
the Horizontalists hastened to profess themselves converted to
whatever opinion the Crown might be pleased to hold, and
Horizontalism took its place among *fides defuncti.*

Zeus, *n.* The chief of Grecian gods, adored by the Romans as Jupiter
and by the modern Americans as God, Gold, Mob and Dog. Some
explorers who have touched upon the shores of America, and one
who professes to have penetrated a considerable distance into the
interior, have thought that these four names stand for as many distinct deities, but in his monumental work on Surviving Faiths,
Frumpp insists that the natives are monotheists, each having no
other god than himself, whom he worships under many sacred
names.

Zigzag, *v.t.* To move forward uncertainly, from side to side, as one car-
rying the white man's burden. (From *zed,* z, and *jag,* an Icelandic
word of unknown meaning.)

He zedjagged so uncomen wyde
Thet non coude pas on eyder syde;
So, to com saufly thruh, I been
Constreynet for to doodge betwene.

Munwele

Zoölogy, *n.* The science and history of the animal kingdom, including its king, the House Fly (*Musca maledicta.*) The father of Zoölogy was Aristotle, as is universally conceded, but the name of its mother has not come down to us. Two of the science's most illustrious expounders were Buffon and Oliver Goldsmith, from both of whom we learn (*L'Histoire générale des animaux* and *A History of Animated Nature*) that the domestic cow sheds its horns every two years.

A NOTE ON THE TYPE

The text is set in Dante, a digitized version produced by Monotype based on a font designed in the 1950s by Giovanni Mardersteig.

Beowolf, the font you see in the running heads and display, was designed by Erik van Blokland in 1990. Its "distressed" look comes from a randomization routine that allows for distortions in the letter forms.

The initial letters are from the Devil Alphabet, a French decorative set dating from 1837.

Design and layout by Adam B. Bohannon.